TZU CHI

Serving with Compassion

16 MAY 2010

TZU CHI

Serving with Compassion

Mark O'Neill

WILEY

John Wiley & Sons (Asia) Pte. Ltd.

Other Wiley Editorial Offices
John Wiley & Sons, 111 River Street, Hoboken, NJ 07030, USA
John Wiley & Sons, The Atrium, Southern Gate, Chichester, West Sussex, P019 8SQ,
    United Kingdom
John Wiley & Sons (Canada) Ltd., 5353 Dundas Street West, Suite 400, Toronto,
    Ontario, M9B 6HB, Canada
John Wiley & Sons Australia Ltd, 42 McDougall Street, Milton, Queensland 4064,
    Australia
Wiley-VCH, Boschstrasse 12, D-69469 Weinheim, Germany

Library of Congress Cataloging-in-Publication Data
ISBN 978-0-470-82567-9

Typeset in 10/13 Sabon Roman by MPS Limited, A Macmillan Company, Chennai, India.
Printed in Singapore by Saik Wah Press Pte. Ltd.
10 9 8 7 6 5 4 3 2 1

CONTENTS

PREFACE

It seemed like an accident. I was in Hong Kong on a regular three-month visit from my post as a business correspondent for the *South China Morning Post* in Shanghai; it was a chance to report to my editors and listen to their advice and criticism. I was sitting in the lobby of a hotel in Wanchai, waiting for my wife to arrive. Out of the window, I saw an old friend, Andrew Tanzer, walking past. Andrew is an American who had been the Hong Kong (Asia) correspondent for *Forbes* magazine, and I had not seen him for several years. I ran out to meet him and we arranged to have lunch. During the meal, he explained that he had written the memoirs of Robert Kuok, a Malaysian Chinese who was one of the richest overseas Chinese in the world and the owner of my newspaper. Mr. Kuok had given Andrew a total of 96 hours of interviews; I was very envious of this inside look at one of Asia's most powerful—and most secretive—men. Andrew told me that for his next project, he had been invited to write a book about a Buddhist philanthropic foundation in Taiwan called Tzu Chi, founded in 1966 by a charismatic nun, but was unsure whether he should take on the project. "My experience is in business journalism, writing about the rich and about chief executives," he said. "Do I have the ability to write about Buddhism and charity?" Even though I had been a journalist in Asia for more than 25 years, I had never heard of Tzu Chi (慈濟). Still, the subject sounded interesting, and I felt more envious of this project than the one on Robert Kuok. "If they are asking you to write it, go for it," I told him. "It looks like a fascinating project, an important subject that no one knows anything about."

I returned to Shanghai and forgot about the Buddhist foundation.

More than a year had passed when, out of the blue, Andrew sent me an e-mail: for family reasons, he had to move back unexpectedly to the United States and would not be able to write the book on Tzu Chi. He recalled that I had shown a fascination in Tzu Chi: would I be interested in taking on the project? I certainly was. Shanghai was an extraordinary city and offered a great deal of news but, after 17 years as a reporter in the mainland, I was ready for a change.

Since I knew nothing about the foundation, I needed to first visit its headquarters in Hualien (花蓮), on the east coast of Taiwan. I was entranced by what I saw. The headquarters sits at the foot of a mountain range overlooking the Pacific Ocean. The staff consists of nuns in grey robes and volunteers dressed in blue and white uniforms. The style was polite and low-key, the opposite of the aggressive and money-centric world that I had been spending my time reporting in Shanghai.

While I understood little about the foundation on this first visit, I realized that Tzu Chi was something extremely powerful and that its founder, Master Cheng Yen (證嚴法師), was an extraordinary woman. I had a brief encounter with her, in the room where she receives visitors. "Thank you for giving me the opportunity to write this book," I said. "Do not write about me, write about them." she told me, pointing at her disciples in the room, "They are Tzu Chi."

I was impressed by the good manners and friendliness of everyone I met. To write a book at their invitation would mean an entry ticket into their world, a rare opportunity to meet their members and ask them at length about their lives, their beliefs and their projects. An outsider writing a book on the foundation would not normally have such access.

A few months later, I made a second visit to Taipei to discuss the details of the contract. Andrew had already drawn one up, so that is what we used. One Tzu Chi member, Kenneth Tai, kindly agreed to pay my salary and travel costs for the 12 months it would take to do the interviews and write the book. Mr. Tai was one of the founders of the Acer computer company, Taiwan's most famous brand; he now runs his own investment firm and gives much of his time to Tzu Chi projects.

Another key person was Rey Her-sheng (何日生), the foundation's spokesman. Rey had been a famous television reporter and presenter in Taiwan, so famous that the island's two biggest political parties had both invited him to run as a candidate for the Legislative Assembly. But he decided instead to join Tzu Chi and has become a fervent disciple, working as the spokesman and writing several books on it. Rey, who became my main contact in the foundation, said I was welcome to interview anyone in Tzu Chi and to visit its foreign operations, which extend to more than 40 countries around the world. It was he who facilitated these meetings and who gave so much of his own time to explain the history, philosophy and operations of the foundation. His staff also helped in these interviews, especially Miss Lai Rei-ling, who accompanied me on many of the trips and provided whatever help I requested.

I chose to concentrate the bulk of the work in Taiwan, where Tzu Chi was founded, where its roots are strongest and projects most numerous, and where it has the largest number of members. I interviewed many Tzu Chi doctors, volunteers, teachers, journalists, specialists at the bone marrow bank, and people in the wider society with a good knowledge of Tzu Chi's activities. What they told me forms the main body of this book and I thank them all for their time and for the honesty with which they answered my many questions. I was also helped by the many media of the foundation, including its Great Love Television channel (大愛台), its monthly magazine and many books, some by Master Cheng Yen and others by volunteers. I also read books by outside scholars and specialists.

The list of foreign countries where Tzu Chi has projects is long. I therefore selected three as the most important—South Africa, Indonesia and the United States. South Africa and Indonesia are the two foreign countries in which the foundation has taken root among the non-Chinese population; so they are important test cases of whether it can flourish outside a Chinese cultural and religious setting. The three trips were memorable, especially to South Africa, a country that could scarcely be more different to Taiwan—a black majority, sparsely populated, the worst AIDS epidemic in the world, and a heavy burden of racial division. As everywhere, the Tzu Chi members received us with warmth and kindness. In Ladysmith, we stayed in the home of Alan Fang and his family. Reluctant to let us take a train or a bus to Johannesburg airport for our return flight to Hong Kong, he and his son drove us the entire journey of 192 miles: wonderful for us to see the splendor of the Drakensberg Mountains and the beauty of a wonderful country—but exhausting for them.

The one interview I did not do was with Master Cheng Yen herself. As she said during that brief first meeting, the book should be about the members and not her. In fact, such an interview was scarcely necessary. Her presence and her philosophy permeate everything at the foundation; no one I interviewed could speak of their life and work there without talking of her and what she meant to them. When I had nearly finished writing the book, I was visiting the Hualien headquarters with a group of Taiwan newspaper and television editors. Mr. Her suddenly invited me into the adjoining room to sit with Master Cheng Yen and two guests—Stan Shih (施振榮), another Acer founder, and his wife. Mr. Shih was giving an excellent presentation about how to create a global brand, something he had succeeded in doing with Acer and from which Tzu Chi wants to learn. I was happy to be present at the table in such company; most members of the foundation do not have such an opportunity.

It was a great good fortune to spend a year on this book, to have the opportunity to spend time with the members of the foundation and learn their experiences and insights. I hope that in writing it, people outside the Chinese world will gain an understanding of the foundation, of their history, their philosophy and their projects. For this good fortune, I must thank many people—Andrew Tanzer for introducing the project in the first place, Kenneth Tai for paying my salary, Rey Her and his staff for arranging the interviews and the foreign visits, the members who gave me their precious time, the many volunteers who gave me cups of tea and a warm welcome and, of course, Master Cheng Yen herself. I would also like to thank CJ Hwu and her colleagues at John Wiley, especially my editor Grace Pundyk, who made the book clearer and easier to read. Lastly, I thank my lovely wife, Louise, who accompanied me on all the trips and explained so many things.

All information are provided and confirmed by Tzu Chi Foundation.

AUTHOR'S NOTE ON THE TRANSLATIONS USED IN THIS BOOK: There are several systems used to transliterate Chinese characters into Roman letters. The most common is pinyin, developed by a group of mainland Chinese scholars in the 1950s, led by Professor Zhou Youguang, used in the mainland and increasingly accepted as a universal standard. But many people in Taiwan use a different system of romanization. In this book, we have decided in general to use pinyin for transliteration; but we also use the transliterations of names and places which Taiwan people have chosen to use. To avoid confusion, we add the Chinese characters of the main people and places at the first reference, so that Chinese-speaking readers will be able to cross-reference them easily. We use the characters in the traditional form that are used in Taiwan and Hong Kong.

Mark O'Neill

INTRODUCTION

A SILENT REVOLUTION

"We should use our time and our abilities to help all living beings. When we give unselfishly to others, we will feel that our lives are real and meaningful. We will not feel that our lives have been wasted."

—Cheng Yen

WHEN SURVIVORS OF SICHUAN'S DEVASTATING earthquake in May 2008 went to seek help in the city of Shifang, they found a group of tents where they were given cooked food, rice, medicines, first aid kits, blankets, medical care and eating utensils. The people helping were middle-aged, retired and spoke excellent Chinese; they wore blue shirts and white trousers, and badges clearly identifying their names. The survivors found not only the goods needed to maintain life in their tents but also a smiling face, someone with whom they could speak about the loss of their family members and of the houses where they had lived since they were born. They had not seen these people in blue and white before and did not know where they came from. But they were grateful that, in their hour of need, they had come. The visitors too were grateful to be there, this place of pain and sadness. They considered it an honor to help: the smile on the face of the elderly woman carrying her sack of rice and the child cured of his stomach ache were ample reward for their work and sweat.

It is the men and women in blue and white uniforms, and the organization they are affiliated to, who are the subject of this book. They are members of the Taiwan Buddhist Tzu Chi Charitable Association for the Relief of Suffering, or Tzu Chi for short. In English, the name may be difficult to pronounce, but in Chinese it is poetic: "*tzu*" means "mercy, compassion," and "*chi*" means "relief, help": you see a person in distress and are moved to help them.

Set up in May 1966, by a Buddhist nun named Cheng Yen and 30 followers in Hualien, a small town in East Taiwan, it has grown into the largest non-government organization (NGO) in the Chinese-speaking world, with 10 million members in more than 30 countries. It is the richest charity in Taiwan, with annual donations of $300 million and an endowment of more than NT$26 billion ($780 million). To date, it has set up the largest bone marrow bank in Asia, built seven hospitals, 100 schools and a university, and runs a recycling program with more than 200,000 volunteers. Its members deliver emergency relief and free medical care each year to more than 11 million people in nearly 70 countries around the world, from North Korea to Paraguay, from Ethiopia to Indonesia.

It is run more like a multinational corporation than a traditional charity. Around the world, members are on call 24 hours a day, connected by the latest telecommunications to the headquarters in Hualien. It has a sophisticated system of managing money: donors can choose dedicated accounts, and each donation and the way it is used is recorded. It has large stocks of food, medicine, clothes, tents and blankets stored in warehouses in Taiwan and abroad, that can be transported at a moment's notice to the area of a disaster.

In fact, Tzu Chi sends volunteers through battle zones, civil war, floods and earthquakes to deliver goods to the four corners of the world. It gives aid to everyone, regardless of race or color, and welcomes people of every belief. It sees the world as one family and everyone who is suffering as worthy of help. This concept of universal love and a worldwide program that acts on it are unprecedented in the Chinese experience.

"Traditionally, Chinese only helped their own family or their own community," explains Richard Madsen, professor of sociology at San Diego's University of California, and a specialist on China and Taiwan. "Tzu Chi helps the whole world and has a global vision. This is a major contribution to the Chinese world. The act of giving has been common to Buddhism for 2,000 years. What is new is a professional organization, a capacity to see the world as one big family."

Tzu Chi is also unique for other reasons. First, it was founded and is headed by a woman, who left home at 23 to establish her own Buddhist community, rather than join an existing one.

Second, it is predominantly a lay organization in which ritual and liturgy play a secondary role; Cheng Yen and the 150 nuns who live at the Abode of Still Thoughts (精舍), their modest home in Hualien, play a minor role. It is the one million volunteers donating their time and energy for no financial reward, who are the driving force. Volunteers distribute aid around the world, counsel bone marrow donors and cancer patients and collect and sort rubbish from food markets, holiday beaches and pop concerts. They include university professors and elderly women who cannot read or write, chief executives and reformed delinquents, lawyers and farmers. Divided by wealth, education and class, they are united in a desire to do something for their communities, both locally and within the greater world. This is Buddhism in action, not a religion confined to temples and monasteries.

Third, Tzu Chi is a movement that combines modern technology with ancient wisdom. Early each morning, nuns recite centuries-old prayers in one room of the Abode. Along the corridor, a high-tech conference room enables Cheng Yen to talk to her members around the world, via satellite telephone and video link-up. She follows world events on dozens of television channels, while her staff surf the internet on banks of computers. The foundation has its own television station, which broadcasts through 12 satellites that can reach 80 percent of the world's population. It has a monthly magazine in Chinese and periodicals in other languages and a website with news of its latest activities, in Chinese and English.

Fourth, the foundation insists that its aid be delivered in person by its own members and not through a third party or government. Tzu Chi believes that the act of giving brings as much blessing to the donor as to the recipient: the one receives needed goods and the other an awareness of their good fortune.

Since starting its international aid program in 1991, Tzu Chi has devoted itself to providing relief goods and medical care around the world, with the aim of bringing the donor and recipient together. Its programs are of particular significance for China and Indonesia: In one of the last, unresolved conflicts of the Cold War, China and Taiwan have yet to sign a peace treaty and Taiwan is becoming increasingly marginalized by it's neighbor's might. Yet in 2008, when the earthquake struck in China, Tzu Chi sent a plane loaded with 100 tons of relief supplies from Taipei to Chengdu, capital of Sichuan province, just three days after the quake. Tzu Chi was the first foreign NGO to arrive in the disaster area and has remained there since. It provided relief goods and temporary houses and is building permanent homes and schools for the victims. Volunteers also give psychological counseling, sing songs and tell stories to the victims to help them through their trauma. In Indonesia, despite the centuries-old animosity between native Indonesians and ethnic Chinese, Cheng Yen has persuaded wealthy Chinese to provide free homes, food, medicines and health care for their less fortunate Indonesian neighbors in the belief that action of this kind is a better form of security than a new barbed wire fence or another team of armed guards.

The history of Tzu Chi is inseparable from that of its founder, Cheng Yen. Born into a modest family in 1937 in the West of Taiwan, then part of the Japanese empire, she was educated only through primary school. At the age of 23, she ran away from home to become a nun, but rather than join an existing order, she decided to establish her own.

Defying Buddhist convention, Cheng Yen insisted that her community work to earn its living, rather than accepting alms from the faithful. In 1966, after witnessing a woman miscarrying simply because the hospital would not admit her without money, Cheng Yen decided to establish the foundation, with 30 housewives as members, to help the poor and sick of Hualien.

An essential part of this story is the leadership, charisma and eloquence of Cheng Yen. At 72, she remains the unchallenged leader of the foundation, its chief executive and its spiritual guide, and she intends to remain so until her final breath. Because of a heart condition, she cannot fly and has never left Taiwan. Even so, members around the world say that it is she who has inspired them to join the foundation, to donate money and take part in its projects. They regard her as an extraordinary individual, the like of whom they will not meet again in their lifetime. She is, they say, their "teacher for life"; her writings and daily talk on her Great Love Television channel serve as their compass.

Cheng Yen was nominated for the Nobel Peace Prize in 1993 and has received many international awards, including the Ramon Magsaysay Award for Community Leadership in 1991, an Eisenhower Medallion Award in 1994 and the 24th Niwano Peace Prize in 2007. Some compare her to Mother Teresa, the Albanian Catholic nun who dedicated her life to helping the poor, sick and dying of Calcutta. Certainly, the two women have much in common—a lifetime devoted to helping others. But while Mother Teresa worked within the structure of the Roman Catholic Church, Cheng Yen established her own doctrine and her own movement, whose scope and activities have reached far beyond those of the Catholic nun.

The philosophy of Tzu Chi addresses the three curses of the contemporary world—violent fundamentalism, the widening wealth gap and environmental degradation. Cheng Yen invites everyone to join her movement; she asks the rich to donate money and time to help the poor; she asks her members to live frugally, devote time to recycling and carry plastic chopsticks and rice bowls, which they use every day. Because she believes in the innate goodness of people, be they poor or rich, and their willingness to help one another, this fragile nun has inspired millions, creating a "circle of virtue" that benefits all.

Tzu Chi: Serving with Compassion traces the extraordinary story of Cheng Yen and how a small group of disciples dedicated to helping the sick and poor grew to become a global movement.

PART ONE

FROM BAMBOO COLLECTION BOXES TO HEART SURGERY

I

BEGINNINGS

*"Why do women always have to hide in the shadow of a family?
Why cannot they raise their head and throw out their chest and
do something for the whole society?"*

—Cheng Yen

Early life of Cheng Yen

Cheng Yen was born Wang Chin-yun (Bright Cloud) on May 14, 1937 in an earthen house with a tiled roof, down a narrow lane that ran through a row of one-story homes. It was a poor, crowded neighborhood, its lanes full of children, dogs, vendors, and women carrying food home from the market. There was no running water and poor sanitation—the life expectancy for a man in Taiwan was 41 years and a woman 45 years, many babies died in infancy, and pneumonia and tuberculosis were widespread.

Chin-yun was the fifth child of a man who made silk and cotton buttons. He shared his modest home with two brothers and their wives and they lived as one large family. All rejoiced in the arrival of the young baby, none more than her uncle and aunt, who were entranced by her clear skin and big, clear eyes.

"I fell in love with her at first sight," recalls her aunt, Wang Shen Yue-gui (王沈月桂), an ebullient 91-year-old, who still works tirelessly for the Tzu Chi Foundation today. "She was a beautiful baby. Her eyes were like two pools of water containing wisdom carried over from a previous life." Her aunt and uncle, childless after several miscarriages, begged Chin-yun's parents to let them adopt her and, when she was 11 months old, they finally agreed. Such adoptions to a childless couple were common practice in Taiwan at that time, yet it would be the experiences with her new family that would help shape the young girl's future. If she had grown up with her birth parents, she would have had another life, and history would have been different.

The adoption of the girl proved to be a double blessing for her new parents. Mrs. Wang finally became pregnant and gave birth to a son, the first of five children. Even so, Chin-yun was the one they doted on. "At 10 months, she could walk and by two she was already smart," recalled Wang, who, as Tzu Chi commissioner number 56, goes by the Buddhist name of Ren De (Benevolence and Virtue). "She was a model child and never any trouble. Merely a child herself, she helped me to take care of the babies. At age five, she was walking around with a baby strapped to her back."

The family was poor—her father did odd jobs, her mother collected firewood and the family lived off sweet potatoes and preserved vegetables. They had no running water, so her mother had to spend hours every day collecting it from outside.

As a child, Chin-yun showed unusual sensitivity to the sick and the suffering. During World War Two, the American bombing of Taiwan, then under Japanese rule, and the ensuing loss of life and destruction of personal possessions profoundly affected her. "Walking among the dead and wounded must have caused her to see the impermanence of life," recalled Wang. "Witnessing the easy destruction of material things, she must have acquired an understanding that no one could hold on to his worldly belongings."

Wang described one raid when she was at home and her daughter at school. After the raid was over, Chin-yun rushed home and embraced her mother fervently, crying that she thought she would not see her again. "I cannot describe her expression at that moment. It was not the expression of a child but of an adult with great wisdom—the wisdom to know that life is fragile and that loved ones can be separated forever by the hands of karma."

During the Japanese era, Chin-yun completed two years of primary school. Before going to school, she rose every morning at dawn to gather firewood in the nearby foothills. She would collect enough for the family to burn in the stove for the rest of the day, and she worked and studied with one of her siblings strapped to her back.

On August 15, 1945, Tokyo surrendered and, with the stroke of a pen, Taiwan belonged to China. In one day, the language of government and education changed from Japanese to Mandarin. And, in less than a year, 200 U.S. ships repatriated the 600,000 Japanese soldiers and civilians on Taiwan.

In 1946, the fortunes of the Wang family took a dramatic turn for the better when they moved to the nearby town of Fengyuan (豐原) where Mr. Wang had taken over a theatre. The timing was perfect. A major junction on the North-South railway line, Fengyuan was the richest town in the area and, after years of wartime austerity and rationing, people longed for entertainment, especially Taiwan opera and the recently introduced cinema. Business boomed and Mr. Wang was soon running seven theatres. He was a gregarious man, so the house was always full of people: in his spare time, he liked to play the saxophone. He worked hard, had high blood pressure and a bad temper—but Chin-yun was his favorite child and suffered less from his temper than the others, who would use her as the go-between.

After the Communist victory on the mainland in 1949, the Nationalist government moved to Taiwan, bringing with it 1.6 million soldiers and civilians and further swelling theater audiences. That year, the family was rich enough to hire maids, relieving Chin-yun of the burden of housework. Mr. Wang spent his new-found wealth on tailor-made clothes, and gold and jewellery for his wife and favorite daughter.

Chin-yun graduated from primary school after six years—two years under the Japanese and four under the new Nationalist government.

"We asked her to attend middle school, because we hoped that she would have the education which we did not," explains Mrs. Wang. "But she wanted to stay at home and help look after the children. I said that others could do this but she was uneasy about this and preferred to be at home."

"She was protective of her siblings. When they had an argument, she would come and ask me to punish her instead of them. She would kneel in front of me and hold her hands out, to be smacked. If I said nothing, she would say that, without my permission, she could not get up," her mother recalled.

After finishing school, Chin-yun also began to play an important role in her father's business. She spent much time in the theatres, studying and keeping her father company and making snacks for customers, collecting tickets and doing the accounts. News of her beauty soon spread among the young men of the town, who came to the cinema in the hope of seeing her.

But by now, it was evident to Mrs. Wang that Chin-yun was not a typical daughter. "She never used cosmetics. Someone brought some from Japan and offered them to her but she refused. She grew her hair very long, up to 90 centimeters." She also had no boyfriends. Marriages were arranged between families and the Wangs received many proposals for their daughter. "She said that she did not want to hear of it or any others," said Mrs. Wang. "I was divided on the idea. I would lose face if she did not marry but I did not want to force her. I cannot explain her attitude toward men. Perhaps it was the days during the bombing that affected her way of thinking or perhaps it was the wisdom she carried over from a previous lifetime. She seemed to realize that, with all the love she carried in her heart, she should not limit or restrain it by the demands of a marriage. Her dreams for the future were different from those of other girls her age—instead of a husband and children, she was waiting for a chance to live in a much grander and holier manner."

In later interviews, Cheng Yen explained that she did not want to live her life for one single family and that, once she had left her comfortable surroundings, she never considered going back.

"I did not consider as hardships what I endured. Why do women always have to hide in the shadow of a family? Why cannot they raise their head and throw out their chest and do something for the whole society?"

In 1960, at the age of 23, she made the momentous decision to leave home and become a nun. It was, in the context of the time and her family circumstances, an extraordinary step. A religious life meant leaving your family, living in celibacy and hardship and withdrawing from society.

There were four major events that prompted her decision. One was the air raids in World War Two, when she witnessed random death and destruction of physical things.

Another came in 1952, when she was 15. Her mother suffered from a stomach ulcer and began to spit blood. The doctor said the ulcer had perforated the stomach lining and that an operation was needed—an operation that, given the medical conditions of that time, could be fatal. Chin-yun went to pray in the town's Buddhist temple for her mother's recovery. She promised that, if her mother's life were saved, she would sacrifice 12 years of her own and become a vegetarian for the rest of her life. During three days of prayers, she had the same dream. This is how she described it: "I saw a small temple with a large door and two small doors on either side, a large statue of Buddha in the center and mother lying on a bamboo bed next to it. I was at her side, cooking medicine in a pot. I heard the sound of wind and from a white cloud flew down a beautiful woman. I raised my head and saw her take out a bag of medicine from a bottle. I said nothing; I knelt down and took the medicine. The shadow of the beautiful woman gradually disappeared. I opened the bag, put the medicine into the bottle and gave it to mother."

Her mother recovered without an operation—in what appeared to be a miracle—and Chin-yun fulfilled her promise to stop eating meat, fish or eggs, for the rest of her life.

The third was the illness of her brother, Ching-feng. In 1954, he went to hospital in the nearby city of Taichung, suffering from meningitis. Over the next eight months, she went frequently to the hospital. The experience left her with a deep respect for doctors and nurses and a sense of the bitterness and mystery of life. Her family was wealthy and able to pay the medical fees to enable her brother to recover, but he continued to suffer from the after-effects.

The fourth, and most important, was the sudden death of her father.

One day in June 1960, her father woke up with a severe headache but still went to one of his cinemas. When she joined him, Chin-yun found him lying on a sofa, in great pain. She called the family doctor, who found his blood pressure to be very high. He gave him an injection and left without further instructions. Seeing her father's discomfort, Chin-yun decided to take him home by pedicab; his condition deteriorated during the short journey. When they reached home, her father could not climb the steps and family members had to help him to his bed. He could no longer speak. The doctor was summoned again and told Chin-yun that she should not have moved her father, because it had caused a brain hemorrhage. He remained unconscious for the rest of that day and died two days later, aged only 51.

The shock and trauma of her father's death was critical in persuading Chin-yun to give up a comfortable middle-class future for a religious life. Mrs. Wang said that, for her daughter, the death was a terrible blow: she stopped eating and was too traumatized to cry. She held herself in part responsible for her father's death by having moved him from the cinema. Tormented by guilt, she ate less and less and became gaunt and pale. "Where did father go? Where is he now?" was her anguished question to everyone.

A friend suggested that she go to a Buddhist temple in Fengyuan, to seek an explanation for what had happened. She went every day to study the scriptures and was very moved by what she read.

In the temple, she met a middle-aged nun named Hsiu Dao (Learning Doctrine) (修道法師), to whom she took an instant liking. The nun recounted the story of an ancient emperor who was grief-stricken by the loss of his wife. He began to pray for her soul and invited monks and nuns to perform litanies for her. He had a dream in which his wife thanked him for what he had done and told him that she must purify her karma by her own deeds. For Chin-yun, the lesson was that nothing lasts forever except karma, which determines the whereabouts of our souls.

In the absence of her father, Chin-yun took over responsibility for the seven theatres and looking after her mother, her brothers, sister and grandmother. (Running the theatres proved an invaluable experience in later years, when she would manage a multi-million-dollar charity.) To prepare for the family's future, she sold two of the theatres, dividing the money between savings deposited in the bank and gold bars, which she stored in a safe place at home.

One day, she asked Hsiu Dao which women were blessed and was puzzled by her answer that they were the ones carrying the vegetable baskets. "I found this reply bewildering because that is what I was doing every day, carrying the basket and cooking for a large family. What was happy about that?"

The next day she went to buy vegetables at the market and, when she came to settle the account, coins and paper money tumbled to the ground. "Then I understood this happiness. I had money in my hand and could use it to support my family. In ancient times, it was no easy matter for a woman to support a family."

After paying the bill and asking the shopowner to deliver the groceries to her home, she went to the temple to speak with Hsiu Dao.

"In the home, society and the hearts of people, women have a low status, so a woman who has the power to carry the vegetable basket is blessed," she said to the nun. "If such a woman is blessed, is not this kind of life too sad? I can be a man among women. Can't I go out and save the world?" Hsiu Dao replied that that would depend on her.

With the sale of the two theatres and income from the others, Chin-yun's family had sufficient means to enable her brothers and sister to look after their mother. Now she could finally follow her true path. Chin-yun asked Hsiu Dao to recommend a temple where she could become a novice and, in the autumn of 1960, without her family's knowledge, she took the train to Taipei and joined Jing Siu (Quiet Meditation), a temple on the outskirts of the city. Unfortunately, friends she had confided in told her mother and, on her third day at the temple, she found her mother in tears in the courtyard. Unable to endure the distress she had caused, she returned with her to Fengyuan.

For the next 12 months, Chin-yun resumed her former life but retained the idea of running away. The moment came one day in the autumn of 1961, when she joined Hsiu Dao harvesting rice in a field. It was a beautiful day and the stalks of rice had bent with the weight of their grains. Working in the fields for the first time, Chin-yun was enchanted.

"Are the stalks not like people?" she said to her friend. "When they know only a little, they are arrogant. The more they learn, the more they become humble and bow their heads."

Hsiu Dao said suddenly: "Do you still want to be a nun?"

Chin-yun thought for a second and nodded: "Yes, right now."

That was the decisive moment. Having failed at the first attempt, she would not turn back this time. Her friend proposed they leave at once, without returning home. She agreed and, carrying nothing with them, the two took a pedicab to Taichung, the largest city in Central Taiwan, and boarded the next train, which took them to the Southern port city of Kaohsiung. From there they went to Taitung, in the Southwest of the island, and to the village of Lu Ye (Deer Country) where they took refuge in a small temple with no water or electricity. The two women lived a spartan life, eating food they found in the fields, reading Buddhist scriptures and praying. As the cold of winter intensified, they moved to a larger temple near Taitung.

Each evening, as the sun set, Chin-yun stared in silence toward the mountains in the West and tears welled up in her eyes. She thought of her family on the other side of the mountains and wished them health and peace.

Her mother came to fetch her daughter a second time, this time bringing Chin-yun's birth father. At first, the nuns denied that there was anyone at the temple matching the description of Chin-yun. Then, 20 minutes later she came out and agreed to return home with them saying, though, "Even if you force me to go back, it is useless. You will only be taking the empty shell and nothing else." They took a taxi to the town of Taitung, where they spent the night in a hotel. Neither woman slept—Chin-yun pondering her next move and her mother fearful her daughter would run away. The next morning they bought three bus tickets and went to the station. Chin-yun let her mother and birth father board and the bus pulled out. Suddenly, her mother saw that Chin-yun had not got on board and began to weep. "Do not cry," said the driver. "You will affect my driving on these mountain roads."

"Do not cry," said Chin-yun's birth father. "It is no use."

A month later, her mother heard a knock on her door and opened it. In front of her was a young woman with a shaven head kneeling and dressed in the clean, gray robe of a nun. The woman bowed respectfully—and Chin-yun had to tell her it was her own daughter. Her mother was shocked to see her in her new clothes, without the long hair, but she was gradually accepting Chin-yun's decision. In the early morning of the third day, Chin-yun said goodbye to her family and left, promising to write once she had settled in a new home. Mrs. Wang was not opposed to her becoming a nun but did not want her to go so far away: she considered monastic life extremely hard. In later years, she said that, when she read about Tzu Chi, she was very happy to have a daughter that had done such service for Buddha and mankind but regretted that, because she loved her too much, she had put obstacles in her way to become a nun.

In December 1962, Chin-yun and Hsiu Dao arrived in Hualien, on the East coast of Taiwan. A small town of 40,000 people, Hualien is the poorest area of the island where around 25 percent of the population are indigenous, Aboriginal Taiwanese, settled on the island prior to the migration of the Han Chinese in the seventeenth-century. By now, Chin-yun had decided not to live according to the rules of an existing community but to establish her own. The two women were introduced to a wealthy retired businessman, Hsu Chung-ming, a devout Buddhist who had financed the building of several temples. He proposed they go to live with the community of nuns at the Tung Jing Shi (Eastern Purity) temple on the outskirts of town. When she saw it, Chin-yun recognized it as the temple she had seen in the dream during her mother's illness in 1952. Her heart leapt and she decided that this was the place she was to stay.

This remote town was to become the headquarters of Tzu Chi, but in those days of poverty and solitude no one could imagine such a future.

Tung Jing Shi temple had no living quarters, so Chin-yun lived in Mr. Hsu's house and went to the temple each day to teach Buddhism to the local people. The health of Hsiu Dao, Chin-yun's companion for the last 12 months, had deteriorated to the point that she could no longer teach and so she had decided to return to her mother temple in Fengyuan.

In the spring of 1963, Chin-yun determined that she must be ordained as a nun. She went to Linchi, a major temple in Taipei, on the day of the initiation ceremony. However, she was told that she could only be ordained with the sponsorship of a master, which she did not have. Then, by chance, in a Buddhist bookshop, she met Yin Shun (印順法師), one of the most famous monks in Taiwan and an internationally acclaimed scholar of Buddhist philosophy. Chin-yun asked him to sponsor her and, against prevailing rules—because she had not studied under him—he agreed, saying that a voice in his heart was telling him that it was his karma to be her master and her karma to be his disciple. This meeting was a critical moment in her life, and one in which Tzu Chi members see as an example of Buddhist providence, a pre-ordained event that was seminal to the birth and development of the foundation.

Yin Shun, who was to become one of Chin-yun's closest advisors and confidants for more than 40 years until his death in 2005, gave her the Buddhist (Dharma) name of Cheng Yen (Master of Discipline). He also gave her a mission: "serve all living beings and enlighten them with Buddhism." The newly ordained nun took it as her mission to put into practice his doctrine of "humanist Buddhism," which means translating religious precepts into action that benefits society.

Cheng Yen remained at the Linchi temple for 32 days, learning the basic rules of an ordained nun, before moving back to Hualien in May. There she left the house of her benefactor, Mr. Hsu, and moved into a small wooden hut, of 120 square feet, which he had built for her next to the Eastern Purity temple. Inside was a picture of the Buddha and a collection of seven volumes of Buddhist scriptures.

It was a spartan existence, living on a pittance and eating one meal a day. Over the next six months, she studied the Buddhist scriptures, especially the Fa Hua Jing (Lotus Sutra). "This became my world. Half a year later, I deeply felt the great mercy of Buddha, allowing me to realize that this world could become a world of Buddhas."

On May 9, 1964, at the age of 26, she accepted her first disciple. By the end of the year she had five disciples, all women. The six of them lived together in the small hut: when they slept, they occupied the entire floor. She laid down three rules—do not accept donations from believers; do not make journeys to read the scriptures; and do not perform funeral services—the three main sources of income for monks and nuns at that time. Instead, the six earned a meager living from knitting sweaters from wool they bought from weaving factories, and sewing baby shoes from sacks used to carry grain. This small group also began charity work; taking care of two elderly ladies, and delivering to them three radishes a day, and flour cakes at Chinese New Year and on festival days.

Cheng Yen began the habit, which she has retained until today, of rising early in the morning to read the scriptures. The six recited and copied the texts and explained them to believers who came to visit. The presence of these women living a solitary life in the hut and burning an oil lamp in the middle of the night aroused the curiosity and suspicion of the villagers nearby. Some attributed it to demonic influences and others thought that it ruined the *fengshui* (geomancy) of the site. Each month, Mother arrived, after a 12-hour bus ride over the mountains from Fengyuan, with a box full of food and daily necessities. Because it was too late to return home, she too would join the others in sleeping on the *tatami* floor.

The three years following Cheng Yen's ordination were a time of study and reflection. She gained a deeper understanding of Buddhism and considered how to implement the ambitious mission Yin Shun had given her. She had already decided that the best way to practice Buddhism was to help the sick and poor. But how? She had no money, no organization and only a handful of disciples.

The birth of Tzu Chi

In early 1966, two events became the catalyst that set her ideas in motion. Cheng Yen went to visit a disciple's father, who had just had an operation at a private medical clinic in the nearby village of Fenglin. Eastern Taiwan was the poorest part of the island and its medical facilities were backward; she wanted to do something to improve them. As she left her friend's ward, she noticed a large pool of blood on a bed but no patient. The staff explained that a pregnant Aboriginal woman had been brought to the clinic, exhausted after a journey of eight hours over the mountains and in need of an operation to save her baby. The clinic had demanded a deposit of NT$8,000 ($250), which the woman and her family were unable to pay, so she had miscarried and lost her baby. Cheng Yen was stunned by the cold-heartedness of the clinic and, weeping, realized the importance of having money to do charity work.

Then, when Cheng Yen was invited by her mentor Yin Shun to join him at his temple in Chiayi, in the Southwest of the island, her disciples were bitterly opposed to her going. They would do anything, they said, if she stayed with them. Moved by their loyalty, Cheng Yen promised to stay in Hualien, asking the disciples to save NT$0.5 ($0.01) per day, to use for charity. The women did as Cheng Yen asked, putting the money into a bamboo tube each day before they went to buy food at the market. (To this day, the foundation continues to use these tubes as a symbol of collective charity. It is a way of saying that the act of giving, however little, is more important than the amount.)

Spurred on by her disciples' efforts and the medical tragedy in Fenglin, on May 14 1966, Cheng Yen formed the Taiwan Buddhist Tzu Chi Charitable Association for the Relief of Suffering. The logo was a ship inside a lotus: the ship goes where it is needed, and a lotus flower, an image of Buddhism, blossoms even in dirty water.

In shaping her organization, Cheng Yen drew inspiration from various sources, including the Christian church in Taiwan.

One Sunday, three Roman Catholic nuns who taught at a missionary school in Hualien visited her in the hut and discussed religion and philosophy. The three saw her as a potential Catholic nun and found common ground on many points. However, they asked her why Buddhists were so inactive in the community, while the Catholic Church built hospitals, schools and cared for the poor. Cheng Yen reflected that, if Buddhists continued only to chant of the misery of mankind but took no action, the tragedy of the Aboriginal woman would be repeated. After World War Two, the United States had helped Taiwan with flour and milk powder, distributed through the Christian churches. Since many Chinese were Buddhists, why could they not do what the foreigners were doing?

Like the Catholics, Protestant missionary churches were also active in Taiwan, building hospitals, schools and homes for the elderly. It was the Presbyterian medical missionaries who first brought Western medicine to the island. In 1865, James Maxwell, a Presbyterian doctor, established the first Western hospital in the Southern city of Tainan. And, in 1895, David Landsborough, also a Presbyterian doctor, set up a hospital in Changhua, in the West of the island, that remains today as the Changhua Christian Hospital. In 1926, Landsborough grafted skin from his wife onto a boy whose skin had been badly burnt, an event that became famous in Taiwan as "the skin-graft of love." The funding for these hospitals came in the form of donations. This, and the work of the missionaries was an inspiration for the medical projects, which became a major part of Tzu Chi's work.

Cheng Yen also drew inspiration from Hsiu Dao, the head of the Fengyuan temple and her first teacher of Buddhism. Hsiu Dao had described her experiences as a novice at a temple in Nagoya in Japan, where the nuns were active in performing charity work in the community. On her return to Taiwan, she was disappointed to find that the Buddhist clergy were socially inactive, engaged only in reading the scriptures and begging for money. Hsiu Dao's observations mirrored those of Yin Shun, Cheng Yen's mentor, who had said that by the early twentieth-century, Buddhism in China had become flawed and distorted, its practitioners only concerned with their personal spiritual advancement and divorced from society. For Cheng Yen, it was vital that this be changed.

"In the eyes of many, Buddhism is a passive religion and an escape from reality," she explained. "Buddhism is also viewed as the superstitious belief of the ignorant poor, who lived in backward nations and belonged to the lower class of society. I decided to bring Buddhism back to its original form, as Buddha had wanted it to be 2,500 years ago. I promised that my followers and I would prove to the world that Buddhism is a positive and active way of living and that we Buddhists would continue with our good deeds to help the suffering masses and bring joy to those who live in sorrow."

Building a Solid Foundation

Cheng Yen created a structure for the foundation, which has remained unchanged until now. Initially, she had decided to only accept nuns into the association, not followers. But she soon realized that in order for the movement to grow, followers were essential. She therefore changed the rules: followers would be welcome as members of the Tzu Chi Foundation but were required to contribute time or money or both. Thus, the foundation developed as a separate financial entity from the temple where she lived with other nuns.

The base of the organization is made up of its members. The second level consists of commissioners, who are unpaid and have three main duties: to raise money, assess who should receive assistance and tend to the sick, the poor, those in difficulty and victims of natural disasters. Commissioners regularly visit donors to collect money and inform them of how it is being spent. They must also ascertain if the financial situation of a family improves and therefore it no longer needs help. The commissioners wear a distinctive dark blue ankle-length dress and a badge on their chest with their name and commissioner number. The third level is made up of those who work directly with Cheng Yen day-to-day, like the managers of a large company. Some are nuns who live with her, some are commissioners and others are specialists who, while being members, receive a salary.

As a result of her own poor health—Cheng Yen suffers from angina pectoris and a weak liver and as a result, cannot fly and has never left Taiwan—she also realized that if she died the foundation would not be able to carry on its work without her. She needed to ensure the foundation was on a firmer footing. One way of doing this was to build institutions, such as hospitals and schools, that were financially self-supporting and that did not depend on external donations, which had been the sole source of revenue in the early years. "It was vitally important to establish a 'fountain' mechanism in order to sustain our perpetual and successful operations," she explained.

Her first disciples were 30 housewives and the small community raised money in the same way that Cheng Yen's first six disciples had, by weaving woolen sweaters and making baby shoes. They were able to save NT$1,070 ($33) per month from the sale of these goods. They also continued to collect money in a bamboo tube. During that first year, the foundation collected NT$28,768 ($900), which it used to support 15 needy people.

Lin Tseng, an 86-year-old mainland widow who was bed-ridden and lived alone in a tiny room, became the first recipient of the foundation's long-term aid. Volunteers supported her with NT$300 ($9) a month, preparing her meals, washing her clothes and caring for her until her death in February 1970. The second recipient was Lu, a vegetable vendor, to whom they gave NT$5,000 ($155) for an operation in May 1966. After an argument with her husband in November, however, Lu took her own life. This taught the members that they must maintain regular contact with those they helped. The members assisted her husband and five children for a year after her death until they were able to manage financially. In November 1967, the movement built its first house, for a blind woman, Li. That year, the number of members grew to 300 and in July they launched a monthly magazine.

In 1967, Cheng Yen's mother gave NT$110,000 ($3,500), which enabled the community to buy 160,000 square feet of land nearby, on which they could grow rice and vegetables for their own consumption. They also wanted to build a new temple, with an assembly hall, altars, a kitchen and a bathroom. One follower agreed to construct it and cover some of the costs. Cheng Yen's mother also contributed NT$200,000 ($6,000). The community still owed NT$240,000 ($6,500), which they had borrowed earlier from the bank. They paid this back over the next seven years, through sales of their products, such as toys, candles, plastic flowers and gloves for the military.

The temple was completed on March 24, 1969, and this modest white building, Jing Si Jing She (the Pure Abode of Quiet Contemplation), has since become the spiritual center and symbol of Tzu Chi around the world.

With the completion of their new spiritual home, Cheng Yen and her disciples began to broaden their mission. On the night of September 26, 1969 a fire broke out in Danan, a mountain village near Hualien inhabited by Aboriginals. The fire killed 42 people, injured 55, left 785 homeless and destroyed the entire village. Tzu Chi's relief mission launched the next day was the first in its history, and was good practice for the thousands more to come. When Cheng Yen and her disciples arrived in the village, they found humans, pig and cattle burnt black by the heat of the flames, giving off a fierce stench. They raised NT$300,000 ($9,500) and bought 148 woolen blankets and several hundred items of clothing, which they distributed, along with cash, to 148 of the worst-hit families, and built new homes for them. Not included were retired soldiers who lived in a compound in the village: angry at their exclusion, they surrounded the railway station, to prevent Cheng Yen from leaving. Her disciples begged her not to meet them but she insisted. "We respect the contribution which each of you has made to the country," she told them. "We are a civilian group, whose main role is to complement the shortfall of the government. You are all veterans of the nation and I am sure that the Defense Ministry will give you the help you need. It is not that we do not wish to help you, but our resources are limited."

On November 27, 1970, another fire broke out, this time sweeping through one of the main streets of Hualien. It destroyed 43 buildings and 300 people lost their homes. The foundation obtained from the city government a list of the victims and 10 days later distributed $863, all the money in the foundation's bank account at that time, in relief money to 72 families. That year, members of the foundation began charity work in Taichung, West Taiwan.

In September 1972, they organized the first free medical clinic in Hualien, on two afternoons a week, with doctors and nurses from the local government hospital: these lasted until 1986, when the foundation's hospital opened. During the 14-year period, the clinic treated 140,000 patients. They extended the clinics to two nearby towns, Yuli and Taitung. In March 1973, the foundation started charity work in Taipei. In December 1976, the provincial government gave it an award, in recognition for its 10 years of work.

After the first decade, Cheng Yen began to consider more permanent institutions. This led to the idea of a major general hospital for Hualien, which is the subject of our next chapter.

2

HOSPITALS

"The most painful thing in life is to fall ill. No matter the sickness of the patient, the doctors and nurses devote themselves wholeheartedly to caring for him. This is great love in its purest form, without selfishness and without blemish."

—Cheng Yen

ONE COLD MORNING IN JANUARY 1983, a group of nuns, housewives and the elderly, wearing hairnets and straw hats and carrying kitchen knives, garden saws and woodcutters, gathered in a field in Hualien. Their task was to clear the land to make way for a hospital.

From this humble beginning, Tzu Chi has grown to become a global medical mission. Today, the organization operates seven hospitals in Taiwan, including the one in Hualien. It manages the world's fifth largest bone marrow bank and has set up an international medical association with more than 10,000 physicians and volunteers who have provided free medical services for 1.4 million people around the world. In 2007, its six hospitals in Taiwan—the seventh opened that year—performed 58,000 operations, with a total of 2.7 million outpatient visits.

Of the seven hospitals, five are in rural areas, reflecting Cheng Yen's desire to bring medical services to poor people who were previously not well served. Her 10 years of charity work had shown that illness was an inseparable part of the poverty trap. When the poor fell sick, they were often unable to obtain medical treatment, their health deteriorated and they could not work and earn a living. If they were the sole breadwinner, their family suffered and their children had to drop out of school. It was a vicious circle.

"Back then, poverty pervaded Taiwan," Cheng Yen recalled. "Many patients would rather save money than see a doctor. Little did they know that what they did not pay with money, they paid with their lives. The money they saved would be spent for their funerals. There were many such tragedies."

She realized the extent of the need when Tzu Chi opened its first free clinic in Hualien in 1972. Hundreds of people crowded in. The foundation found even more people in need when they held outreach clinics in remote, difficult-to-reach areas. "Many illnesses that started out as critical but manageable medical conditions became untreatable or fatal on arrival as precious time was wasted on transportation," she said. Prior deposit before treating a patient was also common practice in most hospitals. "This disheartening rule delayed many time-sensitive treatments. Many lives were lost to this unnecessary hindrance."

Before Tzu Chi built their first hospital, Hualien had two public hospitals—one run by the government and the other by the Mennonites, a Protestant denomination. While these facilities could handle common illnesses and minor surgery, patients who required major treatment had to go to bigger hospitals in Taipei or Kaohsiung, a journey of several hours that some did not survive. Yet, economics dictated that neither the government nor a private company would consider building another hospital in a town with a falling, and largely poverty-stricken population. "Building a hospital is a long, arduous and exhausting undertaking," said Cheng Yen. "But, if I did not do it, who else would?"

A hospital in Hualien (花蓮慈濟綜合醫院)

The Tzu Chi General Hospital today is an imposing 11-story building of gray stone, surrounded by a cluster of apartment blocks for doctors, nurses and administrative staff. It has 2,000 staff, including 320 doctors, receives a daily average of 2,000 outpatients and has 1,000 inpatients. State-of the–art facilities (the surgery wing has been designed so that doctors can continue operations during earthquakes of up to seven on the Richter scale) and equipment ensure the hospital's reputation remains high, and it even operates its own medical school, a nursing college, and a medical research centre with aspirations of becoming the Mayo Clinic of the Far East.

Yet the journey in coming this far has not been easy, and the walls of the hospital tell an extraordinary story: it is the first Buddhist hospital built in China in the two millennia since the religion arrived from India in the first century A.D. It was built not with government money but with donations from thousands of individuals, inspired by the idea of building a hospital in the poorest part of the country. And it was the first hospital that did not require patients to pay a deposit before they were admitted.

Cheng Yen wanted a hospital for the most disadvantaged and thus chose Hualien because it was the poorest county in Taiwan. She conceived the hospital as the first in the country that did not require patients to pay a deposit before they were admitted, and in which staff gave equal attention to a patient's spiritual and psychological health as to their physical condition.

In May 1979, she proposed the idea of a general hospital to her mentor Yin Shun, who was spending the holiday in Hualien. His first reaction was to ask if she would be able to take on this daunting task, given her own poor health; nonetheless he expressed his support. On May 15, to a meeting of all 200 commissioners, most of them poor and middle-class housewives, she announced her plan to build a 600-bed hospital in Hualien at a cost of NT$80 million ($2 million). It was to have a wide range of departments, she explained to them, comparable to a major city hospital. The audience gasped: "How can it be done?" With only 30,000 members in the whole island, they considered the project completely out of reach—how to raise the money and attract qualified staff to work in such a remote and backward area. They also feared for the stress such a project would put on Cheng Yen herself. She told them to trust the love and compassion hidden in the hearts of people. Reaction among the public and the government was disbelief: how would a penniless nun leading a movement of housewives find the capital and management expertise for such a project, and what doctor would work there?

Cheng Yen received her first shock soon afterwards. She called the deputy chief of a major hospital in Taipei, who said that the 600-bed facility she had in mind would cost about NT$800 million ($20 million)—10 times her original estimate. "It gave me a sinking feeling. But I immediately told myself that, to save lives, the hospital needed to be built. I therefore stopped focusing on difficulties."

The first donation came from a professor, Chen Can-hui, a member of the foundation and husband of a commissioner in Taipei. He was also a devout Catholic and admirer of Mother Teresa. Professor Chen gave 15 taels of gold—each tael worth NT$15,000 ($470).

The first challenge was to find a site. Hualien sits on a narrow sliver of land between a mountain range and the Pacific Ocean. Most of the land belonged to government institutions and the military, which regarded the town, with the largest port on the East coast, as a place of strategic importance. Then, as now, it maintained a large air base in the town. In Taiwan under martial law, power was concentrated in the hands of the government and armed forces.

Cheng Yen entrusted Lin Bi-yu (林碧玉), a lifetime associate and now one of the foundation's three vice-presidents, with finding a site. She chose Lin because she was educated, well connected in the town and one of the few members with her own car. A trained accountant, Lin had her own firm and used to spend half the week playing golf, until she decided to devote her life to the foundation. The assignment proved difficult. She found officials unwilling to help, since they did not believe that a group of nuns and housewives with almost no money would be able to complete such a large project. She traveled around Taiwan, visiting hospitals, to learn their organization, recruiting and financing methods. For more than a year, she searched in vain for a suitable site. The breakthrough came on October 16, 1980, when the provincial governor, Lin Yang-gang (林洋港), came to visit Hualien.

"I had heard of Master Cheng Yen from representatives in Hualien," recalled Lin, 80, in an interview. "They spoke of her as a remarkable person, who was giving aid to the poor and lived in a self-reliant community that grew vegetables and made candles. When I met her in person, I was also moved. Tzu Chi was compensating for the inadequacies of the government, doing what the government did not do."

Cheng Yen told Lin that during its frequent typhoons and earthquakes, Hualien was cut off from the rest of the island and sick people requiring major operations could not be treated. That day, Lin gave NT$10,000 ($310) of his own money. Two of his children later became commissioners: Lin and his wife have each given NT$1 million ($310,000) to the foundation. "People in the government, at the central and local levels, supported the project," he said.

Lin sent a report to then President Chiang Ching-kuo, who arrived in Hualien three days later and went to visit Cheng Yen. He was similarly moved and praised the foundation as a model for efficient use of private donations. "You are extraordinary," the president said. "I have been everywhere but have never seen such a small temple able to do so much charity work." This gave the project government backing at the highest level and changed the attitude of local officials who had been reluctant to co-operate.

To promote the project and raise funds, Cheng Yen toured Taiwan each month and held meetings in the homes of her commissioners. In September 1981, a professor who had fallen ill in Hualien and had to be taken to Taipei for treatment sold her family property and donated more than NT$1 million ($310,000). In mid-1981, the government gave Tzu Chi eight hectares ideally situated in the town. Of the land, 80 percent was owned by the county government, 10 percent by the national government and 10 percent by private citizens. Some of them did not want to sell, while some of those holding leases on the public land did not want to move. It took 18 months of painstaking negotiations to persuade them to move and it was only in January 1983—more than three and a half years after the start of the project—that they secured the site. In two days, volunteers cleared the grass, trees and bushes, using tools they brought from home. They saved the foundation the NT$1 million ($310,000) it would have cost to hire professionals to do the job.

They held a ground-breaking ceremony on February 5, 1983, attended by the provincial governor and later president Lee Teng-hui, who himself donated NT$30,000 ($1,000) and promised to become a member. But the financial outlook was bleak. After nearly four years of effort by volunteers, the foundation had raised just NT$30 million ($900,000), less than 5 percent of the NT$800 million ($20 million) needed. On the day of the groundbreaking, heavy rain lashed down on the site, giving Cheng Yen a sense of foreboding. "As I watched the VIPs push their shovels to break the ground, I felt ambivalent. It was wonderful to have acquired the land. But, once the construction got underway, we would need to pay workers twice a month. With construction looming and insufficient money, I felt like a short candle burning at both ends."

She was right to be worried. Two weeks later, a military officer arrived at the Abode and gave her a notice saying that the site was needed for military purposes and had been confiscated. In martial-law Taiwan, there was no appeal against the military. Later, the members learned that, close to the proposed site, the air force was planning to drill tunnels into the base of a mountain, as a place to store planes. At the time the government approved the sale of the land, the plan was a military secret. The air force would not allow buildings close to the new base.

"The news hit me like a thunderbolt," Cheng Yen recalled. "I was totally devastated. I could not eat or sleep. I even thought about returning all the donations because the project could no longer proceed." A single sheet of paper had wiped out four years of painstaking work and the goodwill of thousands of people. For several days, she did not eat or sleep but knelt in grief in front of the statue of the Buddha in the temple at the Abode.

"Those were dark days, with suffering I cannot describe. I could not bear to break the bad news to my supporters. Outwardly, I showed confidence and smiles but, inside, I swallowed the pain and anxiety."

But the goodwill built up in the government paid off. A month later, Lin Yang-gang, now Minister of Interior, called to say he would help to find a new site. He proposed a plot of eight hectares, close to the town's new railway station. A second ground-breaking ceremony was held on April 24, 1984, attended by 3,000 people, including Yin Shun, other senior Buddhist monks and Minister Lin, who personally donated NT$200,000 ($6,000). By then, Tzu Chi had 60,000 members and 600 commissioners, a six-fold increase in five years, largely due to the publicity generated by the hospital. One participant at the ceremony was Lee Teng-hui, who had replaced Lin as governor of Taiwan province. He offered the land to the foundation at a peppercorn rent of NT$1 ($0.02). To the surprise of her disciples, Cheng Yen refused the offer. She thanked Lee for his good intentions but said that, in future, he would go on to higher posts, others would replace him and the decision could be challenged. So she preferred to pay the going rate for the land. It was a prudent decision. With the completion of a railway around the island, land prices in Hualien soared, including the hospital site.

Now construction had begun, the next issue was how to raise the money. A wealthy Japanese real estate developer offered Cheng Yen the extraordinary sum of $200 million. He was a devout Buddhist who had grown up in Hualien and had a great fondness for the town. A Japanese colony from 1895-1945, Taiwan is the only part of its former empire to cherish its colonial past. The donor also wished to show his gratitude to President Chiang Kai-shek for allowing Taiwan's 600,000 Japanese residents to return home smoothly at the end of the war and for not seeking wartime reparations from Japan, a decision which helped toward its swift reconstruction after World War Two. The members were overjoyed, believing that the problem of fund-raising had been solved.

To their bewilderment, Cheng Yen refused the donation, saying that the hospital should be built with the gifts of thousands of individual Taiwanese and would as a result have a broad and strong foundation, with donors feeling a sense of identity with the hospital. "The goodness of one person is different to that of 10 million people," she said in a later interview. "If I had accepted the donation from the Japanese, the hospital would be different to what it is today. It would only have the functionality of a hospital but not its sense of goodness. I hoped to build a hospital that people in Taiwan would care about. It would be a hospital that was not stiff and cold but a hospital that was enthusiastic, caring and people-oriented. What better way to achieve this than to have many people work hard at building it?" It reflected her belief that charity works both ways, helping the giver as well as the receiver. The hospital was the opportunity to awaken the goodwill of thousands of people, who would never have given if she had accepted the money from the Japanese. She was also uneasy about a possible conflict in the future, if the interests of the donor diverged from those of the foundation.

Shocked but accepting, the members moved fundraising into high gear, with charity events, bazaars and auctions. It was not easy. Many Buddhists would donate toward a new temple but needed persuasion that a group of housewives could build a large hospital. Some donated money and others gold, jewelry, works of art, land and buildings. For the more than 200 people who each gave NT$1 million ($31,000), Cheng Yen created a new title of "honorary director" and gave them each a document to mark the donation. Many members took second jobs, including washing dishes and cleaning the streets, and donated this additional income to the project. Members held auctions selling dresses, gold, jewelry and other valuables. Many donors were ordinary people, such as street vendors, hairdressers, domestic helpers and laborers, who found the space in a tight budget to make a contribution. Among them were lepers at the Losheng Sanatorium in Taipei county, some of whom donated their life savings, in the form of coins saved since the end of World War Two. "They were ordinary people with the most extraordinary capacity for love," Cheng Yen commented. The contractors also helped, cutting nine months off the three-year construction period and spending only $14 million or 70 percent of the original $20 million budget.

The next task was to persuade specialist doctors to work in Hualien, which proved to be more difficult than building the hospital. As in other countries, the biggest hospitals and best medical expertise are concentrated in the major cities—Taipei, Kaohsiung and Taichung. Hualien, a poor town connected to the rest of the island by a slow railway only completed in 1980, was unattractive to a young, ambitious doctor who wanted to earn the most money from his specialty, be close to the latest research and have the best education for his children. "The nervousness that we might not get enough doctors before the hospital opened was overwhelming," Cheng Yen recalled.

A year prior to the hospital opening, the organization advertised for doctors; no one applied. Lin Bi-yu had also been spending months pounding the streets of Taipei trying to persuade doctors to go to Hualien. But it seemed that no one wanted to come and work full-time in this remote town. Lin could only get the National Taiwan University (NTU) and other hospitals to agree to send their doctors to Hualien for regular clinics. One evening, after futile hours at NTU hospital, the most prestigious in the island, she knelt in the rain on a street close to a high-speed railway line. This determined lady was close to despair: "I thought of throwing myself onto the track. But then I reflected—the papers would report it the next morning and what would they say? So I did not do it."

The opening ceremony was held on August 17, 1986. The new hospital had five stories, 250 beds and four departments. Two NTU dentists, who had agreed only at the urging of their department head to come to Hualien to work, attended the event. There were no doctors in attendance.

"Each brick and each grain of sand contain the drops of blood and heart of the pure morality of Tzu Chi," Cheng Yen said at the ceremony. "The construction of the hospital is for the interests of all. It is an opportunity for the expression of love. The members of Tzu Chi will, through concrete actions, implement the compassionate ideal of the Buddha." There followed two weeks of free medicine, during which 7,353 people came to seek care, at a total cost of NT$3.3 million ($103,000). To make the hospital less forbidding, Cheng Yen encouraged the playing of music in the large public areas and the wards. This has become a feature of Tzu Chi hospitals.

She appointed as chief of the hospital Tu Shih-mien, deputy director of NTU hospital for 12 years, who was suffering from liver cancer. He was diagnosed as having only several months left to live. "Does the Master know that there is a time bomb ticking away in my body?" Tu asked. To this, Cheng Yen replied that her heart condition was also a time bomb. "If it explodes, then it will explode," she said. "So we must cherish time all the more. If we have one more day to live, we should use it to the fullest." Tu lived for a further six years. His successor was a former director of NTU hospital, Tseng Wen-bin. Less than a month after the hospital opened, the new provincial governor, Chiu Chuang-huan, came for a visit. He was so impressed by what he saw that he made a donation of NT$6 million ($190,000).

NTU finally agreed to give Hualien the same status as Saudi Arabia, to which it sent doctors on two-year assignments. In exchange for working in such a place, they received a promotion to department chief. In this way, the hospital obtained a supply of doctors, if not permanent ones. For the young graduates, the rice paddies and sugar cane fields of Hualien were equal to the deserts of Saudi Arabia!

The shortage of qualified personnel persisted during the first two years. "The number of doctors willing to come was always very limited," Cheng Yen commented. "It was like rubbing the skin to get blood out." Some doctors on short-term assignments did not put their heart into it: they knew they would not stay for long and it was merely a step toward promotion. Some could not be bothered to treat minor ailments and patients who did not require hospitalization. Graduates of a major teaching hospital, they regarded local people with disdain. All this damaged the hospital's reputation.

Then, out of the blue, in 1988 a group of five young doctors from NTU chose to go to Hualien to work, a decision that shook the medical community in Taiwan. They were moved by Cheng Yen's ideals of care—of the heart and spirit of the patient as well as the body. They were uneasy at the growing commercialization of their profession and believed that the Hualien hospital would offer a closer doctor-patient relationship. Other doctors followed: this enabled the hospital to move from providing only basic health care to becoming a research center.

The shortage of staff persuaded Cheng Yen to set up her own nursing college in Hualien. It opened its door in September 1989, with 107 students, the first private nursing school in Taiwan. Her objective was not only to produce well-trained professionals but also to nurture their love and compassion. In 1995, the government named it as one of the top five nursing schools in Taiwan. From 1996, the college offered 50 free places to Aboriginal students. If students agreed to work in the Hualien hospital upon graduation, they did not have to pay tuition fees. But even today the facility still suffers from a shortage of nurses.

To assure a better supply of doctors and ensure that the hospital would be sustainable over the long term, Cheng Yen also decided to set up a medical school. The Ministry of Education initially refused her application, since its forecasts showed a surfeit of doctors. Intense lobbying persuaded the ministry to change its mind and it gave its approval in July 1990. Construction began in March 1993, on a site a short walk from the hospital.

Cheng Yen persuaded Lee Ming-liang, 60, an eminent biologist from Miami University, to give up a well-paid salary and comfortable life in the United States and return to Taiwan as director of the medical school. Explaining their decision, his wife said that Tzu Chi gave them the same feeling of warmth and friendship they had when they left Taiwan 30 years ago. "Our material life is very rich but we felt that Tzu Chi was like going home." The medical school opened on October 16, 1994, at a ceremony attended by 10,000 members.

Today, when doctors and nurses complete their studies, they attend a solemn ceremony at the Abode, attended by Cheng Yen. Wearing their white uniforms, they swear to put the patient's welfare as their priority and to treat everyone equally, regardless of race, religion, nationality, gender or social status. Cheng Yen puts stethoscopes around their necks and tells them that this is their mission for life and that they should not only be good professionals but also warm-hearted people dedicated to the well-being of the patients. She also emphasizes that they should treat the patients as their teachers and learn from them. "The human body is very mysterious and needs years of study. Doctors should be humble, admit that there is much they do not know and be willing to learn from others," she said.

To improve the quality of care and to attract doctors eager to work with new technology, the hospital spent heavily on state-of-the-art equipment and material. In 1992, it also set up the Tzu Chi Medical Research Center, with this objective.

Lin Hsin-rong (林欣榮), one of Taiwan's most eminent brain surgeons and head of the Hualien hospital from 2001 until April 2007 explains, "Our equipment is worldclass, bought from the U.S., Switzerland and Germany. In the last five years, the hospital has invested NT$400 million ($10 million) in such equipment.

"I developed the hospital by raising the medical standards and attracting doctors with the promise of being able to do pioneering work and exploiting their full potential, in fields like treatment of strokes and Parkinson's disease. The Tzu Chi medical system means holistic care of body, mind and spirit."

Lin Hsin-rong's department (he is still a surgeon in the brain neurology department) performs 30 operations a week, in some of which he takes part. He was especially proud of treating victims of strokes, the second leading cause of death in Taiwan.

"Because of the influence of Great Love Television, many international patients with special diseases come to Hualien for medical treatment and assistance. We are working together to create an Oriental Mayo Clinic."

Being head of a Tzu Chi hospital means more than medical duties. As director, Lin worked each day from 5:30 AM to 10:30 PM, with no holidays. His schedule included speeches, television appearances, receiving visiting delegations and Tzu Chi social and community activities. One such activity took place on May 13, 2007, Buddha's birthday, where heads of the foundation's hospitals took part in a sign language performance based on a Buddhist scripture. Some rehearsed in front of a computer in their office, others prepared after an operation, still wearing the white uniforms they wore in the theatre. The hospital chiefs are also expected to take part in volunteer activities, like planting rice and cleaning the homes of poor people.

"Cheng Yen works from 3:30 AM to 10:30 PM every day of the year and asks others to do the same. How can we refuse?" Lin said.

"The dominant culture in Taiwan emphasizes individualism and materialism. We are fighting this by creating our own humanist culture, based on teamwork. If you give, you receive a greater reward. A simple life is enough for me—NT$50 ($1.50) a day for food and a modest apartment. Too much money is trouble."

Low-Key Ambience

Like all Tzu Chi institutions, the hospital in Hsintien, Taipei City, was built and operates according to Cheng Yen's holistic ethic—to give "equal attention to a patient's spiritual and psychological health as to their physical condition."

Opened in May 2005, Hsintien today is a large general hospital, with 42 departments offering the full range of medical services, including community health education and public health work.

Incorporating the work of more than 220 volunteers who serve at the hospital each day was a major consideration for architects, who created a spacious lobby where volunteers greet patients and help them with registration and in finding their ward. On the wall of the lobby is a large mosaic showing the Buddha and his disciples caring for a sick person. The ground floor boasts a large bookshop, manned by volunteers, and space for a grand piano where regular music, dance and sign language performances are held.

Soft music permeates the building to help create a peaceful and harmonious atmosphere, along with the low-key colors of gray, green and white, standard issue for all Tzu Chi buildings. On the mezzanine floor is a Starbucks, the only one of more than 8,000 in the world that serves no meat. On a lower floor is a giant food court, with a wide variety of cuisines and tastes, all vegetarian. While extensive use of sunlight, and widespread use of solar panels aim to save electricity, of the hospital's 18,000 square yards, two thirds is green space, including a large garden in front of the entrance, as well as terraces and roof gardens on each floor.

As per the Tzu Chi way, volunteers also played an important role during the construction of the hospital; they collected donations in Taiwan and abroad, helped in the planning and design, and worked on the site to complement the contractors and laborers. During the six years of construction, volunteers went to the site every day, offering to take the blood pressure of the workers and giving them food and drink. Under their influence, many of the workers gave up smoking, drinking and chewing betel nuts—three of the items Tzu Chi members have to eschew.

A hospital in Talin (大林慈濟醫院)

In the early 1990s, residents of Chiayi in Southwest Taiwan asked Tzu Chi to establish a hospital in their district. Cheng Yen made several visits and, after long deliberation, decided on a site in the small town of Talin, with a population of 30,000 and the center of a district with just eight hospital beds for every 10,000 people. She envisaged a facility with 1,000 beds, including 600 acute-care beds and 400 chronic-care beds, on a site of 46 acres. After three years of lobbying with the state-owned Taiwan Sugar Corporation, which owned the land, construction began in October 1996. The hospital opened on August 13, 2000, at a cost of NT$5 billion ($150 million), raised from Tzu Chi members around the world. This project stimulated an outpouring of donations—through charity banquets, the sale of recycled goods and designer T-shirts, and by singing Christmas carols—and a willingness to help: to landscape the hospital grounds, volunteers planted trees, pulled weeds and paved an area of 66,000 square meters with 720,000 bricks, in just 10 days.

Today, the Talin hospital is 12 stories high with 820 beds, receives about 2,500 outpatients a day, and has a paid staff of about 1,500, including 150 physicians. One third of the staff are members of Tzu Chi, or those who share its ideals.

General Electric (GE), Siemens and Philips all competed fiercely to provide the hospital with state-of-the-art equipment, with GE winning the contract. "Our equipment is better than in the U.S.," boasted hospital director Lin Chin-lon (林俊龍). "We got a good deal from General Electric, which wanted us as a showcase. They wanted to be able to sell to other hospitals so they sold us the whole series below cost."

In 1995, Lin gave up a prestigious post as superintendent of the Northridge Hospital Medical Center near Los Angeles, with a high salary and a spacious house, to work in Tzu Chi's hospital in Hualien. He later moved to Talin.

"At my going away party in the States, a former professor of mine at the University of California said I was crazy to give up all that I had built up in 25 years and move to a remote and backward area. I told him it was an opportunity to do something for Taiwan, for Buddhism and for the medical profession. I could put my 25 years of experience to use. The Catholic church has 6,000 hospitals in the world and Tzu Chi will be like that too."

The hospital's color scheme is gray, blue and green, to give a sense of calm. It has a room for worship, for use by people of all religions, and a ward for the terminally ill. This is equipped with a kitchen, where families can make patients their favorite food, a living room with a piano, and a terrace. Lin Chin-lon has also brought art and culture into the hospital. The spacious lobby contains a bookshop, and musicians and singers often perform here. Patients can listen to the piano, accordion, *erhu* (two-stringed bowed instrument) and dulcimer while they are waiting for treatment.

"Other hospitals are colder," he explained. "Patients feel differently here. They are more at home. The hospital is one family, which is very good. We also have a nursery and kindergarten, and provide patients with 'one-stop shopping' so they can find what they need in one area."

Chin-lon said the hospital was self-sufficient. Of its income, 10 percent comes from the patients and 90 percent from insurance—from the government and also from insurance companies. The government's mandatory health insurance has certainly eased the financing of Tzu Chi hospitals. The scheme, introduced in 1995, has provided coverage to eight million Taiwanese, many of whom are potential patients of Tzu Chi hospitals.

Even so, recruiting staff for this rural hospital continues to prove difficult.

A land of sugar cane fields, tea gardens, fruit trees and small factories, Talin is, like Hualien, a rural community, with a large proportion of elderly people: many young people leave the area to find work elsewhere. "Recruiting staff is a major problem," said Lin. "A lot of people do not want to come here. Some doctors leave and others rise to the opportunity. Most of the staff who have joined us have done so because they agree with Tzu Chi's medical philosophy."

Among them is Chien Jui-teng (簡瑞騰), chief of the department of orthopedic medicine. A native of Talin, whose parents live 10 minutes from the hospital, he graduated in 1990 from medical school in Taipei and, after two years of military service, went to work in the Hualien hospital. He was attracted by the opportunity to work in his hometown: Tzu Chi already had plans to build the Talin hospital.

"It was an adventure. I was not after money and wanted to study. The equipment in Hualien was not as good as Taipei but there was good potential to develop. Many patients meant more possibilities to practice. I spent nine years in Hualien and worked almost seven days a week. The staff was few and the workload large. There were many traffic accidents, as motorcyclists did not wear helmets and drove fast. Accidents were also caused by drink driving and injuries were severe. But Hualien was also more rural, so you could talk more honestly with people. In Taipei, you sometimes have to lie and there is a power hierarchy. Hualien suited my character."

Chien is delighted to return to his hometown and wants to stay for the rest of his life. He prefers a Tzu Chi hospital, he says, because it is not profit making and does not aim to maximize profits from government and patients.

"The management must be sophisticated and calculate the money carefully. The hospital basically breaks even. Other hospitals use improper means to raise money from patients, government and insurance companies. We have back-up from Tzu Chi. Cheng Yen has not changed her core belief, to do whatever is best for the patient."

This translates into a work schedule from 3:30 AM to 9:00 PM almost every day of the year. On call all the time, Chien lives with his family in an apartment building next to the hospital. "Some patients ask for me in person and I cannot refuse."

Working in a Tzu Chi hospital requires a dedication in time and energy over and above that needed in government and other private facilities. And, understandably, the demands are too much for some; Talin, for example, has a higher staff turnover than other Taiwan hospitals. But as Chien explained, "Those who stay can adapt. To work in a Tzu Chi hospital is a blessing for me. I get unexpected feedback: joy from the patients and praise from colleagues and volunteers. If I were in another hospital, I would do more surgery and earn more money. But when I meet my former classmates, I find we are different—they think about how to create more patients and make more money. If doctors stay here a long time, they gradually incorporate the Tzu Chi philosophy into their lives."

Cheng Yen summarizes the task of her medical staff. "The most painful thing in life is to fall ill. No matter the sickness of the patient, the doctors and nurses devote themselves wholeheartedly to caring for him. This is great love in its purest form, without selfishness and without blemish."

This ideal has also inspired tens of thousands of people to work as unpaid volunteers in her hospitals, to help the patients and their families through the trauma of medical treatment and aid the doctors and nurses. No other hospitals in the island—and few in the world— have this abundance of volunteers, who come from all walks of life.

The determination of a single person, the goodwill of thousands of individual donors, and the dedication of those willing to help the poor and those in need is encapsulated in Tzu Chi's hospitals. The next chapter takes a look at the people who selflessly serve in these hospitals and the wider community—the volunteers.

3

VOLUNTEERS

---

*"That day I found the meaning of life. It was a bad moment.
Taiwan had left the United Nations and the U.S. had recognized
Beijing. Of my eight classmates, six had emigrated and property
prices had collapsed. There was a feeling of hopelessness
about the future. My husband had a modest salary, so that we
could not emigrate. Cheng Yen gave us hope for the future of
Taiwan. Other people talked but she was doing something. That
impressed me greatly."*

—Lin Sheng-sheng, Tzu Chi commissioner in Taipei

IF CHENG YEN IS THE BRAIN OF TZU CHI, its one million volunteers
are its arms and legs. It is they who deliver food, clothes and blankets to
victims of floods and earthquakes in Turkey, Indonesia and Argentina,
sit with a patient and his family after a cancer operation and clean
the house of an elderly widow who has given up caring for herself. The
size and range of activities of this unpaid army of students, housewives,
company managers and retired people is what sets the foundation apart
from other religious groups and charities. The volunteers are its core,
with the nuns at the Abode playing a supporting role. It is a Buddhist
organization in which lay people are the main players. Of the one
million, 10 percent work full-time and, for many of them, this means
seven days a week, 365 days a year. The others work as often as job
and family commitments allow. They are inspired by Cheng Yen's call to
become bodhisattvas, living Buddhas: that means implementing unselfish
love in the human world, donating their time, spirit and energy to their
fellow humans.

When Cheng Yen announced the establishment of the bone marrow bank in October 1993, it was volunteers who were on the streets the next day with placards and microphones, trying to persuade a reluctant public to register as donors. When a tsunami hit Southeast Asia on Boxing Day 2004, the volunteers set out at once to collect money at railway stations, schools and shopping centers, to aid the victims. When patients arrive at the foundation's hospitals, it is volunteers wearing brown waistcoats who greet them at the door, guide them through the registration procedure and escort them to their wards. Each morning, thousands of volunteers leave home with pushcarts, bicycles and pick-up trucks and clear the streets of their town of the garbage of the night before. "We are different to other charities," said Cheng Yen. "In most of them, the majority of the members are professionals. In Tzu Chi, the majority are volunteers."

Volunteers were central to Tzu Chi from the day of its foundation. Cheng Yen's objective of "Buddhism in the human world" meant that hers was a movement not of monks and nuns meditating and chanting sutras in a temple but of lay people relieving the sickness, poverty and grief of their neighbors. In those early days, the volunteers visited families in Hualien with a sick parent and gave them money for medical care. They cleaned the house of elderly people living alone with no one to care for them and gave them rice and cooking oil. At Chinese New Year, they distributed blankets and padded jackets to the poor and held a festive meal for those with no family. Today, their work has diversified and gone global—flying overseas to deliver emergency relief and medical treatment, serving as "uncles and aunts" to students at the foundation's nursing college, caring for cancer patients in a hospital, supporting a bone marrow recipient and his family and clearing beaches of the debris left by sun-bathers. But the concept remains the same as it was in 1966: help others and, by so doing, help yourself.

As Cheng Yen explains it, volunteers choose to serve because they benefit as much as the people they help. They are doing it willingly and not out of a sense of duty. They say they gain a sense of happiness and satisfaction that cannot be bought by money.

"People ask me to what school of Buddhism does Tzu Chi belong?" Are we a meditation school or a Pure Land school? I tell them that we take the interaction between humans as our place of cultivation. This is the Tzu Chi school."

In traditional Buddhism, the monk cultivates himself in the temple or monastery by meditating, reciting scriptures or teaching the faithful.

In Tzu Chi philosophy, the hospital, the area hit by flood or earthquake, the recycling center and the old people's home have replaced the temple and the monastery as the places where people practice Buddhism. As the monk learns by reading a holy text and debating with his colleagues in the temple, so the Tzu Chi volunteer learns from bathing a hospital patient, comforting a bereaved relative and distributing aid to flood victims. Cheng Yen's mission is to implement Buddhism in the human world, in the society of today, so the volunteers must go where people are most in need of help.

The largest number of volunteers serve in the foundation's hospitals, where the suffering of humans is most intense and the help of others most needed. "A hospital is like Hell," said Cheng Yen. "As long as there are people in hell, then there will have to be Buddhas." While other hospitals in Taiwan and abroad use volunteers to help doctors and nurses care for the patients, none does so on the same scale as Tzu Chi; in 2007, there were 225,000 volunteer shifts in its six hospitals.

On the day it opened its doors on August 17, 1986, the Hualien hospital set up a volunteer unit. In establishing this unit, Cheng Yen had two objectives. One was to improve the quality of care for the patients and give them a personalized service over and above that provided by busy doctors and nurses. She wanted to make the new facility feel less like a hospital and introduce joy and laughter into a place of death and pain, with music, songs, dance and dialogue. Curing the heart of the patient is as important as curing his body.

Her second objective was aimed at the volunteers: to enable them to see the whole human experience—birth, aging, sickness and death—so that they could understand the impermanence of life and cherish more the blessings they have. So the process would help both the patients and the volunteers.

Volunteers are first given training by doctors, nurses and experienced volunteers, in basic nursing, medicine, psychology, communication and performances. In the single year of 2001, for example, the foundation held 365 training classes, attended by 38,869 volunteers. They continue this training on a regular basis.

They support the medical staff by checking blood pressure, changing sheets, shaving, massaging and cleaning the patients, escorting them from one ward to another, providing spiritual help and comfort to them and their families and cleaning the bodies of those who have passed away. They entertain the patients with songs, dancing and performances, keep in touch with their families and bring them items they need from the outside. They support and encourage the doctors and nurses, especially those who are overworked and under stress. They clean the floors, weed the gardens and work in the kitchens.

They also serve in the anatomy department of the medical school, where they chant sutras as the students dissect the bodies donated by members, to show respect to the spirits of the departed. When the students have finished their work, the volunteers are responsible for taking the remains to the crematorium. It is not work for the faint-hearted. Volunteers say that, initially, they were reluctant to touch the bodies of dead people but that, with practice and the support of other volunteers and the professional staff, they became used to it. The process is an opportunity for the students to learn the secrets of the human body, and for the volunteers an education about life and death.

Some hospital volunteers are full-time but most are people in employment or working mothers, who make the time because they want the experience of serving. Such is the demand that they must apply and wait for the opportunity, often for several months, to serve for several days. They come from different walks of life, from company executives and PhDs to farmers and working people with little education, from children to senior citizens in their 90s, and even some in wheelchairs. This mixing of social classes is part of their spiritual cultivation, a chance to meet people of a different class and background in a setting in which they have a common purpose. However important a post a person holds outside the hospital, once he dons the brown waistcoat, he becomes the equal of his fellow volunteers and must behave accordingly. He must accept the orders given to him by the doctors, nurses and his team leader. It is an opportunity for the company director and university professor to practice humility.

This interaction is part of joining Tzu Chi. It gives the volunteer a social circle outside that of his family and his work-colleagues. It gives him an opportunity to meet people from a wide range of social classes and professions and make friends he would never meet in his normal life.

Yen Hui-mei (顏惠美), who has been head of the volunteer unit at the Hualien hospital since its inception, is a role model for others. After 25 years of full-time service, few know the pain and anguish of the sick and dying as well as she does. She was among the first volunteers to go to the mainland, when everyone feared they would not be allowed to return if they spoke out of turn, and to Indonesia, a country full of hatred against Chinese. She was one of the first volunteers to treat AIDS patients at a time when people feared that washing their wounds or touching their blood would infect the person doing it.

Yen joined the foundation in March 1982 after a meeting with Cheng Yen and the following year was asked to look after a sick Buddhist teacher with a severe leg injury, which she had been unable to treat because her family was too poor. Cheng Yen asked Yen to accompany the teacher to Taipei through the surgery and rehabilitation. What should have been a service of two weeks turned into an ordeal of more than three months. The patient was often in pain and could not sleep and Yen stayed up with her throughout the night. It was a harsh apprenticeship for what turned out to be a lifelong mission of caring for the sick. She oversaw a rapid increase in the number of volunteers at the Hualien hospital—5,490 in 1986, the first year, rising to 9,123 in 1987, 18,230 in 1991 and 30,074 in 1996. In 1993, she published a book of 23 accounts of the patients she had treated. "In my life, there were far too many such stories for me to write them all down," she said.

She was caring for an 87-year-old patient, from the Aboriginal Amei tribe, who had fallen into a coma. Her family, devout Catholics, had given up hope of reviving her. One day, Yen began to sing her a hymn in the Amei language. Suddenly, during the second verse, the old woman joined in. Yen summoned a nurse, who found that her condition had stabilized, and three days later she was able to leave the hospital. As she was leaving, she told Yen, "it was your hymn that awoke me."

There is a long queue among Tzu Chi members to serve at the hospitals, especially the mother facility in Hualien. A typical volunteer was a woman in her 40s who came from Tainan, in Southwest Taiwan, to work there for a week. "I have a normal job and arrange to be a volunteer during my holidays. Today I went to the anatomy room, when they were dissecting the bodies, and chanted sutras to calm the spirits of the dead. They were supposed to linger for 48 hours before going to another place. We wanted to make them calm. It was very moving. I realized how precious my body is and that I do not need to buy make-up," she explained.

This is a common response from volunteers, who say that the experience transforms them as much as it does the patients. Caring for elderly people makes them reflect on how they have cared for—or not—their own parents. Seeing how intensely people with serious diseases fight for life, makes them think of their own health and whether they are doing enough to protect it. When they watch a young person die "before his time," they reflect on their own good fortune and that of their family. Seeing the pain of the patients diminishes the importance of their own troubles at home. Service in the hospital makes them look again at their own life and how to improve it spiritually.

Lin Sheng-sheng, a plump, vigorous woman in middle age who is a commissioner in Taipei, served as a volunteer at the Hualien hospital. "Once my husband lost his temper with me: I smiled and did not react. I thought of a man with a stroke whom I had seen in the Hualien hospital a few days earlier. His body was paralyzed from the neck down, but his brain was clear. I thought to myself: 'How lucky it is that my husband has the strength to criticize me and has not had a stroke.'" Lin said that, after she joined the foundation and became a volunteer, her personality changed. "I felt happier and more motivated. Everything changed in me, except my body. I used to criticize my husband for earning too little. Our family of five lived in an apartment of 320 square feet and I saw people in apartments of 1,000 square feet. But, when I saw a family of six living in a space of 95 square feet, I realized how fortunate we were and thanked my husband. My Tzu Chi membership did not mean that I neglected my family. I organized my time better. My material demands diminished. Before, I liked to wear outfits that were different to others. After, I wanted to wear the same. With a uniform, you do not need to spend much. You must be conscious of the image of the movement and train yourself."

Volunteers have duties outside the hospitals. One is to care for the poor and elderly. This involves visiting poor families and assessing their need for assistance. The volunteers must investigate the circumstances and income of each family and the living conditions of their home. They check information given by the applicant with relatives and neighbors. If they decide that the family merits financial aid, they will give it on a regular basis. They make follow-up visits every three months to ensure that the foundation's money is well used. The aim is to encourage the recipient to become financially self-sufficient so that they no longer require assistance so that it can be given to someone more needy. They keep detailed written records of the families, the payments and the visits. Between 1996 and 2007, the foundation provided emergency assistance to 151,522 households and long-term assistance to 33,334.

Some people live in terrible conditions. One case, in 2006, was an 82-year-old retired lady general living in Taipei with her granddaughter and nine dogs. The volunteers found the floor and bed covered with human and dog urine and feces. The woman had previously been at the top of the social ladder, a general in the Nationalist army whose wedding was attended by then President Chiang Kai-shek. But, after she moved to Taiwan in 1949, her husband died suddenly in his 40s; one of their two sons turned to drugs and the other failed his exams. She became suspicious of and hostile to other people; she would not let her granddaughter go to school. The police gave up on her and passed the case to Tzu Chi. The volunteers came up with a ruse: they told her that President Chiang—who died in 1975—was coming to visit and that they had been ordered to clean the house up. She finally relented. It was a major job. They found that one of the dogs had died, without anyone noticing. They left the old general with a clean house and the granddaughter finally going to school.

Volunteers visit old people's homes, including those of military veterans who left their families behind in the mainland in 1949 and did not marry in Taiwan. They visit homes for the blind, the handicapped and other disadvantaged people. They also go to military bases and prisons. Since 1994, they have been visiting prisons in Hualien and Ilan, in Northeast Taiwan, to sing songs, tell stories and introduce the foundation's philosophy to the inmates. They have helped them to give up drugs and smoking and inspired them to register as bone marrow donors, donate money for overseas aid programs and recycle the waste of the prison. Cheng Yen believes that, in the heart of every person, there is a lotus flower waiting to bloom: "dripping water can penetrate a rock."

Volunteers also play an important role in missions overseas, as medical specialists and distributors of food, clothing and medicines. The foundation aims in principle for volunteers in one country to procure and distribute the aid needed in that country. But often this is impossible, because the number of local volunteers is too few and the scope of the disaster too broad. So volunteers come from outside, from neighboring countries if possible and distant ones if needed. They include members of the Tzu Chi International Medical Association (TIMA) (慈濟國際人醫會), which brings doctors, nurses and dentists from around the world to a free clinic lasting several days. Other missions involve the shipment of the goods needed by the victims of the flood, earthquake, drought or other disaster to the affected areas and their distribution by volunteers.

Another important mission for volunteers is recycling, which began in 1990. More than 62,000 do it on a regular basis in Taiwan, some every day and some on a part-time basis, at 4,500 recycling centers around the island. They have proved especially popular with elderly people, who are happy to find a way in which they can make a contribution to society, while also enjoying the company of fellow volunteers, as a better alternative to being on their own at home.

Volunteers say that the services they perform change them just as the life of a monastery transforms the monks who live there. The spiritual rewards they gain from these services count for more than the monetary benefits they gain during their working life.

One example is Hsaio Ju-chen, a well-known film director, for whom membership meant the difference between staying in her homeland and emigration. "I felt pessimistic and disappointed toward Taiwan and did not want to make any more films. I was not religious at all. Then I was invited to shoot a film about Cheng Yen. It changed my life. When I was with her, I felt very ashamed. In one day, she visited 10 schools and everyone asked her questions. She was very diligent. I felt that I had done nothing. I had found my life teacher. I found that there was no end to what I could film. I had thought that there were no good people in Taiwan and then I realized that it had many. I did not imagine that I would enter Tzu Chi. My friends were very surprised."

Hsaio joined the foundation's television station where she continues to work. She was sent to Guizhou, Southwest China, to film a poverty-alleviation mission. "I was carrying many biscuits and gave some to an old man. He said: 'no one has been so good to me, you are a Buddha.' I then knew the meaning of life."

4

RICH IN MONEY,
RICH IN LOVE

*"In terms of creative spirit and enterprise management, Cheng
Yen can compare with Bill Gates, except that they are in different
sectors. Compared to other corporate and charitable groups, Tzu
Chi is outstanding in terms of organizational culture, training
manpower, implementation and efficient use of resources."*

—Stan Shih, founder and former
chairman of Acer Computers

IT STARTED WITH A GROUP OF HOUSEWIVES putting NT$0.5 ($0.02) into
sticks of bamboo and has evolved into the richest charity in Taiwan,
with an endowment in 2005 of NT$26.3 billion ($800 million) and
annual donations of NT$10 billion ($300 million). Tzu Chi combines
simple charity with sophisticated fund-raising and money management
worthy of a multinational corporation. Its members include company
chairmen, chief executives and senior managers who want the same
value for the dollars they donate as from businesses they invest in. As it
expands around the world, the need for money will grow. The continued generosity of its donors will be essential—and this will depend on
their trust in Tzu Chi's probity and efficiency. This could be destroyed
by a financial scandal or a misuse of donor funds.

To ensure Tzu Chi's future, Cheng Yen set up an independent foundation for each of the four missions—charity, medicine, education and
culture—and aims to make them financially self-supporting. Its hospitals
and schools earn income from their patients and students, like other
private institutions in Taiwan, and have achieved or are close to achieving
financial independence. But other parts of the foundation, such as its

bone marrow bank, overseas aid, charity and television station, need substantial capital, as do construction of schools, hospitals, homes and other building projects at home and abroad. Fund-raising is essential for the survival and growth of the foundation.

What has enabled Tzu Chi to become the wealthiest charity in Taiwan is the scale of its donations and its ability to raise large sums in a short time. Of its 10 million members worldwide, about six million are in Taiwan, providing a network of donors that other charities cannot match. Commissioners, who are friends and neighbors, collect donations each month from members in their homes, providing a personalized and convenient service.

When floods strike in Nepal or New Orleans, within hours the foundation can put thousands of volunteers on the streets with collection boxes. Two disasters demonstrate its financial muscle. After the major earthquake that struck Central Taiwan in September 1999, it raised NT$10 billion ($300 million), at home and overseas. After the Southeast Asian tsunami on Boxing Day, 2004, it raised NT$2.7 billion ($85 million). These enormous sums covered short-term aid and long-term reconstruction of homes, schools and other infrastructure.

Donations, large and small

In 1982, the founder of a shipping company donated NT$2 million ($60,000) toward the hospital in Hualien, supported other projects, and donated his body after his death to its medical school.

In March 1986, a man gave Tzu Chi his publishing company, which four years later became that of the foundation itself.

In the late 1990s, a computer firm donated valuable land in Taipei, on which the foundation built its television station and humanities center. A farmer in Southwest Taiwan gave a plantation that grows San Yi, a well-known brand of green tea, without pesticide or fertilizer, which the nuns drink at the Abode and the foundation sells at its shops around the world.

In the late 1990s, Hou Bo-wen, senior adviser to Tung Ho Steel, the island's second largest steel company, provided NT$500 million ($15 million) worth of steel for the frame of the new hospital in Taipei.

In 1998 and 1999, Duh Chun-yuan, founder of two semiconductor companies, donated land and stocks worth NT$2.8 billion ($87 million).

In 2001, a 93-year-old leper who had lived for 50 years in a leprosy rehabilitation center, donated NT$300,000 ($9,300), in addition to NT$130,000 ($4,000) he had given earlier.

The wife of a Taiwan businessman had advanced cancer. Members of Tzu Chi cared and prayed for her and she was cured, one way or another: her husband donated NT$11 million ($350,000).

Others have also donated hundreds of thousands of dollars, as well as factories, land, homes, offices and stocks.

All were touched by Tzu Chi and believed a donation more important than buying a new property, putting the money into the family firm or giving it to their children.

One of the reasons for this remarkable generosity is the personal charisma of Cheng Yen, who, for more than four decades has convinced people of her benevolence and honesty and that their money will be well spent on projects that will bring real benefit to others. This trust and belief in Cheng Yen herself is the single most important factor in the high level of donations.

"Buddha told his disciples to divide their savings into four—one for their parents, one for their own family, one for their business and one for charity," she said. "I do not ask for 25 percent, 10 percent is enough. You give this money and you are still rich and do business. Rich is rich in love. . . The rich who work in Tzu Chi earn more respect and love and can still do business. If they did not, they might not be respected. Freedom comes from within your heart and not from money.

"Wealth is like a bubble on the water. Our basic needs are simple. You buy an expensive diamond and put it in a safe deposit box in the bank. Does it belong to you or to the bank?"

The second reason is the effective use of the money. Of every NT$100 ($3) given, less than NT$5 ($0.15) is spent on administrative costs. The foundation has set up a system of dedicated accounts, for overseas aid, medical work, education, its television station, charity or a particular construction project. Donors can choose into which account their money is paid and are given a receipt. They can monitor how it is spent, through their commissioner's report and the foundation's television station, radio and print media. The foundation has a finance department and system of internal control that ensures the money is used for its stated purpose and not spent on expensive cars and lavish banquets—as is the case in some other Buddhist charities.

The Buddhist faithful in Taiwan, as in other countries, give money to monks, to be spent at their discretion, believing the gift will bring blessings, and do not ask how it will be spent. Such donations to the *Sangha* (community of monks and nuns) have been a Buddhist tradition for more than 2,000 years, and an important source of income for Buddha's disciples. But, when Cheng Yen established her community in 1964, she decided that she and her nuns would not accept such money and that donations go only to the foundation.

Donors can see what their money has been used for—blankets for victims of a fire in Manila or a new Tzu Chi secondary school in Taiwan. They see volunteers give relief goods directly to victims of floods and earthquakes. This transparency and system of dedicated accounts has greatly helped the foundation's credibility. There has been no known incident of misuse of the foundation's money or theft by its employees. However, its success in fund-raising has also drawn criticism in Taiwan that it attracts too much of the charity pie, drawing money away from other institutions.

To help maintain probity and effectiveness, Cheng Yen has, since 1979, instituted two long-term policies. One is that expenditure is the same or more than income: projects drive the flow of money and not the other way around.

The second is that the foundation does not invest in real estate, stocks or other financial instruments, however good the rate of return, and instead puts its money into projects or the bank.

This is to ensure that Tzu Chi focuses on its missions and does not become an institution that concentrates on increasing the value of its assets. Also, it wants to ensure its one million volunteers are not left idle and that their energy and their talents are fully utilized.

Many members from the business community did not agree with these two policies. After all, why should Tzu Chi not act like any other financial entity and earn as much as it could and generate more revenue?

Ho Kuo-ching, a commissioner and manager of a property company, raised the issue in 1989, when the foundation was looking at sites for its medical school in Hualien. He proposed to Cheng Yen the purchase of land around the site where the school was to be built. Once it was finished and with a new railway station nearby, he argued, the commercial value of the land would rise: sale of the land would enrich the foundation and give it more money for projects.

"Do not speak to me about this again," she replied. "You are not the first to make such a proposition. I am not willing to do this." She explained that, while the foundation would need more funds, its objective was not to accumulate money but to awaken the desire in everyone to express love and concern.

"I hope to plant a seed in everyone, as in a fertile field, so that they can express this love constantly. Our aim is not only to help the poor but to educate the rich, arousing the love of everyone and educating everyone to do good."

Rather than creating an institution whose assets were based on financial growth, Cheng Yen's most precious asset is the trust and confidence of her members and the public. While a smart stock or land deal would yield a high short-term return, it would make the public suspicious of the foundation's real intentions—charity and wealth creation, or the well-being of its members and leaders. In the long term, she believed, the foundation would be able to raise more from the public if it retained that trust and confidence.

The experience of the Hualien hospital, as described in chapter two, showed her strategy. Cheng Yen believed thousands of people wanted to donate to the hospital, even if they did not know it. They needed to be given the opportunity to show that willingness. She believed the process of fund-raising would make thousands aware of Tzu Chi and its work and turn them into members. And so it turned out, thanks to the hard work of her members who raised the additional NT$770 million ($24 million) between 1984 and 1986.

Most successful was the idea of "honorary director," a title given, along with a certificate, to anyone who donated NT$1 million ($30,000). It is a directorship only in name, since it gives the donor no authority or decision-making power. One of the first honorary directors was a woman named Hsiu Kuan, the owner of a Buddhist lecture hall, who had become ill when visiting Hualien and had to be sent to Taipei for treatment: so she understood the logic for building a general hospital in Hualien. In September 1981, she sold her family property and donated the proceeds of more than NT$1 million. In the 27 years since, this practice has become very popular, with thousands donating NT$1 million and earning the title. Donors include many on modest incomes, sometimes with several honorary directors in a single family.

With the completion of the hospital, it became easier to attract money. Potential donors could see for themselves what had been achieved through the charity of thousands of individuals. The success of the fund-raising also gave Cheng Yen confidence to launch larger projects—the bone marrow bank, a network of hospitals across Taiwan and expanding overseas, including aid and building hospitals and schools. These are long-term and capital intensive, especially the bone marrow bank, whose charges to the patient cover only a fraction of its cost.

Funding a Foundation

Of the four separate foundations, two have their own sources of income. The medical foundation, with the largest number of professional staff—about 3,000—at its seven hospitals, earns money from patients who pay rates comparable to those at other private hospitals in Taiwan. Its doctors and nurses receive salaries that are at market levels. The financing of the hospitals became simpler after the introduction in 1995 of a mandatory universal health insurance scheme by the government. Since then, the hospitals have received most of their income from this insurance scheme. But they still require a subsidy from the mother foundation, because they provide drugs and treatments not covered by this government scheme. The hospitals required substantial investment at the beginning, to acquire land, construct the buildings and buy the equipment, mostly imported. Similarly, the schools, college and university charge fees to their students but need capital for new buildings and facilities.

The other two foundations, charity and culture, are weaker financially and require a substantial subsidy from the mother foundation every year. Charity has no income of its own and culture only a limited amount, from money earned from recycled goods, sales of books, DVDs and other items at its bookshops. The Great Love Television station does not carry advertising and receives a small income from sponsors who have their names announced between programs. Twenty-five percent of its revenue comes from the money earned by Tzu Chi's recycling program, and it also appeals to viewers to donate money to Tzu Chi's bank account.

Overseas aid is another major expenditure. In principle, the foundation aims to cover the costs of aid in a country from revenues raised there or in neighboring countries. But this is impossible in a country with few or no Tzu Chi members, or if it is a major disaster, like the earthquakes in Turkey (1999), Iran (2003) and Pakistan-administered Kashmir (2005).

Each year, the four foundations report their income and expenditure to the government ministries that oversee their sector. The officials review the accounts to ensure that they fulfill the conditions of a foundation and can retain their tax status and privileges. Neither the ministries nor the foundation make the figures public.

Like the chief executive of a corporation, Cheng Yen assesses plans on the basis of current and future revenue. "Future revenue" however is not the income from sales or investments but the goodwill of Tzu Chi members and the public. While a CEO believes in the quality of his future products, so Cheng Yen believes in the benevolence of the public, that they will support future projects. On this premise, she has continued to expand the organization and accept new projects, confident that the finance and members will follow. Indeed, between 1986 and 2009 membership has surged from 80,000 to 10 million, and today Tzu Chi is recognized as the richest charity in Taiwan.

The foundation itself has two sources of income. One is from the public, including members, who donate a fixed sum each month, starting at NT$100 ($3). The second is interest on its endowment deposited with the banks, which reached NT$26.3 billion ($800 million) in 2005, up from NT$25.1 billion ($780 million) in 2003. Under Taiwan law, foundations like Tzu Chi cannot spend the principal in their endowments but only the interest they generate. The endowments are regarded as the financial base of the foundations. In 2005, Tzu Chi's spending was NT$12.7 billion ($400 million), up from NT$8 billion ($250 million) in 2003. In 2000, the total endowment of the island's 300 largest foundations was NT$50.8 billion ($1.5 billion), an increase of 37.3 percent over 1999. Of this, Tzu Chi ranked top, with an endowment of more than NT$12 billion ($350 million), and that of seven other foundations exceeded NT$1 billion ($30 million).

In global terms, Taiwan's people are generous. According to government figures, they donate about $1.3 billion a year to charity, a per capita ratio of $57: the number of donors is 5.5 million, 18 percent of the population. The Norwegians, the most generous people in the world in terms of foreign aid, give an average of $99 a year, followed by the Irish with $71 and the Americans with $36.

The foundation has succeeded in attracting money from the rich and famous as well as from ordinary people. It is business-friendly, like Taiwan, which has become wealthy through the hard work and initiative of tens of thousands of small businessmen and women who have sold their products around the world. Taiwan society celebrates entrepreneurship, in charity as in business. So the foundation encourages business people to use their talents and experience as well as their money.

Stan Shih, the founder and later chairman of Acer Inc., a computer firm that is one of Taiwan's few global brand names, is an enthusiastic Tzu Chi member: "In terms of creative spirit and enterprise management,

Cheng Yen can compare with Bill Gates, except that they are in different sectors. Compared to other corporate and charitable groups, Tzu Chi is outstanding in terms of organizational culture, training manpower, implementation and efficient use of resources. Volunteers have two roles, as a participant without pay and as a donor. They give not only money but also time and find a high rate of return, in terms of happiness and sense of achievement." Shih said that many non-profit organizations had good intentions but lacked business expertise, making it difficult to accumulate funds and develop, unless companies or individuals continued to put in money. Tzu Chi's growth, on the other hand, is due not only to religion but also the satisfaction of customers, the return to shareholders and the achievements of its staff.

Certainly, Tzu Chi has developed a philosophy around money that appeals to corporate executives and rich heiresses as well as taxi drivers and street vendors. It is this combination that has enabled the foundation to become wealthy, to attract donations large and small and make each donor feel that he or she has made an equal contribution. "To give willingly is the expression of non-exclusive love," said Cheng Yen. "Starting with five cents, Tzu Chi was formed by the accumulation of miniscule resources. Therefore, we should not underestimate the power of 'smallness.' Do not refrain from doing good deeds just because they appear minor. Any good deed, regardless of its significance, is worth doing."

Finance was certainly simpler in the early years of Tzu Chi, when the community earned money through the sale of sweaters and baby shoes they made. Then, there were no difficult questions on what to invest in and no need for complex accounting systems. Even so, the notion of simplicity remains fundamental to Tzu Chi's financial success today. To reinforce that notion, the Great Love Television station broadcasts programs on model people who live simply and donate what they can to the foundation. For example, it portrayed a 90-year-old woman who used to be an aid recipient but declined the money when she was able to support herself. She does recycling work 364 days a year as well as giving NT$1,200 ($35) a month to the foundation. Another, a retired school teacher, said that he had a home and a pension that covered his daily living expenses. He did not need the rest of his money, so he donated it to the foundation.

"The happiness of personal achievement is transitory and you will always feel distress if you only cling to your self-interest," said Duh Chun-yuan, the founder of two semi-conductor companies who gave land and shares worth NT$2.8 billion ($80 million), making him one of the foundation's largest donors. "There is something more meaningful in life than material purposes. Now I sweep the streets every morning. I feel very good, very calm. I feel that it is helping me spiritually."

As Tzu Chi's fame has grown, it has received more requests for help, in Taiwan and abroad. Cheng Yen, driven by a sense of mission that becomes more intense as she grows older, accepts many of them, seeing new projects as giving volunteers and members motivation and focus and an opportunity to donors, old and new, to show their benevolence. Likewise, as the foundation's membership grows, it must take on more and more projects and not slow down. Cheng Yen believes that the energy of members and volunteers must be utilized, to give them the opportunity to cultivate themselves and relieve the suffering of the poor, the sick and the victims of disasters. Once asked by a weary commissioner why the foundation continued to expand, she replied: "Fine, I will retire and cultivate myself but what about the rest of you? What will you do with no projects—just recite the scriptures?"

5

MEDIA

"Cheng Yen is very reserved and does not even like to look into the mirror. After she became a nun, she only allowed one portrait of herself. She did not like to appear in the media and in the early years always refused interviews—but then she set up a television station."

—Gary Ho, chief executive of Tzu Chi, Canada

WHEN CHENG YEN LEFT HOME TO BECOME A NUN, she looked forward to a life of quiet study and charity work that suited a shy and retiring character. Now, four decades on, she finds herself at the center of media attention like that of a Hollywood film star. Television cameras follow her wherever she goes and record her every step. Secretaries write down every word she says in meetings, and publish most of them. This hi-tech world of glaring spotlights and video cameras is not what you expect to find in a community of nuns. Yet the Abode has become a combination of centuries-old Buddhist learning and twenty-first-century telecommunications.

What persuaded a shy woman who does not like to look into the mirror or to be photographed to submit to this kind of treatment? It was a decision in 1995 that, if Tzu Chi was to spread its message to a bigger public, in Taiwan and abroad, it had no alternative but television. It is the dominant medium of our era. If the foundation was to get its voice heard in a cacophonous world where people have hundreds of media choices, it needed its own channel. The foundation began with a production center, which provided programs to cable channels. But this was insufficient so it decided to set up its own channel. *Da Ai Tai* (Great Love Television) went on the air on January 1, 1998 in Taiwan and overseas in October 1999. Today, its signal can reach 79 percent of the world's population, through the rent of 12 satellites at an annual cost of NT$250 million ($7.5 million), and it ranks sixth in popularity among Taiwan's 80 television channels, with 7.13 percent of the audience.

Going into television meant changing the habits of a lifetime. The core content of the channel is the life, work and philosophy of Cheng Yen and the members of Tzu Chi. These have to be put into a form suitable for television: almost everything they do has to be recorded and broadcast. So the Abode, where Cheng Yen lives with her fellow nuns, was wired up with video screens, cameras and spotlights. Cameras record the morning prayers, her meeting each morning with volunteers, her speeches, her meetings with visitors and visits to schools, hospitals, branches of the foundation and recycling centers.

This exposure is uncomfortable for Cheng Yen and the 150 nuns who live with her. Their culture is one of reticence and self-effacement: they shave their heads, eschew make-up and wear plain, gray smocks, to minimize the importance of the individual. But the imperative of television forces them to do the opposite—everything must be shown, every word must be heard and the differences between people emphasized. It is a heavy price to pay. Another downside of television is the concentration on Cheng Yen herself. As she watches the channel, she sees everywhere images of herself—on the walls of the branch offices, in the living room of her members and the classrooms of their schools overseas. When members come to greet her, they often kneel on the ground, their foreheads to the floor and their palms facing up. She does the same when she meets masters who are higher in the Buddhist hierarchy. To critics, all this looks uncomfortably like a cult of the personality and the pursuit of individual fame. The foundation emphatically denies this: it insists that there is no alternative to a television station if they want to spread the message of Tzu Chi, especially overseas, and that the focus on Cheng Yen is a means to achieve this and not the end.

The decision to go into television was difficult but strategically necessary. While Cheng Yen herself would prefer a private role and work behind the scenes, she decided this high profile was essential to spread Tzu Chi to a global audience. This round-the-clock exposure, however, takes a heavy toll on Cheng Yen's health and privacy. Cheng Yen's nuns control the level of flash that can be used, to prevent damage to her eyes. As her disciples see her on television, they are watching for any sign of age, illness or change in routine. Long gone are the days of private contemplation and prayer.

Her disciples persuaded her to accept the intrusion of television for the long-term development of Tzu Chi. It allows them to have a comprehensive record of her words, public activities and speeches. They consider this material invaluable for the history of modern Buddhism and will use it as the basis to teach Tzu Chi philosophy after the passing of Cheng Yen. The television station is also essential to spread the movement to foreign countries: currently, it is heavily Taiwan-centered. The island accounts for about 60 percent of its 10 million members and 90 percent of its 33,000 commissioners. The station enables those who watch to see and hear what the foundation is doing and how the money they have donated is being spent, at home and abroad.

For Cheng Yen herself, it is a delicate balancing act between ego and self-effacement. As the founder and leader of a mass movement, she must make herself available to her disciples, who want to see and hear her every day. Believers want to identify with a person as well as a creed. But she does not want her personality to overshadow the Buddhist message she is teaching: she tells journalists and researchers not to interview her but to talk to her volunteers and participate in their projects. "Write about them and not about me," she says. So Liu Soung, a well-known Taipei director, discovered when the U.S. Discovery channel hired him to make a 45-minute profile of her, one of six profiles of Taiwan people. "She gave us three and a half hours of her time but not an interview on camera. It was the biggest obstacle in our film. She wanted to change the viewpoint that the achievements of Tzu Chi are due to her. She wanted to give the credit to others." As a result, the film contains interviews with many foundation members but not Cheng Yen herself. "She told us that, instead of using all the resources needed to make the report, we should work in Tzu Chi for two days and then we would know what it was."

Cheng Yen defines the goal of Tzu Chi's media in messianic terms: "My ultimate goal is to purify minds. Only when the human mind is purified will society be peaceful. Therefore, we need to deepen the influence of our culture, from the two-dimensional Tzu Chi monthly magazine to the three-dimensional Great Love Television station. Everything must be deepened and refined. If human minds are not purified, hell will never be empty. If the task of purifying people's minds is not accomplished, even after becoming a Buddha, one still needs to return to the ordinary world."

The beneficial results of Tzu Chi's other three missions—poverty relief, medicine and education—can be measured on a daily basis, like food to a flood victim in Indonesia, treatment of a stroke patient in Taipei and teaching a primary school student in Thailand. But the objectives of the "humanity" mission are harder to measure. This is how Cheng Yen defines it:

"The media should exert a positive influence. They should report the positive aspects of society and spread the seeds of love in the hearts of man and lead them into the path of love and good works. I hope that everyone will speak, behave and think in a good way and lead society toward truth, goodness and beauty.

"I hope that the media will always report good things and not only Tzu Chi. The purpose of *Da Ai Tai* is to cleanse the hearts of people.

"The influence of culture is as enduring as the universe. It can last for as long as 10 years, 100 years or even thousands of years. If we fail in this historical mission, we are laying many difficulties in store for future generations."

For Cheng Yen, the solution to global crises lies less in political negotiations and international treaties than in the hearts of individuals. "One mind creates the world we live in. . . One thought can destroy the world and make many refugees."

The television station, with two channels, one domestic and one foreign, is the most important of a range of media, that includes radio programs, a publishing company, a website in Chinese and English, dozens of books by Cheng Yen and Tzu Chi members, which are sold in 26 foundation bookstores in five countries, and magazines in Chinese, English, Japanese, German, Spanish and French.

Tzu Chi's media work began 15 months after the foundation was born, with a four-page monthly magazine that explained the charity work, how recipients were chosen and the overall mission. Since its creation, the now 100-page magazine has remained the principal written record of the movement, containing stories about the foundation's major projects and individual members, in Taiwan and overseas, as well as an account of Cheng Yen's activities, meetings and sayings during the month. More than 300,000 copies are now published and distributed free each month, and Tzu Chi chapters in the U.S., Malaysia, Argentine, Brazil, Canada, Australia, the Philippines, Hong Kong and South Africa are also producing free magazines for their members. In the autumn of 2007, Cheng Yen began to encourage her disciples to read the monthly magazine on line, to reduce the amount of paper used to print it. This is not easy for older members unfamiliar with computers so branches have been holding classes to encourage them to learn. Chen Yen's aim is to reduce the monthly print run from 300,000 to 50,000.

The foundation's foray into publishing received a boost in March 1986, after three members donated a lecture hall and publishing house, which one of them had set up 14 years earlier. This became Tzu Chi's own publishing house and enabled it to improve the quality of its printed works and appeal to a more educated readership. The Tzu Chi Cultural Publishing Company was formally established in October 1990. In February 1998, it changed its name to Jing Si Publications. The company publishes the sayings and speeches of Cheng Yen, profiles of and books by its senior doctors and major figures in the foundation as well as accounts of its major projects. It also produces magazines, books, music CDs and DVDs in English, German and Japanese, as well as in Chinese, and has opened bookstores across Taiwan, Malaysia, and the U.S., as well as in Singapore, Jakarta, Auckland and Suzhou.

Undoubtedly, the most important and widely read of the publisher's titles is *Jing Si* (Still Thoughts) *Aphorisms* (靜思語), a collection of Cheng Yen's sayings. Compiled by two groups of disciples who had written down her words over many months, the book was first published in 1988 by Jiu Ge (Nine Songs) house. In 1992, under the foundation's own moniker, a second volume was published and the books soon became best sellers, selling more than 400,000 copies in Taiwan alone. Today, there are three Still Thoughts volumes, and they have been translated into many languages including simplified Chinese, Japanese, Korean, Bahasa Indonesia, Thai, Vietnamese, English, Spanish, French and German. Members use the aphorisms as a guide for their daily lives. The works are also used as a textbook in Tzu Chi schools where students memorize the aphorisms and are encouraged to put them into practice in their daily lives.

For Cheng Yen, the opportunity to reach out to a wider public came in 1980, when, at the invitation of the Ministry of Interior, she gave her first speech at the Sun Yat-sen Memorial Hall in Taipei, one of the most important venues in the country. The government had come to regard her and her movement as an important force for social cohesion, and the speech, delivered on June 18, was televised live. The next year, Cheng Yen delivered many public speeches around Taiwan, at the invitation of the Government Information Office and the Labor Commission. In this way, thousands of people became aware of the slender nun and the work of her foundation. For Cheng Yen, it was an important step in turning from the leader of a local Buddhist charity into a national figure.

By 1985, the foundation had begun a regular morning radio program, *Tzu Chi World*, that today broadcasts an average of 10 hours a day over

16 stations to Taiwan, mainland China and North America. However, it was not until 1987, when martial law ended in Taiwan, that the organization was able to launch itself fully into broadcast media. Under martial law, Taiwan's government did not allow private enterprises to own media. With its end, however, dozens seized the chance to set up their own newspapers, radio and television stations. Taiwan soon became one of the most competitive media markets in the world, with more than 80 terrestrial cable and satellite channels for a population of 23 million. This explosion of new media, especially cable stations, and the content of their programs were also factors that influenced Cheng Yen's decision to go into television.

She was alarmed by the quality of the output, especially sex and violence, as commercial channels competed with each other to provide extreme and bizarre images. Dramas caused copycat behavior in real life—people threw themselves off buildings and kidnapped businessmen and their children for ransom. "The media carries a big responsibility for the chaos in the world," said De Fan (德凡法師), the nun who has recorded Cheng Yen's words for the last 13 years. "One article can bring great stability and also cause chaos. People of culture have a mission."

Tang Jian-ming (湯健明), current director of Great Love Television, said that at the time, he advised against setting up their own station because of the high cost. "I proposed that we sell programs to other stations. But she insisted. The station is her eyes and ears to Tzu Chi in the world.

The channel recruited professionals from other stations, paying them salaries close to market levels, as well as unpaid volunteers, and raised money from donations.

In January 1998, Great Love Television began broadcasting in Taiwan. In October the following year, it also started broadcasting overseas. On January 1, 2005, it moved into a new 230-foot-high state-of-the-art facility in a Northern suburb of Taipei, built on land donated by the owner of a software company. The station is entirely digitalized, using no tapes, and employs 535 people. The decision to go digital followed a flood, which inundated the basement of the building it had used previously and had threatened to destroy the tapes stored there. Hundreds of volunteers rushed to the scene to save the tapes, the precious legacy of 40 years.

From this new facility, the station broadcasts two channels—one for Taiwan and Asia and the other for the rest of the world. Since the majority of the programs are in Chinese, some with subtitles, the audience is mostly the 10 million members of Tzu Chi around the world.

The programming includes a daily address by Cheng Yen, news coverage, talk shows, documentaries, drama, educational and children's shows, medical programs in which viewers can call in and question doctors and nurses, cartoons, cooking demonstrations, music and culture.

Nonprofit-making, the channel has no advertising. Of its income, 25 percent is generated from the sales of Tzu Chi's 4,500 recycling centers around Taiwan, 20 percent from 100,000 "Friends of *Da Ai*" who donate an average of NT$300 ($9) each per month, donations from companies who have their names broadcast, and sales of DVDs of its programs. The station broadcasts daily appeals for donations. Where once it received a subsidy from the foundation, today the Great Love Television channel makes a modest profit, which it then gives back to Tzu Chi.

The channel ranks sixth in popularity in Taiwan, with 7.13 percent of the audience, compared to 17.18 percent of the market leader, the private Minshi channel, and 13.49 percent for the second, Home Box Office, the U.S.-based film channel. Tang Jian-ming said that they did not buy programs from abroad. "We broadcast touching stories. There is so much conflict on other channels. People like to watch ours and feel peaceful. The media has a big responsibility in society, to report good news, promote manners and awaken the goodwill in people. Most of the mainstream media do not broadcast good news."

All this makes the channel unlike its competitors. Cheng Yen likes discreet colors and simplicity, so presenters dress conservatively, in blue, white and grey and do not wear lipstick or earrings. It avoids the sensationalism and gossip about politicians and celebrities that fill much of the airtime of other stations, and shows no sex or violence.

Instead, the station shows acts of love and kindness. One program, for example, presented people with physical disabilities and showed how they were able to overcome their disabilities and lead near-normal lives, as teachers, painters, dancers and singers, through determination and hard work. In the program, Cheng Yen praised them for concentrating on what they were able to do and for not dwelling on what they had lost, telling them they were an example to able-bodied people who should rejoice in the faculties they have. Other programs show content that mainstream stations would balk at: the funerals of Tzu Chi members, for example, especially those who have donated their bodies to medical science, including the anatomy room where students dissect their bodies, while nuns and volunteers chant Buddhist sutras.

Great Love Television's news program, broadcast with segments in Mandarin, Taiwanese, English and Indonesian, must also give proper guidance. Tang Jian-ming cites an incident where two members of Taiwan's national legislature threw water onto each other. "We considered broadcasting this, with a comment that this was inappropriate behavior," he said. "But we decided not to, fearing that people would ignore our message and imitate the legislators. We must give a message of love and goodness."

The station also records what the foundation has done at home and abroad. When teams go abroad on relief missions, a team from the station goes with them. It sends back images from the scene of the flood or earthquake, which the station broadcasts to show what the foundation is doing and how the donors' money is being spent. These help Hualien evaluate how to help the victims of the disaster and move viewers to make donations.

The global reach of Tzu Chi is clearly evident in Great Love Television's growing popularity outside Taiwan. In 2006, the foundation's branch in Jakarta obtained a license from the government to launch a television station, which in February 2007 began producing a four-hour program in Bahasa Indonesian, repeated during the day. In addition, Great Love Television's mother station in Hualien has also initiated a project to increase the range of material from abroad. So far, 2,000 foreign members of an expected 8,000 have been trained to shoot film of their work and send it, electronically or by post, to the station for broadcasting. This will enable the station to show footage of Tzu Chi activities around the world, at no charge. "Our station is spiritual food for our members overseas," explained Tang Jian-ming. "They have little chance to see Cheng Yen in person. If we change the times of the programs in which she appears, there is a big reaction."

The focus on humanitarian Buddhism sets Great Love Television apart from Taiwan's other Buddhist foundation channels, which mostly broadcast lectures and the reading of scriptures by Buddhist monks. Indeed, Cheng Yen believes that it is the stories of individuals, not the reading of scriptures, that attracts and moves viewers. Her theory is perhaps best illustrated in the popularity of the channel's long-running drama series. Broadcast during peak evening hours, these dramas attract up to 600,000 viewers and rank third among the Taiwan audience.

"We are not the mainstream but aim to become the mainstream," said Pang Yian, 68, the executive producer of the station's drama department, and who has been making plays and films for 45 years. After receiving the assignment from Cheng Yen, who personally selects a disciple's story for it to be turned into a television drama, Pang and his crew visit the person to conduct lengthy interviews about his or her life, family and ancestors. They also meet with the family and friends of the subject. Around five dramas a year are produced by Great Love Television, with 18-24 months needed to complete them. Cheng Yen also insists that everything in the story be factual. For example, drinking and smoking can be shown, however, they must be portrayed in a negative way.

PART TWO

A GLOBAL MISSION

6

OVERSEAS MISSIONS

"I was so moved. These people were so poor but were as smart as me. If they had the same opportunity, they would do as well as me in the United States. I thanked God for the opportunity I had been given."

—William Keh, a successful doctor and businessman in the United States, describes a relief mission in Guizhou, China

IT BEGAN IN JUNE 1991 WHEN TZU CHI donated money to victims of heavy flooding in Bangladesh, its first aid outside Taiwan. Since then, its global mission has helped 11 million victims of war, flood, earthquakes and other disasters in more than 60 countries around the world. It has developed a sophisticated logistics operation, with warehouses full of relief goods in Taiwan and abroad and volunteers ready to go to the scene of a disaster at a moment's notice.

The rapid expansion of foreign aid has been made possible by the increase in membership to 10 million members and 50,000 commissioners in 29 countries worldwide, up from 1.5 million members and less than 3,000 commissioners in 1991, when it had only one foreign branch, in the United States.

In global terms, Tzu Chi is small compared to the giant charities of the U.S. and Europe established after World War Two. But it has become the biggest foreign NGO in China and a significant player in Indonesia, the Philippines and Malaysia, countries where it has a large number of members. It is also active in the United States, where it has 62 branches and 100,000 members, the biggest number in any country outside Taiwan, who also do charity work in Latin America and the Caribbean.

In spring 1991, Cheng Yen received a request from the foundation's U.S. chapter to approve a donation for flood victims in Bangladesh. She decided giving such aid was in line with the principles of Buddhism, to assist people abroad as well as at home, so she gave her approval. She asked children in Taiwan to donate the equivalent of one loaf of bread a day to their fellow children in Bangladesh. Within a month, the foundation had raised $157,000, which it gave to the International Red Cross in Los Angeles, for use in Bangladesh. The foundation set up a new bank account—the "international emergency aid fund."

"Our mission is to shelter all those on earth who are suffering, with a network of Great Love that has spread worldwide," explained Cheng Yen regarding her decision. "We see natural and man-made disasters occurring frequently, putting countless lives in danger and causing souls to lose direction. Since we all share the same earth and breathe the same air, it is our inescapable responsibility to help and care for each other." She did not consider whether the foundation had sufficient funds for such missions but acted out of a sense of charity.

Cheng Yen conceived the missions differently to those of other charities. Volunteers would deliver the aid directly to the victims of a disaster: they would not use professional employees, a third party or a government. The volunteers would pay all their own costs. When they handed over the aid, they would bow and thank the recipient for the chance to give. They would show respect and care toward the recipient and present the aid like a gift to a friend or family member. The act would be an exchange between equals, not the gesture of a rich person disposing of something he does not want to someone he regards as beneath him. It would bring equal benefit to both parties—the recipient would receive goods he needed and the donor would realize his good fortune in being able to make the gift. So Cheng Yen turned the mission into a form of Buddhist practice. This method has the advantage that those who give to Tzu Chi know that the money will be properly used, and not disappear en route into the hands of corrupt officials and middlemen; it also means that administrative costs are kept to a minimum. The money given to the Red Cross for Bangladesh was an exception, because it was an emergency and the foundation had not yet developed its own relief system.

Cheng Yen set out other principles for missions abroad. One was the three "Noes"—do not talk politics or business, or proselytize. The aid was without conditions, a gift from one person to another, with no political or religious overtone, no requirement to convert to Buddhism or give anything in return. Cheng Yen told volunteers that on aid missions abroad they must act as ambassadors of peace, their hearts full of love and gratitude. They must respect local customs, lifestyle, religion and cultural traditions. The quality of relief goods, be it clothing, food, medicine or shelters, should be as good as if they were for the volunteer themselves to use. Nearly all those on foreign missions, including doctors and other medical staff, would be volunteers who pay their own way. The only ones to receive pay would be a small number of professional staff from Tzu Chi. Everyone would wear its uniform of blue shirts, white trousers and a white baseball hat, bearing its logo, in Chinese and English, so that they were instantly recognizable.

Participation would be limited to Tzu Chi commissioners and not ordinary members. After two years of training, commissioners would conduct themselves appropriately and follow the foundation's rules. As it turned out, there would be no shortage of people volunteering to go on the missions, despite the cost, harsh conditions and potential danger.

Cheng Yen said that her aim was not only to give material goods but "more importantly to spread the seeds of love. Touched by the unprejudiced and genuine concern shown by fellow human beings, suffering people will open up their hearts and find love within." This would encourage mutual help among victims and help local people to become independent by involving them in rebuilding their own communities. She aimed to inspire disaster victims to contribute to others, when they can, and move from being helped to helping others.

These were ambitious goals for an organization with no foreign experience, except in the U.S. In Taiwan, over 25 years, the foundation had built up members in every corner of the island, good relations with government and business and the ability to react rapidly and effectively to crises. Overseas aid, however, raised new questions: How to deliver aid to countries which were unfamiliar, had different religions, social and political systems and no Tzu Chi members? How to deal with governments and people who had never heard of Tzu Chi and knew nothing of Taiwan or Buddhism? Many were suspicious of foreign religious groups, especially those they suspected of proselytizing. Would governments face pressure from China to exclude it? Would it able to raise the additional funds? Did it have the skilled personnel, management and know-how to carry them out? Could it protect its volunteers in countries hit by war, a guerilla uprising or a breakdown of government? Since Taiwan was expelled from the United Nations in 1971, the number of countries recognizing it has shrunk to less than 25. If members were kidnapped or wounded, would their government be able to help them?

Tzu Chi was a late arrival to the international aid scene. Since World War Two, the big charities of Europe and the United States had built dense networks of contacts, official and unofficial, in the countries where they operate. Tzu Chi would have to start from the ground up, building its own networks.

On the positive side, however, Taiwan had no history as colonizer, meaning the members would carry no burden of history and the foundation would be able to preserve the political neutrality it strived for. Charities from Europe and the United States suffer, to a greater or lesser extent, from an association with their country of origin and its diplomacy. Politicians and people in receiving countries often read into their actions a political agenda, which may or may not exist. For example, during the presidency of George Bush from 2000-2008, an American charity could not help the citizens of Iran or North Korea, because of the stance of its government.

In addition, Tzu Chi could call on the Taiwanese diaspora around the world. With the boom of the island's economy from the 1980s, thousands of its entrepreneurs went overseas, to Southeast Asia, Central and South America, South Africa and China. Since the 1950s, there has been a significant emigration to the United States, where today an estimated 1.5 million people of Taiwan origin live, including 600,000 in California and 360,000 in New York. Tzu Chi grew among these expatriate Taiwan communities and could count on their help in its overseas missions. With their knowledge of local languages and conditions and personal networks, they would become an invaluable part of the foreign aid mission.

Tzu Chi abroad grew fastest when it found people who were well established and used their connections and energy to help.

One is Chen Chiu-hwa in Jordan, a former marine in Taiwan, who trained members of its royal family and knows them personally, including Prince Hassan, uncle of King Abdullah. Another is Lucio Tan, one of the richest men in the Philippines, chairman of the national airline and dozens of other companies with an estimated worth of $20 billion. Born in July 1934 in Xiamen, Fujian province in Southeast China, he moved to the Philippines with his parents when he was a child. In Indonesia, the foundation attracted two tycoons, Kuo Tsai-yuan (郭再源) and Huang Rong-nian (黃榮年), who have mobilized their companies and connections for the sake of Tzu Chi projects.

In its foreign aid since 1991, Tzu Chi has remained faithful to the guidelines Cheng Yen set out. The aid is to be given directly, in the form of food, clothing, medicines, schools or homes but not money, to ensure that it reaches the victims. Given its limited resources, Tzu Chi sends it said to the area where it is most needed, in the quickest and most efficient manner, and ensures that it is what the victims want. For example, goods given to people in Mongolia on New Year's Day 1993 were purchased in China, the nearest country where they were available, instead of being brought from Taiwan, to save delay and transport costs. In 1993, when the foundation built 1,800 new homes in Nepal, it brought in architects and planners for the design but used a local company and local workers to construct the homes. It also avoids areas where other charities are operating.

But the foundation cannot provide meat even if disaster victims request it—as a Buddhist organization, it only gives vegetarian food.

Which countries to aid and how, is a dialogue between headquarters in Hualien and members on the ground. Every day Cheng Yen monitors the international news, in the newspapers, on television and the internet, and talks to her members around the world. If she decides to send a mission to a country, she will convene a meeting attended by officials of the humanitarian aid department and members of her secretariat, often nuns, responsible for research on that country and region. They will ask members in that country or countries nearby about the logistics of an operation. Alternatively, the initiative may come from the members in a country who know more quickly and directly about a disaster.

In the early years, when the foundation had few branches abroad, it sent personnel and materials from Taiwan. As the branches increased, so it passed the responsibility to them. From the mid-1990s, branches were established in Japan, Hong Kong, the Philippines, Indonesia, Thailand, Canada and the U.S., and members became active in mainland China. But, when there was a major disaster, like the Taiwan earthquake of September 1999, the September 11, 2001 attacks in New York and Hurricane Katrina in August 2005, the foundation organized a global response. After the tsunami of December 26, 2004, for example, it raised NT$2.7 billion ($80 million) around the world.

What distinguishes Tzu Chi from other charities is the large-scale use of unpaid volunteers and the person-to-person distribution of material. Recipients express surprise at the man or woman in a blue and white uniform bowing in front of them and thanking them for accepting the items. Often at the bottom of the social ladder, these people are unaccustomed to such civility.

One condition, however, is that missions do not put the lives of the volunteers at risk, which has ruled out Sudan. Hsieh Ching-kuei (謝景貴) said that, to date, no Tzu Chi volunteer had been wounded or killed during an aid mission. "Cheng Yen's first consideration is safety for volunteers. To help others, you have to be safe yourself. If there were one accident, the risk would increase and the number of participants willing to go would fall."

Despite the risks, discomfort and the fact that they must cover their own costs, there has been no shortage of volunteers for these missions. In fact, there are usually too many applicants. Those who take part express their joy at being able to help others at first hand.

It was such an experience that persuaded William Keh (葛卓言), the current chief executive of the U.S. branch, to close a profitable sports-wear business in New York and devote himself full-time to Tzu Chi. In 1997, he took part in a mission to distribute aid in Guizhou, a poor province of Southwest China. The air ticket from New York cost $2,200 and the trip took 36 hours, including three flights and seven hours in a jeep over rough mountain roads.

"As we distributed the rice in big sacks, I fell tired and numb. In the evenings, volunteers cried as they described their joy. As I thought of this, I did not sleep well. But, the second evening, I had the same experi-ence and cried because I was so moved. These people were so poor but were as smart as me. If they had the same opportunity, they would do as well as me in the United States. I thanked God for the opportunity I had been given. Why should I complain? This mission was the turning point of my life. It saved me. Tzu Chi is not a charity or volunteer group so much as a group of practitioners, to understand the meaning of life. It does not lie in possessing wealth, nice clothes or spacious homes but in renouncing one's attachments and making the best of one's life to serve and help others."

Hsieh Ching-kuei, director of the department of religion and humanitarian aid, said Tzu Chi provided people with a channel for their charity. "Volunteers come back from missions abroad, find the experi-ence to be rewarding and tell others, who also want to give money and participate. A majority of Taiwan people have no prejudice. This is an island of love."

Hsieh said that, on the first day of a mission, rich wives who had volunteered could barely bring themselves to open the dirty doors of homes where the recipients lived but, by the second day, had adjusted and were distributing aid. "They change very quickly and want to come again. Cheng Yen tells us to respect and thank the recipient. You could be like that. You count your blessings. In the mainland, we found old men with hands like tree bark, who had not eaten for several days."

The missions take one of three forms: One is to send people and material from Taiwan; the second is to use Tzu Chi members in the affected country or nearby; the third is in co-operation with foreign charities, like the Atlanta-based Christian Action Research and Education (CARE), which in 2005 disbursed more than $514 million to poor communities in more than70 developing countries. With CARE, the foundation provided aid to victims of an Indian earthquake and fertilizer to farmers in Kosovo. Another partner was the Paris-based *Medicins du Monde* (MDM), set up in March 1980, which sends medical professionals to care for the sick, in war and disaster zones, in poor countries. Tzu Chi has carried out joint missions with MDM in Kosovo, Ethiopia and Rwanda. "It is hard to find partners with the same principles as ours," said Hsieh.

Cheng Yen declared 1992 "Tzu Chi's international year," to let the international community understand that Buddhism was not passive but was playing a positive role in the world. In August that year, East China again suffered serious flooding and the foundation was quick to offer help. In August, the head of the Red Cross in Mongolia came to Hualien to ask Cheng Yen for help. His country's economy had declined after the collapse in 1991 of the Soviet Union, which had supplied it with expertise and goods, on preferential terms, since 1924. Cheng Yen sent a senior member to Mongolia in early October: he saw for himself the severe shortage of daily necessities ahead of winter, when the average temperature in the capital, Ulan Bator, is 3°F. The foundation launched a major operation, delivering 8,700 cans of powdered milk, 5,000 blankets, 10,000 pairs of gloves, 10,000 hats and 20,000 pairs of socks. It purchased these items in China and took them to Ulan Bator by plane and truck in the middle of winter. The costs were met from money left over from the relief operations to flood victims in East China the year before.

In 1994, the four aid destinations were Cambodia, Nepal, Rwanda and Alaska. The organization was invited to Cambodia by overseas Chinese living there. Looking to help people in the long term, it gave to 82,000 flood victims, 20 water pumps, 600 tons of seed, 2,600 gallons of diesel oil and 80 gallons of petrol, to irrigate rice paddies. In addition, the foundation distributed 1,640 tons of rice. Such distribution was dangerous, since the country has an estimated eight million land mines. In Nepal, it started a form of aid it would repeat in many countries— construction of 1,800 homes in three counties worst hit by flooding that displaced over 400,000 people.

In Alaska, the recipients were American Indians in Allakaket who had lost their homes to floodwaters.

In 1995, the number of recipient countries increased to nine, including Chechnya in the Russian Republic, Cambodia, four countries

in Africa—Guinea-Bissau, South Africa, Lesotho and Swaziland—
Mexico, the Philippines and Thailand, where Tzu Chi launched a
three-year relief plan for former soldiers of a nationalist army and their
descendants.

In 1996, Tzu Chi continued its aid to Cambodia and, in Cote
d'Ivoire, worked with MDM to set up a shelter for street children that
provided vocational training and counseling. It donated 1,500 tents,
100 wheelchairs, winter clothes and mattresses to some of the one million
Azerbaijanis left homeless after its war with Armenia, in a joint project
with two British charities. The help came after a request from the country's deputy prime minister. In June 1997, the foundation provided them
with a further 100 wheelchairs, 1,500 insulated tents and 156,000
blankets and winter clothes.

In 1998, the foundation started large-scale aid in South America,
with projects in Argentina, Brazil, Peru and Paraguay, most carried out
by local volunteers. In Argentina, they set up 15 distribution centers in
two provinces badly hit by floods. They gave out 1,183 blankets and
500 packs of food.

In 1999, the foundation worked with a Los Angeles-based Christian
charity, Knightsbridge International, to send $300,000 worth of anti-
biotics to camps in Albania, Macedonia and Montenegro, and to house
630,000 refugees from Kosovo. It also signed an agreement with MDM to
run a five-month medical assistance program for five cities inside Kosovo.

It was here that Hsieh Ching-kuei found a deep hatred equivalent
to what he had seen in Afghanistan. "Serbs and Albanians used to live
together as friends before the politicians poisoned their minds. Each
day, in Pristina, I saw the homes of Serbs burning. I asked why no one is
doing anything about it and people told me: 'keep quiet and do not talk
of love or forgiveness here.' The only places where Serbs and Albanians
could shake hands were in our medical clinics and in the mental asylums.
The world was turned upside down. The children in Kosovo could not
speak. They drew pictures of a scene in red, with tanks and guns, of
a Serb soldier killing a baby in a cradle. As in World War Two, it will
take the second and third generation to resolve the hatred. Our ability
is limited."

After 18 years in the overseas aid business, the foundation has sophisticated logistics operations, with dedicated warehouses in Taiwan full of
food, clothes, blankets, daily necessities and medical supplies ready to
be shipped at a moment's notice and teams of volunteers on standby
around the clock. It researches how to improve the goods it provides,
such as tents, inflatable boats and food. For example, a 15-kilo bag

of rice is too heavy for many people to carry, so it is working on dried rice, which weighs only five kilos and becomes rice when mixed with hot water.

But not everything has gone smoothly. In some cases, a mission has been impossible because a government insists that it alone can handle the distribution. For example, the foundation offered aid to the Indian state of Gujarat, after an earthquake measuring 7.9 on the Richter scale in January 2001 left 30,000 dead. However, the government declined the offer, saying it did not want outside aid. In India to date, the foundation has only been able to do three joint projects, with CARE India. At other times, political obstacles get in the way. When a devastating earthquake struck Pakistan in October 2005, its government, a close ally of Beijing, initially refused Tzu Chi's aid. Foundation members in Hong Kong lobbied the consul there until he gave his permission. They told him: "Your people are dying of cold and hunger and you are not allowing us to help them."

So, too, in the case of Tzu Chi's operations in Nepal, where the government is also a close ally of Beijing. Once it understood that there were no politics at stake, however, it was happy to accept.

The foundation's UN status as a certified NGO obtained in December 2003, is especially useful in entering countries where it is not known. However, politics also threatened to get in the way of Tzu Chi's application to the UN. Initially, Tzu Chi's U.S. chapter proposed applying for the status, but Cheng Yen insisted that Taiwan be included in the name. Fearing that Beijing would object to this, the foundation did not apply. Finally, it applied under the name "Taiwan Buddhist Tzu Chi Foundation (USA)," which the United Nations accepted. Members say that, in its overseas work, the foundation has not suffered interference by the embassies of China, because they know that it is neither connected to the government nor involved in politics.

The Tzu Chi International Medical Association (TIMA)

An important part of the foundation's overseas aid is provided by doctors, nurses, dentists and pharmacists who belong to the Tzu Chi International Medical Association (TIMA). They charge no fee and pay their own costs. The TIMA was set up in October 1996 by Tzu Chi volunteers and medical professionals from hospitals and clinics in Taiwan. Their model was the French charity *Medicins Sans Frontieres* (Doctors Without Frontiers), which was set up in 1971. Like Tzu Chi, it raises most of its funds from the general public. Since its inception, TIMA has grown rapidly to 33 branches in 19 countries, with more than 10,000 physicians and volunteers, who have provided medical services to over 1.4 million patients around the world. It requires them to be available at short notice, to go to areas hit by floods, earthquakes and other natural disasters and offer medical care to the victims for a limited period. Conditions are difficult: they treat patients in a school, a community building or a tent as well as in a hospital. Sometimes there is no power or water and no facilities to conduct operations. They must carry as many medicines and equipment as possible. Such conditions are a world away from the well-equipped hospitals and operating theatres where they spend their professional life. But nowhere else do they find themselves so valued and appreciated, by people who rarely have access to modern medicine. The experience is usually no more than two weeks, but intense. Participants say that any frustration at the poor working conditions is overwhelmed by the deep gratitude of the patients and a sense of making a contribution at a critical moment.

The volunteers include many who do not work in Tzu Chi hospitals but have been inspired by its ideals. In Indonesia, for example, some of the 100 volunteers are superintendents of military hospitals and even military generals. Doctors from Vietnam, Iran and Ecuador have joined TIMA clinics in disaster-hit countries.

The branch in California has a free clinic in Los Angeles, which provides regular sessions and home visits to low-income patients. TIMA volunteers in Brazil hold monthly clinics in Sao Paolo and surrounding areas. Each TIMA branch regularly conducts free clinics at fixed sites. When it holds a large-scale free clinic, members from neighboring countries come to take part. TIMA has held clinics in China, Cambodia, Vietnam, Thailand, Malaysia, Singapore, Indonesia, the Philippines, Sri Lanka, Pakistan, Afghanistan, South Africa, Rwanda, Ethiopia, Chechnya, Azerbaijan, Papua New Guinea, Samoa, Micronesia, the United States, Brazil, Paraguay and Australia. The association also conducts long-term programs to recruit local medical and non-medical volunteers, to nurture medical resources in areas where they are inadequate.

A typical operation was conducted at the end of May 2006, in the South Indonesian city of Bantul, which had been hit by an earthquake of 6.2 on the Richter scale five days before. A local hospital set aside an operating room for the use of the Tzu Chi team, who brought surgical equipment from Taiwan and a foundation clinic in Jakarta. "Bringing the equipment proved to be worthwhile. Other foreign medical teams, who had not brought their own medical equipment, were frustrated by the severe shortage of equipment and medicine in local hospitals.

During their eight-day mission, the team treated 3,000 patients, some in hospitals and some in their homes, which they would not or could not leave because of their injuries after the quake. One of the patients was a woman in her 70s, whose left thighbone had been broken by a fallen roof. Her family had used cotton balls and two pieces of plywood to stabilize the injury. She did not dare to make the slightest move, for fear that the jagged edges of the broken bone prick the surrounding tissue and cause excruciating pain. She lay still for several days and ants built nests in the cotton rolls covering her wounds. "When we removed the plywood, ants ran out of the dressing," said Dr. Su Quan-fa, chief of neurosurgery from Tzu Chi's Hualien hospital, who performed the operation. "Having been bed-ridden and motionless for several days, the poor woman had bedsores on her buttocks. You can imagine the pain she must have endured." The team fixed her broken bone with steel plates.

In one hospital, with 125 beds, more than 600 patients arrived on one day after the quake and 63 passed away during that day. Beds were placed in the hallways and in big tents set up by the military.

Since there was so little space, male and female patients were placed together, with no privacy. Family members sat or lay by the beds of their loved ones. Volunteers went to outlying villages and treated anyone who needed help. Unaccustomed to medical care, many villagers were skeptical and watched from a distance. A few came forward. As the news of the treatment spread, so many came that the doctors had to work into the night by candlelight.

TIMA teams also played an important role in Sri Lanka, in the aftermath of the tsunami that devastated the island on December 26, 2004. For a period of 35 days, medical teams took turns to provide emergency medical treatment and psychological counseling to 27,000 people. Many suffered from chronic illnesses and psychological traumas that will require long-term assistance.

A typical member of TIMA is Ling Sing Yew, an oral surgeon and university teacher in Singapore. A devout Christian, he enjoyed a comfortable life as a doctor and father of four children. In 1999, a surgeon friend invited him to a free clinic in Jakarta. The team first stayed in a five-star hotel in the city, complete with swimming pool and golf course. The next morning they left their hotel and the wide, clean avenues and drove over pock-marked roads to a building next to a filthy river, which the residents used to wash and do laundry in and throw rubbish and urinate into. Used to the order and cleanliness of Singapore, Ling was shocked. The clinic was held in a community center, where an operating room consisted of two tables and the patients came in their ordinary clothes. There was no running water; volunteers had to scoop water from a nearby well and bring it to the surgeons. "There was not enough light," Ling said. "Everything was makeshift and simple. It was the first time that I had ever conducted operations this way. I was scared and paid a lot of attention to sterilization procedures, in which I probably doubled the usual dosages."

It was a life-changing experience. Ling became a devoted TIMA member, participating in free clinics in Indonesia and the Philippines for the next three years, which involved hundreds of medical professionals and thousands of patients. "Buddha was the son of an Indian king," Ling commented. "He lived happily in a palace and knew nothing about the illness and suffering in the world. One day he walked out of his palace and saw poverty, sickness and death. He never returned to his normal life in the palace. He had walked out and could never return again."

Dr. Lin Chin-lon, superintendent of the Tzu Chi hospital in Talin, has taken part in many overseas clinics. He said that it was only because of the international recognition of Tzu Chi's work of the last 40 years that it was allowed to enter Islamic countries like Iran and Pakistan.

"Doctors, nurses and pharmacists from Tzu Chi hospitals fight for the opportunity to go," explained Lin. They know that, while it is tiring, it is a great spiritual inspiration." Taiwan hospitals provide a wide range of medical facilities but emergency missions confront the doctor with a severe shortage of facilities and manpower. "The doctor has to work with the facilities at hand and realizes the close relation between poverty and medicine. Free treatment is not only about providing medical care, it is even more a rare opportunity to provide love and concern. It is a great benefit for the practice of Buddhism."

7

CHINA

---

*"The people in the mainland and Taiwan are innocent. The
tensions between the two sides are the result of politicians. Love
can ease the tensions and avoid war. The people there are very
polite to us. We do not talk of politics or religion."*

—Kao Ming-san, a Tzu Chi volunteer from Taiwan,
who has been working in the mainland since 1997.

ON THE AFTERNOON OF MAY 12, 2008, a devastating earthquake
struck the Southwest province of Sichuan, killing 70,000 people and
injuring 375,000: it was the worst earthquake in China for 32 years. On
the afternoon of May 15, a China Airlines cargo flight, with 100 tons of
supplies and a relief team from Tzu Chi, flew from Taipei to the Sichuan
capital of Chengdu. The foundation was the first foreign NGO to
reach the disaster zone. In the absence of regular flights between Taiwan
and the mainland, the relief mission required special permission from the
two governments. It was the start of a long-term mission to Sichuan
that continues today, including distribution of food, daily necessities
and medicines, medical care and construction of schools and homes,
temporary and permanent. By mid-August, it had provided hot meals
to 818,600 people and medical care to 45,000. Tzu Chi's rescue and
reconstruction work received widespread coverage in the Chinese media,
giving the foundation a prominence it has never enjoyed before.

This access and the coverage it received is a sign of how far Tzu Chi
has come in its 18 years in China, its largest and most controversial
overseas mission. China is the country in which it has invested the most
money, resources and manpower since it first delivered aid to victims of
severe flooding on the Yangtze River in 1991. Since then, it has given

food, clothes, blankets and medicines to hundreds of thousands of victims of natural disasters.

It has built 40 schools, 4,100 homes, 158 nursing homes for old people, 13 day care centers, two hospital buildings and 13,400 water cisterns for farmers in the arid province of Gansu. It has provided scholarships to more than 7,000 students. Its bone marrow bank has made more than 580 donations to patients in the mainland, the largest of any single country and accounting for nearly 40 percent of total donations. Staff from Tzu Chi hospitals in Taiwan, together with doctors and nurses from mainland hospitals, have held free medical clinics. All this has made it the biggest foreign NGO charity in China.

In March 2007, the Chinese government named Tzu Chi one of the top 10 philanthropists of 2006. State television broadcast a 90-minute program nationwide about the 10, with a five-minute segment on the foundation's work in the mainland, including a brief clip of Cheng Yen speaking. It broadcast the program twice and the news was also carried in the People's Daily, the mouthpiece of the Communist Party. In February 2008, Beijing gave it permission to establish a foundation in China, the first non-mainland NGO to earn such a right. It was a sign of the government's appreciation of its contribution and its confidence that Tzu Chi has no political, religious or social agenda.

The mission to the mainland has a double significance. Hostility between China and Taiwan is one of the last legacies of the Cold War. The Nationalist government withdrew to Taiwan after losing the civil war in 1949 and there was no direct contact between the two sides until 1987. Since then, Taiwanese companies have invested $45 billion in 74,000 projects in the mainland and about one million Taiwanese live there on a long-term basis. Political relations were bad until the election of Nationalist President Ma Ying-jeou in March 2008. Beijing insists that Taiwan is part of its territory, a concept rejected by the vast majority of Taiwanese. The two sides have not signed a peace treaty: since 1949, politicians on both sides have been incapable of ending the conflict.

Cheng Yen sees her mission in China as a contribution to ending this conflict: "We must arouse love as a bridge and soften the enmity. The people of Taiwan and the mainland are from the same source and the same race. Their joint roots are very deep and should not be enemies."

Tzu Chi carefully avoids politics. Its relations with the mainland are with individuals—farmers who use its water wells, children who receive its scholarships, families who live in the houses it has built, old people who live in its nursing homes and victims of disasters who receive its food, clothes and medicines. It has relations with the officials who supervise these projects, at the local and central level. In their dealings, members of Tzu Chi are careful not to discuss politics and other sensitive subjects, so as not to arouse suspicion of ulterior motives. They focus on the projects at hand. They have won the trust and confidence of these Chinese officials who have seen that there is no secret agenda and no political sub-text. Its cross-straits policy is of love and engagement, one that aims to show the volunteer a farmer in Guizhou as an individual struggling to make a living in the face of poverty and drought, and show to the farmer a Taiwanese willing to share part of his wealth and good fortune with him. It is an interaction between two individuals, not political entities. If politicians cannot make peace, individuals must do it.

The second significance of the mainland mission is that, if there is one people in the world who can comprehend and accept Tzu Chi's philosophy, it is the people of China. The Buddhism Cheng Yen teaches is rooted in the mainland, where the religion arrived from India 2,000 years ago. Her mentor is Yin Shun, a famous scholar from Zhejiang, East China, who trained at monasteries in the mainland and lived there for the first 40 years of his life. She draws extensively from Confucius, one of China's most famous philosophers. The language in which Cheng Yen speaks and in which her books are written is Chinese. If Tzu Chi is to become a world movement, then it must take root in China.

The moment could not be more propitious. Three decades of prosperity in China have created an urban middle class numbering tens of millions—lawyers, teachers, businessmen, bankers, stockbrokers and computer engineers—similar to the class that provides the backbone of the foundation's membership in Taiwan. Many have the education, surplus income, and sense of service that makes them ready to donate to the foundation and participate in its activities. Millions of Chinese are also becoming increasingly troubled by the country's widening inequality. According to a 2007 survey by the Chinese Academy of Social Sciences, the richest 10 percent of Chinese families own more than 40 percent of private assets, while the poorest 10 percent share less than two percent. Income distribution in China is more unequal than in India and the United States. In June 2007, Chinese were stunned to see slave children working in brick kilns for no pay and little food in the provinces of Henan and Shanxi. The children, some as young as eight, had been sold to the employers for 500 yuan ($60) each.

Tzu Chi members see the enormous potential of China, as well its needs among the population, and how much more they could do if they could mobilize local money and volunteers. However, the foundation is unable to grow at the speed it would like. All foreign NGO operations are restricted in the mainland and Tzu Chi, despite its achievements, is no exception. It is not allowed to raise money in public, even for victims of disasters in the mainland. It cannot run its own schools and hands those it builds to the local government. It cannot publish a newspaper or magazine. When it sends a relief mission, the government still has to approve each member in advance. China's government will also not allow its people to watch Tzu Chi's satellite television channel—unless they can find it on the internet or illegally install a satellite dish. Nor can mainland Chinese join the organization, although they can take part in its projects unofficially. So the vast majority of the population have no idea what Tzu Chi is or what it is doing.

Despite this seeming setback, however, members are diplomatic: get on with the work they can do and see the cup as half-full, not half-empty. After all, they can do so much more today than 10 years ago, so how much more will they be able to do 10 years from now?

The work of the foundation in China was a major reason the people of Taiwan donated NT$21 billion ($420 million) toward the victims of the Sichuan earthquake, the largest amount of any foreign country. "When people on the mainland are hit by natural disasters, people in Taiwan express their loving care," said Cheng Yen. "This leaves a common feeling in the hearts of both, which can be a bridge of love and promote a cycle of love between the two sides."

She sees individuals not politics, saying that, whenever she had come into contact with mainland people, she had felt their goodness and honesty. "Even if they are leaders, there is love in their hearts. If there is true sharing of the heart, then everyone will have love in his or her heart. . . Politics involve a small number of people but influence the common people. They are truly innocent. From the religious point of view, we should love everyone on earth. Life is equal. Criminals, even those sentenced to death, receive the same treatment at the Tzu Chi hospital as others."

Li Feng (李逢) is an example of how Tzu Chi has transformed the life of an individual. She was abandoned by a father, a poor farmer in Sichuan, on a country road at the age of five because she was blind. She is one of thousands of baby girls in China abandoned every year by their families, who regard them as a burden: when they marry, they become part of the husband's family and owe their loyalty and earnings to that family. The fact that Li was blind and unable to do manual labor was another reason to discard her. Li was sent to a state-run welfare institute for orphans and abandoned children in Wuhan, an industrial city on the Yangtze River. It was an old, dilapidated building, with a leaking roof and the children packed there in a single bed. When volunteers from the foundation visited the institute, they were shocked by its poor condition and said they would build a new one. In October 1997, it opened a Tzu Chi Children's Welfare Institute in Wuhan, on 17.4 acres of land, with space for 500 orphans. It includes facilities for medical care, rehabilitation, teaching and recreation.

During the construction work, the volunteers discovered Li. At the age of nine, she had been sent to a special school for the blind, where she developed a talent for the piano, winning a special prize in an Asian piano competition in 2003. Despite her handicap, she was talented, intelligent and determined. The volunteers saw a talent that could be developed: they encouraged her to study for the highly competitive university entrance examination and offered to pay her tuition and living expenses if she passed.

Without this, Li would have been unable to go. She became only the second student from the institute to pass the college exam and in autumn 2006 went to Changchun, in Northeast China, to study acupuncture and massage, a skill that will enable her to earn a living for the rest of her life. Before going, she went to Hualien, during celebrations for the foundation's 40th anniversary. She met Cheng Yen, who gave her a set of chanting beads.

The Great Love Television channel covered widely Li's achievements, to show how a person with a positive outlook and hard work can overcome a severe handicap. Her life is an example of how the love and concern of the foundation has transformed the life of a person who, as a blind village girl abandoned by her family, had no future. She has developed to the point that she can give love to others. "We are no longer aid recipients," she wrote to Cheng Yen. "We have learned to become givers, each according to our abilities. Our hearts carry a lot of love, which is transformed into power strong enough to prompt us to move forward. We will share this love with people who love us and with those who need it." This is a remarkable sentiment from a young person with a terrible handicap and, for the foundation, the realization of its ideal—the person who is helped is able to help others, starting a circle of virtue.

First mission

Tzu Chi began its aid to the mainland in the summer of 1991, a few months after the start of its international relief in April that year, to Bangladesh. From mid-June, the worst flooding in a century hit more than a dozen provinces in East China and continued for over two months. In Hualien, Cheng Yen watched on television the footage of burst dams, fields and villages covered with water and thousands of people living in tents and in the open air. She was deeply distressed, wept and could not sleep or eat. On July 15, she received a message from members of the U.S. chapter of Tzu Chi, who wished to contribute money for mainland relief and asked for her judgment before going ahead.

It was no simple decision. She knew that extending aid to the mainland would be, for her members and the Taiwan public on which they depend for funds, more controversial than help to any other country. More than 40 years after the end of the civil war, political relations between Taiwan and the mainland remained hostile. Neither government recognized the other and while Taiwan people had been allowed to visit the mainland since 1987, they traveled on a "Taiwan compatriot" document issued by Beijing, which gave them no consular protection in the event of arrest or legal disputes. The People's Liberation Army had a large concentration of land, naval and air forces in the Southeast, including 1,000 long-range missiles, able to attack Taiwan at a moment's notice. Beijing threatened an attack in the event of the island declaring independence.

When Chiang Kai-shek retreated to Taiwan in 1949, he brought with him 1.6 million people. Most had lost all their goods and property to the new Communist government, not to speak of family, friends, colleagues and comrades-in-arms killed, imprisoned or persecuted in war and political campaigns. How would they react to the news that Tzu Chi was giving aid to the "enemy"? Another reason for caution was the knowledge that, if aid were distributed through official channels, much of it would not reach the people for whom it was intended but end up in the pockets of local officials. In addition, the Communist government severely restricted freedom of religion, not allowing Buddhists to open schools, hospitals or help the poor—the very activities which Tzu Chi did in Taiwan and overseas. In 1989, Beijing had issued an order expressly forbidding Buddhists from proselytizing. The mainland was one of the few countries in the world with a large Chinese population but no Tzu Chi organization.

There were also logistical problems. Since Taiwan did not allow direct flights to the mainland, Tzu Chi volunteers and materials would go through a third country, increasing time and expense. The work would be difficult because the disaster-hit areas were not in major cities but in rural regions that were difficult to reach. To deliver relief goods would require days of traveling and an enormous logistical effort. Working in the mainland would impose on the volunteers stress they did not encounter elsewhere—fear of detention or interrogation, with no access to consular help. How would mainland officials, raised for four decades on anti-Taiwan propaganda, react to them?

Opinion within the foundation was divided. Some argued that, if it wished to help victims of natural disasters abroad, there were many other countries apart from China. Faced with such a complex decision, Cheng Yen did not hurry. The first question was whether her own government would allow such aid and whether Beijing would accept it. Her brother and foundation vice-president, Wang Duan-cheng (王端正), contacted the government's mainland affairs council, headed at the time by Ma Ying-jeou, who was elected President of Taiwan in March 2008. To their surprise, he said that the government would have no objection: "We were waiting for a civilian organization like Tzu Chi to offer such relief to disaster victims on the mainland."

Ma Ying-jeou approached the mainland government, through a prominent Taiwan scholar, who was told the aid would be welcome. After receiving these assurances, Cheng Yen decided on August 2 to proceed. She had to explain her decision to her members. "The teaching of Buddha is to extend love and compassion to everyone on earth, without conditions. We have ties of blood with the victims of the flooding in the mainland that are thicker than water. Can we stand idly by and do nothing?"

Cheng Yen set up a team, headed by Wang Duan-cheng and Tseng Wen-bin, director of the Hualien hospital, to take charge of the aid operation. The two men led a six-man team that flew to the mainland to visit the affected areas and decide what aid would be most appropriate.

Wang and his team told local officials that they wanted to find the worst-hit area and deliver the aid directly to the victims, who would feel at first hand the love and concern of Tzu Chi. They promised they would not speak of politics or proselytize Buddhism or the philosophy of Tzu Chi. They would give cash, medicines, clothing and foodstuffs, including six months' supply of rice, to help the victims survive the winter. The talks were difficult and the two sides could not reach an agreement. The Chinese officials proposed that Tzu Chi give money, which they would spend on aid items. Some suspected the visitors of a secret political and religious agenda. Wang's team returned, disappointed, to their hotel and prepared to go home, their mission a failure. Suddenly, due to intervention by Yan Ming-fu, Deputy Chairman of the China Disaster Relief Association, and who was familiar with Tzu Chi and supported its work, the mainland side had a change of heart and accepted the foundation's offer.

The team selected Anhui province as the target of its aid. On August 25, Cheng Yen chose a speech to major donors at the Sun Yat-sen Memorial Hall, one of Taipei's biggest meeting halls, to launch her appeal for the mainland. It was one of the most important speeches of her life, to persuade her own members and the public at large. She explained they had a moral duty to help the flood victims on the mainland, as worthy of Buddha's compassion as people suffering elsewhere in the world. They could not distinguish between a flood victim in Anhui and another in Argentina. "It is easy to love your friend, it is difficult to love your enemy." The speech was widely covered by the Taiwan media and provoked a fierce response.

It sparked a flood of protests, which the foundation would never experience in any future foreign aid program. The first criticism was that Tzu Chi should not spend such money abroad when there was much to do at home. The second was that it was aiding "the enemy," who maintained the daily threat of an attack or invasion. Providing help to the victims would save the government from having to do so and enable it to save money to buy more arms and missiles to target Taiwan, they argued. In response, Cheng Yen explained that they were giving aid not to the Communist Party but to innocent victims. "In addition to providing physical aid, we will move their cold heart. The good fortune (fubao) of man is not diminished by the giving of alms. It is like water in a well. If the source does not provide water, then the well will dry up. If everyone awakens the love of their compatriots, it will soften their hatred, awaken their intuition and arouse their sense of warmth toward others. This awareness of blessing will create blessing."

Fifteen years later, she recalled that her decision had made her a criminal in Taiwan. "Even until today, they have not forgiven me, but I have not stopped breathing." Cheng Yen said that those who opposed the project had not deeply reflected and had politicized people and events. "From the religious point of view, we should love everyone on earth. Life is equal and we should respect life."

The weight of her moral authority and organizational ability of the foundation won the day. In December, it held an auction at National Taiwan University to raise money for the mainland and, by February 1992, it had collected NT$412 million ($13 million) for the mainland operation. The opposition remained, but a majority of Tzu Chi members and the public were persuaded by her arguments and supported the decision.

Given the sensitivities involved, the foundation prepared the first mission with meticulous care. The members chosen were instructed to take no newspapers or magazines from Taiwan, to be as discreet as possible in their language and behavior and not talk about politics or other sensitive issues.

After three evaluation trips, Cheng Yen addressed the first 30 commissioners who were to go. She told them that their mission was for Buddha and for humanity. "While the mainland has forbidden religion for many years and does not know the essentials of Buddhism, we hope that this relief mission will, without words, enable them to know the importance of Buddhism to mankind.

"You must treat them equally and must not display, in word or action, any sense of superiority as a result of the wealthy lifestyle of Taiwan, or hurt their feelings even if you do not intend to. You must show the character, education and appearance of Tzu Chi, be well-mannered, soft in your language, smile and show them the dignified culture of Taiwan."

She said that the relief operations in the mainland represented a major new step for the movement and each member must be conscious of his or her responsibilities. The success or failure of this mission would depend on Tzu Chi's future involvement in the mainland.

During this first mission, in October, 43 members went to 22 counties and towns in Anhui province and distributed 19,687 cotton coats and trousers, blankets, seeds, fertilizer and 100 yuan ($12) in cash to each of the victims. In December, members delivered 1,635 cotton coats and trousers and 984 pieces of bedding in Xinghua, Jiangsu province. In January, they continued large-scale aid, including 35,000 pieces of cotton clothing, 2,220 pieces of bedding, 1,230 tons of rice, 900 tons of fertilizer and 80 tons of seeds, to more than 40,000 flood victims in Henan and Anhui provinces. These large-scale relief projects became the hallmark of Tzu Chi operations in the mainland, which suffers every year from floods, typhoons, snowstorms and other natural disasters.

Tzu Chi has continued to expand and now has projects in almost every corner of China, from Harbin in the far North to Hainan in the South, Shanghai in the East to the far West region of Xinjiang, close to the border with Kazakhstan. In addition to building schools, homes, old people's homes and day care centers, it has each year delivered emergency aid to tens of thousands of victims of floods, typhoons, snow storms and other natural disasters, as well as providing animal feed, pesticide and fertilizer. In April 1996, for example, it provided 55 lbs of wheat each to 16,000 people in Qinghai province, West China, suffering from food shortages as a result of snow falls that cut off one region for several months and left 60,000 households suffering from food shortages. In June and September 2001, it distributed three months' supply of relief goods to 20,000 herdsmen in 10 remote townships in Inner Mongolia and held a free medical clinic for them. This vast region, with 706,000 square miles, or 12 percent of China's land area, is a huge prairie on the country's Northern border with Mongolia.

These are major logistical operations, involving shipment of enormous quantities of material by air, road or rail to remote areas and mobilization of hundreds of volunteers, whom are each paying their own way. Most destinations and projects are in remote, backward locations, with poor transport links, little touched by the economic prosperity of the last 20 years. For the volunteers, the missions are costly, time-consuming and exhausting. The mainland side would prefer the foundation give funds directly, saying that it would be easier and more efficient for the local government to disburse the money. But Tzu Chi insists that its members distribute the goods themselves and express their thanks to the recipients, in this way it remains an exchange between two individuals.

The volunteers come from Taiwan and the communities of Taiwanese living in China, which have grown rapidly since the early 1990s. More than one million Taiwanese, about five percent of the island's population, are long-term residents of the mainland. Among them are many members, whose involvement has greatly facilitated the growth of its operations in China. As residents, they have a detailed knowledge of the mainland, its laws, regulations and officials, enabling them to react quickly and effectively to natural disasters.

One of the places with the largest concentration of Taiwanese investment is Suzhou, an ancient city with beautiful classical gardens that is also a center of the IT industry. The foundation has a large number of members in Suzhou, which is the first, and so far the only, city in China to receive permission to open a branch, in 2006. The next year, it opened a bookshop, again a first, which employs 10 graduates from universities in the city.

According to official mainland figures, Tzu Chi has invested two billion yuan ($260 million) in its projects in China since 1991. They have earned the trust and support of the authorities, so that its missions are no longer followed by the police and are welcomed by the communities they benefit. In Taiwan, the public debate over whether Tzu Chi should help the mainland has subsided. Two decades of people-to-people contact have melted much of the hostility and suspicion that followed Cheng Yen's speech in August 1991.

Even so, opposition remains among the Taiwan public. Hsieh Ching-kuei, director of the department of religion and humanitarian aid, explains: "Our account for international aid does not distinguish between the mainland and other countries. This hostility (toward the mainland) diminished after the September 1999 earthquake in Taiwan, when 20 countries sent 37 rescue teams to help. Many did not know Taiwan and did not need to come. But some people still complain. We do not talk politics. Love is the only way to resolve conflict."

Water in the desert

There are few places on earth less fit for human habitation than the Loess Plateau of Gansu province in West China. The land has no grass and is covered by loess, a thin yellowish-brown deposit of soil left by the wind. With almost no groundwater, the inhabitants depend on the small amount of rain that falls between July and September. Most live in homes built of mud and their only furniture are brick beds, and pots and pans. They eke out a living by raising two or three sheep, and growing potatoes and other vegetables on small patches of land.

Like much of West China, Gansu suffers from desertification and an acute shortage of water. It is one of the poorest provinces of China, with a per capita income of 5,000 yuan ($650) a year.

On the plateau is Dongxiang county, four hours drive from the provincial capital of Lanzhou. Most of its inhabitants are Dongxiang, a Moslem ethnic minority, descendants of Arab and Persian traders who came to China about 700 years ago. With poor roads, they live remote and isolated from the rest of the world.

Tzu Chi learnt of the plight of these villages and their need for water. Better-off families built their own water cisterns; primitive ones lasted only three years before the soil made the water dirty. The poor had no cisterns and had to walk several hours a day to bring water home from wells, in buckets or on the backs of donkeys. Water is so scarce that some people never take a bath in their entire lives: they make do with a towel soaked in water used by the whole family. Others take a bath twice in their life—before they marry and after their death.

The foundation began its work in 1997, when volunteers from Tainan in Southern Taiwan built 300 cisterns in two counties. It was an enormous journey, flying first from Taipei to Hong Kong, then Beijing and onto Lanzhou, followed by a drive of four hours. In 1999, volunteers from Shanghai took over the project and built cisterns in Dongxiang county. The place left a deep impression on them: "It happened to be winter every time we went there," said Lin Pi-yu. "All that met our eyes were endless stretches of bare loess. Not a single blade of grass was in sight. Almost every child had scabies on their head and their skin was covered with ringworm. Just looking at them made my heart ache. Only one in 10 families can afford to eat food made from wheat. The rest have only potatoes to eat."

The poverty and resolution of the people to survive in such a difficult environment moved the volunteers. Construction of a cistern costs 1,000 yuan ($120) and can last 20-25 years. The system collects water on the roof and the courtyard and runs it through a filtering pond into a bottle-shaped cistern for storage. For a family of five, the water collected during the rainy season is enough to sustain them for half a year. This water improves the hygiene of the family and increases the number of livestock they rear. It saves them the hours spent to fetch water, which they can use for other activities and earn money. So the residents call them "water of happiness, cisterns of wealth."

In Dongxiang, the foundation has also built two schools, repaired 18 homes and delivered rice to 4,500 families during the winter of 2007.

As of the end of 2007, the foundation had built 13,415 water cisterns in six counties in Gansu. It provides building materials, including bricks, sand, cement and water-collecting pipes, while the household does the building. Kenneth Tai, who was one of the founders of the Acer computer company and now runs his own investment firm, is one of the Tzu Chi volunteers responsible for the Gansu project. "In business, we speak of return on investment. Each well costs 1,000-1,200 yuan ($125 to $150) and will bring an annual return of 1,000 yuan to the farmer, because he knows that he has water for his crop, which he does not have now. If there is no rain, he has no harvest.

"When I am with the farmers and their children, I receive a happiness that I cannot describe. A rich man stays in the best hotels and has the best goods, but is not satisfied. He wants more. This experience is something else," he said.

Scholarships for poor children

"The more time we devote to the program, the more suffering children we find."

Xu Juan-juan, a Tzu Chi volunteer living in China

In 1997, Tzu Chi started a scholarship program for needy children and began to build schools in poor provinces, including Jiangxi, Guizhou, Henan and Gansu. The scholarship project was born after the completion of the foundation's first school in China, the Baizhu Elementary School, in an impoverished county in the Southwest province of Jiangxi, in September 1997. The school was funded by foundation members in Shanghai and elsewhere in China, but they discovered that, while they had built a proper school, more than 30 percent of the pupils were too poor to attend. Since the scholarship program began, it has helped 7,000 students in remote areas. In 1986, China introduced a system of nine years of free and compulsory education. In theory, that means that a child can attend six years of primary school and three years of junior middle schools without paying. But, in reality, schools charge a variety of fees, which many students, especially those in rural areas, cannot afford. A lack of education and low literacy mean that they can only do low-paying jobs and spend the rest of their life at the bottom of the social ladder.

The foundation decided to offer scholarships to children with talent and potential, who would benefit from higher education but were unable to continue school because their families are too poor.

First, volunteers identify potential candidates and assess the financial situation of their families. Once they have picked the candidates, they visit the family on a regular basis and give the money in installments to the student in person. They monitor their progress and ensure that the money is being spent on education and not on something else. Since many families live in poor, remote areas, this means extensive and time-consuming travel by the volunteers, with the journey often ending with a walk up a mountain because there is no road. They form a close bond with the families of the recipients.

One of them is Qiu Yu-fen, a Taiwanese who has lived in Shanghai since she went there on business in 1992. To distribute the money, she visits the home of each student, so that she can understand their family situation and help them apply for the appropriate subsidy. "Education is especially important for children living in remote, backward areas," she said. "I always remember what my mother said to me, 'Only through incessant effort can a poor country girl change her fate.'" This is especially true of a girl in rural China, who will, without education, spend her life working the land and looking after her husband and his family. Her husband is likely to leave home to find work, leaving her to carry the domestic burden alone. Rural families consider the education of a son more important than that of a daughter: if money is short, they will withdraw her from school before her brother. So an education is the only way to give a rural girl an alternative choice in life.

Qiu has a particular sympathy for the children because she came from a poor family. After the family grocery shop closed and her father could only find work as a security guard, her mother had to beg friends and family to lend money to put Qiu through school. "My family had to put up with a lot of sarcasm when they tried to borrow money. I swore to myself that, one day, if I were able to, I would help poor children to continue receiving an education.

"Helping a child go to school is like giving hope to his or her family and may even change the fate of the child's descendants. Our determination to help these students is greatly strengthened when we hear some of them say that their greatest wish is to help those in need in the future— just as Tzu Chi volunteers do."

8

INDONESIA—EASING
CENTURIES OF HATRED

THE MISSION OF TZU CHI IN INDONESIA has a special meaning: a Buddhist charity founded by Chinese is helping the poor and underprivileged in a Muslim country with a history of violence and discrimination against its Chinese population.

Many Chinese in Indonesia enjoy wealth and a standard of living which their compatriots cannot dream of. Accounting for two to three percent of the country's 220 million people, ethnic Chinese own about 70 percent of its private corporate wealth.

This gap between the wealth of a few and the poverty of the many has nourished a hatred that has led to regular attacks on the Chinese and their property over the last 100 years. The most violent came in May 1998, when the country was suffering the full impact of the Asian Financial Crisis, and left 1,200 people dead.

From that great evil, Tzu Chi has sought to find good, in persuading the Chinese in Indonesia that they and their children will have a better future by earning the love and respect of their compatriots rather than putting their money into bank accounts in Singapore and Switzerland.

The foundation has built housing for the poor of Jakarta and victims of the tsunami in Aceh, distributed rice to over two million families, helped earthquake victims and tuberculosis patients and held free medical clinics for tens of thousands of people.

"All conflicts between people are caused by selfishness," Cheng Yen told a Tzu Chi delegation from Indonesia in December 2003. "The power of love can soothe many prejudices. If everyone can open their heart and express the greatness of love, then there will not be conflict.

"Around the world, Chinese business people have earned people's respect, because they have given this love. So many people are suffering and need their help. If everyone who is rich can reach where they are needed, that is a life that is valuable."

Never was this love more needed than after the riots in Jakarta and five other cities in May 1998, in the country's worst communal violence of the twentieth century, mainly targeted at Chinese.

According to the Asian Human Rights Commission, 1,188 people were killed, 101 seriously injured, 40 shopping centers were burnt and 2,479 houses and shops, 1,119 cars and 1,026 civilian houses were destroyed. A total of 66 women, mostly ethnic Chinese, were raped.

The rioters stopped trams and cars, searching them for Chinese, and targeted shops owned by Chinese. Thousands of Chinese fled, some permanently, to the United States, Australia, Singapore and the Netherlands.

But the majority of Chinese could not or did not want to leave the land of their birth, their family and their business. So what could they do to stop the riots happening again and end a cycle of hatred and violence lasting more than 100 years?

Cheng Yen's answer was that the Chinese must win the trust and confidence of their fellow citizens by showing their love and concern and change their image of a people driven only by money, family loyalty and accumulation of material goods. They should put back into the community some of the profits they had made from it.

Her appeal touched thousands of people, including business leaders. Since the 1998 riots, the size and scope of the foundation's activities in Indonesia have grown rapidly; out of a great tragedy can come an unexpected good.

Tzu Chi arrived in Jakarta in the early 1990s, when wives of Taiwan businessmen began to visit orphanages, old people's homes and leprosaria and provide subsidies for poor students.

In the summer of 1993, six of the wives, all members of Tzu Chi, went to Hualien for a week of voluntary work in the hospital, the prison and visiting aid recipients. They met Cheng Yen, who told them to give love and compassion to the people where they lived.

Later that year, the leader of the group returned with her husband to Taiwan. The others chose as her replacement Liu Su-mei (劉素美), the 37-year-old wife of a shoe manufacturer who had moved to Indonesia in 1991, setting up a factory in Bekasi, East of the capital. Since then, she has been chief of Tzu Chi in Indonesia.

"In the beginning, we were acting in the dark. We did not know the language, we did not have a network and sometimes could not find the places we wanted to go."

During the Suharto era (1966–1998), it was illegal to have material in the Chinese language, so they had to smuggle in Tzu Chi books at the bottom of their suitcases. In addition, Chinese needed official approval to hold meetings; police used to watch their gatherings in the city's Taipei school. Sometimes police knocked on the door of Liu's home to make sure that there was no illegal activity.

In November 1994, a volcano erupted on Mount Merapi, in Central Java, and, with the aid of Taiwan businessmen, the members organized shipments of tents, blankets, food, water and medicine to the victims on the side of the mountain. They visited the site eight times and built 12 homes for the victims.

In November 1995, the members started to co-operate with two health bureaus West of Jakarta, to provide tuberculosis medicine and nutritional supplements to villagers. TB has been the second major cause of death in Indonesia; in poor villages, those suffering from it could not obtain the long-term treatment required. In one area, Tzu Chi's efforts enabled 88 percent of the patients to recover.

In November 1996, the members set up a Tzu Chi liaison office in Jakarta; it became a branch in September 1999. In 1997, they offered free clinics to poor people who could not afford to see a doctor. (Indonesia has no national health insurance policy and medical fees are high.)

Their activities were modest until the arrival of two Chinese tycoons who run multi-billion-dollar businesses employing thousands of people and have connections from the top to the bottom of society.

The first was Franky Oesman Widjaja, whose Chinese name is Huang Rong-nian, the eighth child of one of Indonesia's richest men, Eka Tjipta Widjaja (Huang Yi-tsong), the founder of the Sinar Mas Group. The secretary of the elder Huang was a Tzu Chi member named Jia Wen-yu, who had studied at Taiwan Politics University and had joined the foundation in 1995. Jia persuaded the two men to visit Hualien in May 1998 and call on Cheng Yen.

The elder Huang told her how the Asian Financial Crisis had worsened living conditions of the poor in Indonesia. She encouraged him to return to the community some of what he had earned.

For the younger Huang, it was a life-changing experience. "The first time I saw Cheng Yen, I immediately dropped to my knees and asked to be converted," he recalled. "My brain is simple and did not really understand the meaning of conversion. I just felt deeply happy."

His father, a Protestant, approved the decision but on condition that he did not neglect the family business. "That is our responsibility. So many people depend on us for their living."

That was May 9, 1998. Just four days later, rioting broke out in Jakarta and five other major cities, mainly targeted at Chinese people and their businesses, in the most widespread anti-Chinese violence in Indonesia since independence in 1950.

Among the mansions burnt down was that of Liem Sioe Liang, Indonesia's richest man and a close confidant of President Suharto. The riots occurred in cities with large military garrisons and police forces who did little or nothing to protect them. Many had paid money to the security forces, as insurance for just such a crisis. To guard their properties, Chinese formed self-protection brigades which patrolled 24 hours a day.

Even Liem, who had the ear of the president, could not save his property. Later investigations showed complicity by sections of the security forces in the riots, part of a struggle to overthrow Suharto, who resigned on May 21.

The violence caused thousands of Chinese to flee. Liem moved abroad and left his business empire to his children. Huang Rong-nian took shelter in Singapore and chartered planes to fly his family, friends and the managers of his company to safety in Singapore and Taiwan.

The riots were a turning point for many Chinese. Some concluded they had no future in the country and made the difficult decision to emigrate with their families.

Others reached a different conclusion. "Indonesians are not anti-Chinese, they are simply too poor," said Huang. "They are sincere and good-natured people. Proportionally, Chinese are better off and run many shops. As life became more difficult for the poor, people instigated them to loot and burn shops that were well-stocked with goods."

For him, poverty and not racism was the cause of the riots. On January 22, the value of Indonesia's currency, the rupiah, fell to a low of 17,000 to the U.S. dollar, from 2,450 in July 1997. The financial crisis pushed the number of those in poverty—on less than $2 a day—to 60–70 million or one third of the population.

For Tzu Chi, the lesson was not to leave Indonesia but to improve ethnic harmony and give the poor hope in the future.

In June 1998, Liu Su-mei went to Hualien to seek guidance. Cheng Yen told her that they must prepare relief supplies for Indonesia, saying that only love would cure hatred. "I did not realize that she was talking of a major effort. Our ability at that time was limited."

The entry of Huang, backed by the resources of his giant corporation, made the difference. In August 1998 and January 1999, Tzu Chi organized distribution of 100,000 bags of rice and other goods to soldiers, police and civilians at 34 collection points.

Huang set up three committees within his company to do the work and sent several hundred staff to train as volunteers: they were not enthusiastic since they had to do it in their own time. Huang established a computerized control center to monitor the distribution minute-by-minute.

In January, the headquarters in Hualien sent two nuns to supervise the operation, aided by 80 Tzu Chi volunteers from Taiwan, Malaysia, Australia and the United States.

The day the visitors arrived, the streets of Jakarta were full of demonstrators burning buildings and throwing stones, but they decided to proceed. Fearing the rice would be looted en route and that they would be unable to keep order among people desperate for food, the military sent soldiers armed with machine guns to accompany each truck loaded with rice. The volunteers were told that, if looting broke out, they were to leave the materials where they were and evacuate. In the event, they were able to distribute the rice and other goods without incident.

Next was medical care. In March, July and September 1999, Tzu Chi conducted free medical clinics that treated more than 14,000 people, for illnesses such as harelips, thyroid tumors, hernias and cataracts.

Soon, more Chinese businessmen in Indonesia began to join Tzu Chi. Liu Su-mei said that the 1998 riots were a turning point for the Chinese in Indonesia and, in Buddhist terminology, predestined.

"They realized that, if they did not show their love, the next generation would receive the same treatment. So the number of our volunteers increased and the level of our donations."

She said that Indonesians were sincere and good-hearted people but simple and easily misled. "Master Cheng Yen told us that we must use our love to overcome misunderstanding. We must show them thanks and respect."

This is no simple matter for many Chinese, who live separate lives from their native compatriots. Chinese are Buddhist, Christian or Confucian and few are Muslim, the religion of 86 percent of the population. Marrying a Muslim means converting to Islam, a step most Chinese are unwilling to take.

Ethnic violence has encouraged Chinese to live in their own areas, which offer some protection in times of civil unrest. Many attend private and not government schools.

The riots were a warning to both the government and the Chinese. The government saw how much they had damaged Indonesia's international image, discouraged foreign investors and hurt the most economically productive segment of the population.

As a result, President Abdurrahman Wahid (1999–2001) lifted the ban on Chinese media and publications and designated the Chinese lunar new year as a national holiday. He allowed Chinese to learn freely Mandarin at home or at school, publish Chinese books, newspapers and magazines and celebrate their own festivals. They were also now allowed to form their own associations and political parties.

In July 2006, the parliament passed a new citizenship bill that recognizes as Indonesian anyone who is born to Indonesian parents and has never changed citizenship. This should, if implemented, end the status of second-class citizenship for Chinese and open careers in the military and other government sectors that were previously closed.

For the Chinese, the riots were a warning to improve their reputation among their fellow citizens. "The concept of Cheng Yen is correct," said Huang Yi-tsong, founder of Sinar Mas. "If the gap between rich and poor is too wide, it will sooner or later lead to problems. I had always wanted to do something but did not know what this should be. I thank Cheng Yen for showing us the way."

The next tycoon to join Tzu Chi was Sugianto Kusuma, whose Chinese name is Kuo Tsai-yuan. He is a major shareholder in the Artha Graha Group, a large property, finance and trade conglomerate.

He and his wife, who formally converted in 2002, went to Hualien at the end of 2001 and were profoundly impressed. "When I saw the Tzu Chi hospital and school, I felt that Buddhism has a future," he said. "I had never seen a Buddhist school or hospital."

While most of Tzu Chi's 100 commissioners are ethnic Chinese, the foundation is working to increase the number of native Indonesian members: it currently has a total of 10,000 members, both Chinese and native. For this purpose, and after a protracted approval process, Tzu Chi obtained a rare license for a satellite channel. The channel, which reports on the foundation's work in Indonesia in the national language, is the best way to reach the wider public and build up membership outside the Chinese community.

Red River and Great Love Village

Serious flooding in Jakarta in January 2002 led to Tzu Chi's next major project. The floods were the worst in 20 years and lasted for four weeks. Tzu Chi volunteers brought relief supplies to the victims, provided free medical care and helped in the cleanup.

They saw that the damage was due to both the heavy rain and serious pollution of 13 of the 16 rivers that run through the city.

Domestic and industrial waste dumped in the rivers had reduced their depth and flow, so that the water soon overflowed the banks and ran into the surrounding areas.

One of the worst hit districts was Kapuk Murua Village, on the Kali Angke river. The village consisted of illegally built wooden homes on stilts above the river. Over the years, the residents had dumped personal and household waste into the river, turning it black.

Originally at a depth of 23 feet, it had reduced to only three feet. The waste came from residents, who did not have public toilets and factories on the banks that discharged their waste directly into the water. Twice a month the tidal river flooded, bringing filthy water into the homes on the banks, damaging furniture and spreading disease.

On March 6, in Hualien, Huang Yi-tsong asked Cheng Yen what they should do. She laid out a five-point plan of action—pump out the water; clean the river by removing the rubbish and dead animals; kill the poisons in the river; provide medical care to the residents, especially for infectious diseases; and build a new village for the residents, since the floods would simply recur because they threw their waste into the river.

The river resonates with historical meaning for Chinese. *Angke* means "red stream," so named after Dutch rulers in 1740, fearing a rebellion by the Chinese, who had lost their monopoly of trade to the European colonists, massacred 10,000 Chinese residents of Jakarta and dumped their bodies into the river.

Cheng Yen asked the volunteers if they would clean the river. They did not wish to, because it was so dirty, but did not dare to refuse; so they agreed.

It was a filthy, laborious task. On March 24, the branch mobilized 1,000 people, including volunteers, soldiers and local residents. They boarded shallow boats and used long poles to remove nearly 100 tons of mobile telephones, electric batteries, shampoo bottles, dead animals and other rubbish, put them into white plastic bags and loaded them onto trucks. The foundation built public toilets on the site, to change the living habits of the residents.

The work continued during the summer. In late September, the city government sent excavators to remove garbage from the river. On November 4, to celebrate the cleaning, the volunteers organized a dragon boat race for the residents, an event held every year since.

The next task was new homes for those who lived on the river. The project, named Great Love Village, would cost $8 million. Kuo Tsai-yuan and Huang Rong-nian were ready to fund the construction on their own. But Cheng Yen insisted they raise the funds from a wider range of people. "I was not accustomed to doing this," said Kuo. "When it was my turn to solicit donations, I found it really hard to open my mouth. In the past, I was always the one asked to make the donation."

He made a list of entrepreneurs. "They found it strange for me to ask for money. I explained the thinking of Cheng Yen and they read her book and came to understand it. I told them that they were saving themselves. As I told one banker, it was a time bomb for us. Maybe, because I had maintained good relationships with them when doing business, they all trusted me and agreed to donate money," he said.

The city government provided five hectares in a northwest suburb and construction work began in July 2002, undertaken by Kuo's Artha Graha Group. However, squatters were already occupying the land and had to be persuaded to leave. "Tzu Chi puts a lot of emphasis on communication," Kuo said. "We were taught not to take a tough stand. So I have gradually learned to put myself in others' shoes."

The volunteers also had to negotiate with the residents on the river who were to be moved. Suspicious of officialdom, they did not believe they were being given new homes for free, especially by a Buddhist organization; they feared the move would be conditional on converting to Buddhism.

The foundation visited each household, insisting that no conversion was necessary, and set up a special unit to communicate with the residents.

The village was completed in July 2003. It consists of 1,200 housing units, each of 387 square feet, in eight five-story blocks, with gray walls and red roofs. Each unit has a living room, kitchen, bathroom and two bedrooms and a window facing the exterior, to ensure good ventilation. The village contains a primary and secondary school, a clinic, a community center, a 30-bed nursing home, an Islamic prayer room and a room to handle the dead before a funeral.

There are two sites for street stalls, a small factory making paper and a job-training center. There are also dormitories for school staff, medical professionals and volunteers.

Each block is named after a fruit, which is painted at the top of the building. This makes it easier for residents, half of them illiterate, to identify where they live. Their only cost is a monthly maintenance fee of 90,000 rupiah ($9).

The village was officially opened on August 25, 2003 by Indonesia's then president, Megawati Sukarnoputri, who thanked Tzu Chi, saying the government had wanted to improve the life of the river residents but had not been able to do so.

The village has transformed the life of the 3,000 people who moved there. They live in clean, well-built apartments, with a level of comfort and hygiene they had never known. For the first time, they have access to a modern, well-equipped school and hospital.

"After living here for a year, I still wonder from time to time whether it was real, especially when I take out my key to open the door," said a woman named Tuti, 47, who lives in a unit with her husband Edy and their seven adopted children. "This is the first time in my life that I have lived in a house with a door key."

Prior to this, the family lived for 24 years in a wooden house on the river and could not afford to move elsewhere. Like many of Jakarata's poor, they come from outside the city. Edy worked in a Jakarta factory for four years, took up sewing and rented a car to drive as a taxi. But bad health has prevented him doing a full-time job for the last 10 years: Tuti has supported the family by making and selling food.

"Now the children can eat anything they want," she said. "I never dare to think about our past. We had to share very little food. Sometimes a meal would be just rice with a few pieces of shrimp cake. In the past, my children had to stay in a tiny room filled with garbage. Now, they have stronger homes and can go to school. We do not need to worry about the health of the family. My life has improved and I have a permanent place for my business. I have been poor since I was little but now feel very fortunate. I do not have to think about floods or worry that the children might be falling into the river again."

The family is typical of those who moved to the village. With little formal education, they have limited job options. They do whatever work they can, often in poor and filthy conditions, but prefer to stay in the capital, because job opportunities and living conditions at home are even worse. Of the parents, half work as maids and laborers, earning 350,000 rupiah ($39) a month, less than half the average for Jakarta residents.

The village school, up to junior high, is the principal way to escape poverty. It has 668 students, most of them from the village, and 59 teachers: its fees are very low—10,000 rupiah ($1.1) a month for the first three years, 20,000 rupiah ($2.2) a month for the next three years and 30,000 rupiah ($3.3) a month for the final three.

It has a library, activity centre, language laboratories, music room, computer classroom, basketball field and convenience store, making it far better than many schools in Indonesia, which have no facilities. The school follows the standard Indonesian curriculum, with additional classes in Chinese and Tzu Chi philosophy, as approved by the Ministry of Education.

Since 90 percent of the students are Muslim, there are four teachers of Islam. On Friday, the holy day, the school closes at 11.20 AM, to allow students to attend prayers in a nearby mosque.

In July 2005, the foundation completed a second phase of the village on a site nearby, with 600 housing units.

Liu Su-mei, director of the Indonesian branch since 1993, said that, when she saw the residents move into the Great Love Village, she wept with happiness. "One's life consists of only a few decades. I am glad I can do something good for society in the fourth decade of my life. I am grateful for all that our volunteers have given and for the support of my family. Thanks to them, I have not lived in vain."

Tsunami

The next major project followed the tsunami, which devastated the province of Aceh, on the Northern tip of Sumatra, on December 26, 2004, killing more than 200,000 people.

Tzu Chi was the first foreign aid agency to reach the disaster. On that Boxing Day, Kuo was in Shanghai when he received a telephone call from Hualien to tell him the news. He flew back to Jakarta on December 27 and, at four the next morning, flew in a chartered plane to Bandar Aceh, the provincial capital, with four doctors and 12 tons of relief supplies.

Kuo was stunned by what he saw—a city covered with corpses, without water, power or transport. Survivors were walking in shock, with bare feet and wearing pajamas, clutching a small bag of belongings and searching desperately for family members. "What frightened me most was not the dead but the living. What had happened to make them like that, to drop everything and run away?" he said.

By December 31, doctors belonging to the Tzu Chi International Medical Association began to provide free medical care in Bandar Aceh. On January 5, Stephen Huang (黃思賢), head of the foundation's international affairs, signed an agreement with Indonesian Vice President Jusuf Kalla in Jakarta to send 33,000 tons of rice, 3,000 large tents and two sets of water purification equipment to Aceh.

As Tzu Chi kept 3,000 tons of rice in Jakarta for relief purposes, it was able to distribute that shipment quickly. The large tents were able to accommodate eight people, with two windows and equipped with simple beds and desks.

The foundation launched a major fundraising campaign, with 35,000 volunteers in Taiwan and 25 other countries taking to the streets in the first four days of January to ask for donations. The campaign in Taiwan lasted until March 31, 2005. More than 100,000 tsunami victims received help from the foundation, in food, goods or medical aid.

On January 8, Kuo led a team from Indonesia to brief Cheng Yen in Taiwan on the aid effort and work out a long-term strategy.

The foundation decided, in co-operation with the government, to build 3,700 permanent homes, in three "Great Love Villages." The villages would include power and water supply, sanitation, schools and mosques. To qualify, a family member must have a stable job and its original residence must have been made uninhabitable by the tsunami.

The first 230 units opened on December 24, 2005. Two days later, on the first anniversary of the tragedy, volunteers from Indonesia and Taiwan distributed 2,000 bags of rice to residents of the village and poor people nearby. They also gave out gas stoves, Muslim prayer rugs and blankets.

Among the visitors that day was Indonesia's President Susilo Bambang Yudhoyono, accompanied by his foreign minister and joint chief of staff. He signed his name on a memorial that records the completion of the village.

He thanked Tzu Chi for its help. "I remember that Tzu Chi volunteers arrived in Aceh on the day after the tsunami," he said. He appreciated the fact that the views of the residents had been consulted in the design of the village and said the Tzu Chi form of aid was a model for Indonesia.

To those living in tents, the gift of a secure, new home was a dream come true. "I used to pray to Allah for a new home," said Junaedi, one of the fortunate ones, moving in with his wife and daughter. "Now Tzu Chi is helping me with my new home. I think that Allah has granted me my prayers."

Islamic school

Tzu Chi has crossed the religious divide in working with the Nurul Iman boarding school, in Parung Bogor, a 90-minute drive from Jakarta. It was founded by a local Muslim teacher, Habib el Saggaf, who wanted to provide a religious education that preached tolerance for all. Habib accepted abandoned and homeless students, many of them orphans, and used money from donations to pay for the education. Practical courses in agriculture and economics account for the half of the curriculum, with the other half Islamic law, doctrines and teachings.

In 2003, Tzu Chi volunteers visited the school and found that it lacked proper food and medical services. In October that year, they agreed to provide 50 tons of rice every month and to hold a free clinic every six months. In the summer of 2005, the school completed construction of a two-story building, with 24 classrooms and 40 bathrooms, paid for by Tzu Chi.

At the opening ceremony for the new building, Habib El Saggaf said that "Still Thoughts," the sayings of Cheng Yen, would be included in the curriculum, saying that the ethics and morals they advocated were shared by Buddhism and Islam alike. He announced that a photograph of Cheng Yen would hang in each classroom—a rare presence of a Buddhist master in a Muslim religious institution. It has over 7,000 students, from the elementary to university level.

The next major projects are construction of a Tzu Chi International School, a building to house the Jakarta branch and a Hall of Still Thoughts on a 10-hectare site, part of a 216-hectare project of 2,000 luxury homes called Bukit Golf Mediteraina in Northwest Jakarta. Agung Sedayu Group, one of Kuo's companies, is carrying out the construction of the project.

The school will be private and follow the Taiwan curriculum. When the new branch is complete, the volunteers will move from their current premises, an office in a building owned by the Sinar Mas group in North Jakarta.

9

SOUTH AFRICA

*"On the day of judgment, when God comes to take His people
home, I would prefer not to go to heaven but to Hualien."*

—Gladys Ngema, a Zulu woman who was Tzu Chi's
first black commissioner in South Africa

IN A TOWNSHIP OUTSIDE DURBAN, seven Zulu volunteers in blue and
white uniforms sway gently and sing as they enter a one-room house: it
is dark but for a single candle. The mother of the house, with five children,
has just died of AIDS, the second such death in the township that day.
"All we can do is comfort the family," says one of the volunteers.

In Ladysmith, 155 miles to the North, more than 3,000 students
gather each morning at seven primary schools in rural areas around the
city. All were built by the Tzu Chi Foundation. Without them, the students
would be taking classes on stubble grass below a tree in the hot sun or
not attending school at all.

Tzu Chi has reached out beyond the Taiwanese who brought it to
South Africa to inspire thousands of local people to help the poor, the
sick and victims of AIDS and to educate thousands of poor children.
The mission has inspired people who are neither Chinese nor Buddhist:
most volunteers are devout Christians who see the message in harmony
with their own faith.

Since the first liaison office was established in Johannesburg in 1992,
the foundation has grown to 3,600 members and 70 commissioners,
with activities in seven cities, and food, clothes and blankets given to
more than 200,000 people. It collects 1.5–2.0 million rand ($227,000–
303,000) a year in donations. In Durban, it has set up 52 vocational
centers, which have trained more than 14,000 people. In Ladysmith, it

has built seven elementary schools and one kindergarten and plans an orphanage and school for 200 AIDS orphans. In Johannesburg, it has distributed food and necessities for 10 schools and carried out large-scale winter relief distribution. In Capetown, it has given aid to refugees, the poor and the homeless. It has given scholarships to poor black students.

The first black commissioner was Gladys Ngema, a 55-year-old Zulu woman in Durban, who received her badge from Cheng Yen in November 2006. A recipient of Tzu Chi aid during the winter of 1994, she was moved to help others. Since early 1995, she has worked full-time as a volunteer and leads a team of 1,200 volunteers, in poor townships in the city suburbs. "When I was at the bottom, it was Tzu Chi who saved me," she said. "Cheng Yen has sent us these messengers. We are doing God's work."

Ngema and her volunteers provide lunches two to three days a week to 1,500 AIDS orphans at 50 locations, run classes to train women to sew and knit clothes and provide help and psychological support to thousands of people who are HIV-positive. Many of her volunteers are themselves HIV-positive: they have found in the work a release from suffering and a way to turn their pain and anguish into something positive.

Tzu Chi has grown during a period of extraordinary change. In 1994, the first election with universal suffrage brought an end to 340 years of white rule and the African National Congress (ANC) to power. Blacks account for 76 percent of the population of 45 million. The ANC abolished the apartheid system in place since 1948 and promised to redress the inequalities of the past. Since then, the government has achieved GDP growth averaging three percent, built 1.9 million new homes, connected 4.5 million homes to electricity and provided 11 million homes with running water. But unemployment remains high, at 27 percent by the narrowest official definition and close to 40 percent by other estimates. Crime is serious, with 215,000 murders between 1994 and 2004: tens of thousands of skilled people, mainly whites, have emigrated.

Most tragic is the AIDS epidemic. According to estimates by the Actuarial Society of South Africa and AIDS/WHO, the disease killed 320,000 people in 2005 and 345,640 in 2006, with more than 800 people dying each day, and has left more than 1.2 million orphans. South Africa has 5.5 million HIV-positive people, the largest number of any country in the world, out of a population of 45 million. This tragedy is in part a result of policy by the government, whose leaders refused for several years to accept world medical opinion on the cause and treatment of the disease. Only in 2003 did it start to take the necessary measures and distribute the anti-retroviral drugs.

It was against this complex background that Tzu Chi began its work in 1992. Doing charity among the poor, overwhelmingly black, was difficult. Under apartheid, Taiwanese were "honorary whites"—they lived in white areas and only met blacks in the work place. Whites rarely entered black areas, which they regarded as hostile and dangerous. The number of Taiwanese in South Africa, the best support base for Tzu Chi, was only several thousand. Millions of blacks lived apart from their families, many in single-sex dormitories full of drugs, alcohol and violence. The legacy of this and the AIDS epidemic have left thousands of families without a husband or father, with only the mother or grandmother left to raise the children alone.

"When I first came to South Africa, I saw the expensive mansions of white people everywhere I looked," said Shih Feng-chi, a Tzu Chi commissioner in Taiwan who moved in 1990 to Ladysmith, a city of 80,000 in the Eastern province of KwaZulu-Natal. "I could not believe I was in Africa. Later, when I visited the countryside, I saw how impoverished the black people were. They had nothing to eat, no houses to live in and no warm jackets to shelter them from the cold." He began to seek members and donations from the few thousand Taiwan people in South Africa. With a fellow member from Johannesburg, he delivered aid to those in need in their two cities and in poor villages.

Another Taiwan migrant was Michael Pan Ming-shui (潘明水), a computer importer who moved in 1990 to Durban, the country's third largest city on the East coast. Pan spent his spare time as a volunteer at nursing homes and orphanages. Through his wife and other Tzu Chi volunteers, he became involved in the foundation's work.

In 1994, Tzu Chi launched a "Send Love to South Africa" campaign, which shipped two containers of used clothes from Taiwan to South Africa and distributed them to 200,000 poor blacks. Pan covered thousands of miles in his van to visit villages and select those eligible. "The shacks of the very poor had a soil floor and the roofs were built of scrap metal. Through the holes in the metal, they could see the sun during the day and the stars at night." Often he could not deal directly with the poor but had to obtain the approval of the village chief. "We had to use our money with extreme care," Pan said. "We had to present the goods to the recipients directly and extend our gratitude to them."

The donations were so well received that the foundation held the campaign again in 1995, collecting 15 containers of clothes, distributed in six cities in South Africa and Swaziland. The experience convinced Pan that job training would be more useful than donations: "Instead of giving them fish to eat, we should give them fishing rods and teach them how to fish." He found that some aid recipients knew how to sew and, after consulting other members, decided a sewing class would be the most useful.

He started in May 1995 with three sewing classes in Umbumbulu, a one-hour drive from Durban, using second-hand sewing machines donated by Tzu Chi and scrap cloth given by garment factories. The classes took off. Those who had been taught decided to become teachers themselves and impart their skill to others. Pan decided to expand the lessons to carpentry, farming and production of handicraft and admit men as well as women. Durban now has 53 such vocational centers, which have trained more than 14,000 people. In 1999, the Ruentex Construction Group of Taiwan donated two containers of cloth to the foundation in South Africa. The students sewed them into winter garments that were delivered to needy families. The women use the items themselves, sell them to local schools and markets and donate them to the poor.

It was an enormous challenge to launch the classes. First, Zulu communities are scattered, involving Pan in hours of traveling in his four-wheel-drive, nine-passenger van over poor roads. Second, most people advised Pan not to enter the black areas at all. Not only was there a high incidence of crime, but also political violence between the ANC and the Inkatha Freedom Party, under Mangosuthu Buthelezi, a Zulu leader. In the decade from the mid-1980s, 15,000 people died in fighting between rival Zulu groups in KwaZulu-Natal. One Taiwanese volunteer visiting a black village had his van stolen by bandits, who fired a bullet that grazed his cheek. Because Pan was brave enough to enter black villages, Zulus called him "warrior." He had to negotiate with local chiefs and political factions suspicious of any challenge to their authority. He told his volunteers to stick to the Tzu Chi principle of not being involved in politics.

The classes changed the lives of the students financially and spiritually. It gave them a means to earn money and improve the life of their families and inspired them to help others as they had been helped. Most of the 1,000 volunteers in Durban come from among these students.

An AIDS pandemic

KwaZulu-Natal is the most seriously AIDS-affected place in the world. The disease has spread fast because people do not understand how it is caused and transmitted, and the government has been slow to educate the public and provide the necessary medicines. Sexual promiscuity and the refusal of men to use condoms are major factors: inequality between the sexes means most wives cannot refuse the demand of their husband for sex.

The impact of the pandemic is evident everywhere in the townships outside Durban where Pan and his volunteers work. These are sad and remote areas, without proper roads, shops or community facilities. Many homes do not have running water, electricity or telephones. The townships are home to thousands of AIDS orphans, who live with their grandmothers or other relatives. Many families consist of elderly people and young children, with no one in the 20–45 age group. One grandmother in the district looks after 37 children, most of them AIDS orphans. Families such as these survive only on a modest government pension. In many families, there are no adult men—they have died of AIDS, been killed in political and criminal violence, have left to live with a second woman or to work elsewhere.

The T-section of the Mlazi township has 17,000 residents, including 2,200 AIDS orphans. Accompanied by six volunteers, Gladys Ngema visits the home of Myeza Zodwa, 42, mother of seven children, who suffers from tuberculosis and is HIV-positive. She used to live in Johannesburg but was thrown out of her house when her husband discovered that she was HIV-positive. Now she lives in Durban with two of her children. Her home is a two-room concrete structure, with a corrugated iron roof and rubbish scattered on the grass outside. Listless and emaciated, she lies on her bed in a dark room, with paper flapping in the window in place of glass. The volunteers help her out of bed and onto a bench in the sunshine outside. Putting on rubber gloves, they give her a massage and listen patiently as she speaks of her pain. She explains that one of her daughters has died, leaving a one-year-old baby: she does not know where she is and asks if they can help to find her. They promise to do their best and check that she is receiving the proper medication.

Next stop is a one-story corrugated shed lined with cardboard on a slope that is home to dozens of illegal homes, put up by people who have moved to the township. The volunteers received word that morning that the mother of the house, Dudulize Swetebetkawala, a single woman of 46 with five children, had died of AIDS. She came to Durban in 2005 from a rural area. The volunteers went at 6 AM to wash the body and prepare it for burial. Now they return to comfort the family. The home is dark except for a single candle and the woman's clothes, neatly ironed. "I had known her for eight years," said one volunteer. "She was a good woman and a good mother. She had been sick for three years and was receiving medicine. One of her daughters, who is 28, is also HIV-positive. "The children will be looked after by their grandmother." Ngema bows her head: "Such a death is very common. There were two in this area today. All we can do is comfort the family."

The volunteers go to one home where they give free lunches to AIDS orphans. Women in the house have been boiling rice and beans, which they serve on plates and hand out to 30 children sitting in the sun outside. "There are thousands of such orphans in the district," says one of the volunteers. "Some come from here and their mothers have passed away. Others are collected from the street and taken in by the community. It is poor but full of sympathy. The children sit and remember their mothers. We talk to them and give them games. We try to make them like other children. The community is very strong and people grow food which they donate to the children."

The volunteers explain to the families that it was God's will that their loved one should pass away. "As a Tzu Chi member, we want them to die in peace," said Ngema. "We tell the relatives that they must learn to be free in their heart. We talk to them until they accept the death and release their loved one." In January 2006, she herself lost a son, 36, who passed away suddenly. "With other Tzu Chi members, I was able to accept it. When he was sick, he gave me money to buy a cellular phone. He died in peace. Three weeks later, he appeared in a dream to my daughter and comforted her. He told her that there was no heaven in the sky. When she asked him where it was, he laughed. Heaven is the secret of God. My son will not come back. Nothing is ours."

The next day the fight against AIDS takes the form of a presentation to 50 people, young and old, crowded into a township home. A 27-year-old volunteer steps forward to speak. Siyabonga Dlamini, HIV-positive since he was 15, was thrown out of the family home after his father learned of his condition. With nowhere to go, he lived on the streets, begging. "I got HIV from sleeping around with many girls. I do not know who gave it to me. I tried to kill myself several times. Sleeping with a virgin is no cure, as is widely believed. A condom is only 99.1 percent safe." The presentation aims to inform the audience of the dangers of AIDS and, by telling them of Tzu Chi's work, to recruit new members.

Like Gladys, Dlamini received aid from Tzu Chi. In the winter of 1995, he received food and, in 2005, joined the foundation as a member. "I want to teach others about Tzu Chi and teach the young about HIV, not to use drugs and to love one another. Before, nobody helped. I lived on the streets begging and surviving somehow. I did not know what a normal life was."

"We are doing God's work," said Ngema, a fervent Protestant. "Master Cheng Yen has great love. Jesus and Buddha are the same. Tzu Chi people are like angels. In the hour of our greatest need, they brought clothes to us. From them, I have learnt the way of love. Now I hope I do the same thing and love my own people."

She urges her listeners to follow her example, accept their grief, leave their loneliness at home and turn their energy into helping others. "God does not like lazy people. You must work. It makes no sense to cry. You see your neighbor sick and hungry and you do nothing? Sick and hungry people need your help now."

Tzu Chi members in Durban spread the news of their work through a Zulu-language radio station, which was set up in 2003, using old equipment donated by the South African Broadcasting Corporation. Although 80 percent of KwaZulu-Natal's people speak Zulu, all but one of its eight radio stations are in English or Afrikaans.

Money for the Durban projects comes from the 300 Taiwan families who live there, of whom nearly half contribute money, and the city's Rotary Club, which donates food, clothing and wheelchairs. It is happy to give because the foundation provides a clear accounting of how its goods are used and it knows that they all reach the poor.

In November 2006, Pan brought four African volunteers, including Ngema, to Hualien to attend a meeting of foreign volunteers. In her speeches, Cheng Yen picked out the four women for special praise. "They are from poor families and live in very difficult circumstances but go happily in their work, visiting the sick and AIDS patients. They have to walk from three to eight hours to attend meetings, which are held in churches. They told me that, while walking over hills to visit people, they were not tired because they walked not with their legs but with their hearts. They are materially poor but very rich in spiritual terms. They do not have diplomas and formal education but have enormous wisdom. Buddha came into the world to end the caste system and proclaim that everyone is equal. No one is above or below another."

For the four, it was a time of intense emotion. When they met Cheng Yen, they told her in Mandarin that they were "her children." One of them was weeping as she spoke to her. Before going, Ngema composed a song, in which she said that, on the day of judgment, when God came to take His people home, she would prefer not to go to heaven but to Hualien. "When they left, they were weeping because they did not want to leave me and other Tzu Chi members, because this is their home," said Cheng Yen.

Ngema said that, when Cheng Yen met her for the first time, she asked her in Taiwanese if she was tired. Without waiting for a translation, she answered "no." "When I am with her, something touches you, which I cannot explain and put into words. It touches you. When she talks, you feel it inside spiritually. When I see her, so humble, sick with a heart attack and looking after the whole world, I want to work more. She cannot visit South Africa, but I feel that she is here now. Sometimes I speak to her and my grandchildren ask me where she is. I often read her book *Still Thoughts* and receive advice."

Ladysmith

Another important part of the mission in South Africa are the schools in Ladysmith, a small town in the center of KwaZulu-Natal best known for battles fought nearby between the British, the Boers and the Zulus. One, on January 22, 1879 at Isandlwana, was the worst defeat ever suffered by the British Empire—every single soldier in an army of 800 was killed by Zulu soldiers armed with spears and assegais in broad daylight, aided by a partial solar eclipse.

In the early 1990s, Taiwan businessmen moved their factories there, to take advantage of investment incentives and labor costs cheaper than at home. One was Shih Hung-chi (施鴻祺), a Tzu Chi volunteer, who set up a factory to make audio equipment and cassette tapes. He is the senior Tzu Chi commissioner in South Africa.

In March 1996, while delivering food to a local kindergarten, he and a friend saw a group of children in tattered clothes running out of a ramshackle building: it turned out to be an elementary school. They discovered that all six classrooms had two walls and no roof. With no desks or chairs, the students had to stand during the lessons. Moved by the plight of the students, the two decided to build a school for them.

They went to the 40 Chinese families in Ladysmith to solicit contributions but received a mixed reception. Many said that it was pointless, since residents would steal the construction materials before the school could be built. In 1994, students had set fire to their own schools. But they were able to raise $57,000 from Tzu Chi volunteers there and in other cities. They used the funds to build a school with 10 classrooms in November 1997. Thanks to its good condition and the addition of English to the curriculum, more students came and they added six classrooms. Now there are 1,062 students, nearly five times the original 217, in 18 classrooms, with three more being built. The foundation provides the school with books, stationery and bursaries for the poor.

It has offered 20 computers, in addition to the one the school has. The members have planted 80 trees around the school and hope to add a sports ground on a piece of vacant land next door.

Buthelez Jabulani, the principal, said that, previously, the school had held classes in rooms and kitchens made of mud in nearby houses. "We did not have a building, furniture, books and stationery. We did not know where to start." He wanted a transfer because he could not raise the funds for a new school, until Tzu Chi arrived. "What distinguishes us from other primary schools is that we have better discipline. Tzu Chi emphasizes love and respect for elders. Also we have continued support from them. They visit us regularly and I can say what I need. This gives us hope for the future," he said.

The schools are in rural areas outside Ladysmith, the townships set aside for the blacks in the apartheid era. The setting is a world away from the city's high school, one of the most famous in Natal, with spacious brick buildings and meticulously trimmed sports fields, in the center of town. With a pass rate of 100 percent for university, it would not be out of place in a U.S. or European city. The rural areas, however, are different—two- and three-room homes in the middle of open fields, with earth roads and many without water and electricity. Families grow their own vegetables and maize on small plots. AIDS has taken its deadly toll—many families have no parents and orphans live with their grandmothers. Some children arrive at school with an empty stomach.

In April 1998, the foundation built a second school and later a third. Then nearly 400 schools wrote to ask for help. But, with limited numbers and resources, the members in Ladysmith decided that they could only build schools within a 50-kilometer radius of the city. To date, they have financed seven elementary schools, costing two million rand ($303,000) and one kindergarten, with more than 3,000 students, and provided books, supplies and scholarships.

Nhlanhla Hlongwane is principal of Mthandi, the second primary school, with 341 students. "Without Tzu Chi, there would be no schools and no buildings. If you apply to the government, it could take nine years. Most of the students are orphans and some have single mothers. Their grandmothers cannot help them with their studies. At home, they have no electricity and do their homework by the light of candles or paraffin or wooden stoves." Classes in the first three grades are taught in the Zulu language and from the fourth to the seventh in English.

In October 2004, the members paid for 16 children from the schools, accompanied by their principals and Nsibanyoni Dumazile, a mathematics teacher, to attend the Tzu Chi world education fair in Taiwan.

It was the first time they had left South Africa and flown in an airplane. In Hualien, they sang songs in Mandarin and Taiwanese, to thunderous applause from the astonished audience. "It was the highlight of my life," said Jabulani. Dumazile said that she cried a lot because of the love shown to her. "We are not used to this. We need to love others and this needs to come from the heart. We have to change the way of thinking of blacks that expect to receive. I need to give." She said that she needed to practice what Tzu Chi said and help her family and community. "I wish to be a Taiwanese and move to Taiwan."

In addition, the members in Ladysmith have organized distribution of food, blankets and daily necessities to 13,000 households, and visited orphanages and homes for the physically disabled. In 1999 and 2000, they also drilled 38 wells in the area around the first primary school, to save residents a walk of two-three hours to the nearest well. They proposed drilling a further 1,000 but the government suddenly imposed a charge of 5,000 rand ($758) per well, plus stringent approval procedures, so they dropped the idea.

The next project in Ladysmith will be an orphanage and school for 200 AIDS orphans, at a cost of 10 million rand ($1.43 million), with money raised from local companies and foundation members in the United States and Canada. It will be a major undertaking, morally and financially, with each student costing about $100 a month for living and school fees. "We should have done this 10 years ago," said Shih. "Sadly, it is very easy to get such orphans. There is a lot of land in Ladysmith and the mayor will give us some. Security is better here than in Johannesburg. The school will be the same as the Tzu Chi school in Hualien. The government is flexible—we will have the national curriculum, with the Tzu Chi classes in addition."

The sharp fall in the number of Taiwan people, the base of Tzu Chi, living in South Africa casts a shadow over its future there. The number has declined from a peak of 40,000 in 1997 to 6,000–7,000 now. This is due to rising crime, the difficulty of Taiwanese graduates to find work, when government policy favors the hiring of blacks, and the flood of cheap imports from mainland China, which have badly hit local factories, including those owned by Taiwanese.

To prepare for the future, Tzu Chi gave badges to nine black African commissioners in November 2007, making a total of 10, including Gladys Ngema.

10

USA—WEALTH AND POVERTY

IT IS A HOT SUMMER SATURDAY morning in downtown Los Angeles, the center of the American film and music industry—the city of dreams. Cruising down the road are Mercedes and Cadillacs carrying their passengers to a business lunch at the Biltmore Hotel, the campaign headquarters of John F. Kennedy in 1960. Behind the Biltmore are elegant skyscrapers that are home to banks, investment houses and multinational corporations. This is the nation's richest city, after New York. But the people who walk the streets this scorching day belong to another world, far from the pinstriped men in the Cadillacs, and their only dream is to fill their stomachs with a hot meal.

These are the homeless, who live in tents and cardboard boxes on streets downtown. They eat at McDonalds and Subway, where the toilets are locked to prevent drug addicts using them, and whose staff fear the violence of their customers. Residents from outside the city come to the center and complete their business as soon as possible: they jump back into their cars to return to the peace of the suburbs. Cheek by jowl in these few square kilometers are dazzling wealth and shocking poverty.

Each Saturday, the homeless line up to receive a free lunch prepared for 350 of them by members of the Tzu Chi Foundation in Los Angeles. Dressed in their blue shirts and white trousers, the volunteers lay out the dishes on tables next to the pavement. The meal consists of a vegetable burger—which looks and tastes like meat—fresh vegetables, fruit and water. Most of the homeless are dirty and unkempt, the uniform of life in the gutter, but a few wear a suit and carry a briefcase: the volunteers do not ask for identity cards or proof of income, it is first come, first served. "They think we are religious Buddhists," says Daniel Hickey, a volunteer who is a native of Britain living in Los Angeles. "Thousands live on the streets. My feeling is 'there but for the grace of God go I.'"

Los Angeles is one of 12 cities across the U.S. where Tzu Chi provides free meals to the homeless. It was the first city in the world where Tzu Chi established an overseas branch, in December 1989, and is where the foundation has its U.S. headquarters today. The country has the largest number of overseas members and branches. Since that first office, the foundation now divides its U.S. chapter into eight regions, with operations in 27 states, including Arizona, California, Hawaii, Nevada, Illinois, New York, New Jersey, Texas and Washington. It has opened branches in 62 cities in 27 states, recruited 100,580 members, with 6,600 active volunteers and 1,184 commissioners. It has given help to more than 13,000 individual American families. It runs over 20 community programs, including services for families and the homeless, food banks, visits to pensioners' homes, medical and dental services, recycling, and reading to children. It has set up schools and kindergartens, donates books to inner-city children in four major U.S. cities and provides scholarships to outstanding high school graduates who need money to help them continue their studies at university.

It was the only organization to provide immediate cash relief to families affected by the attacks of September 11, 2001. Its volunteers regularly go on the streets of the cities where they live to collect litter and waste and recycle it. And, since 1994, volunteers from the U.S. have gone on foreign relief and medical missions, to Central and South America, the Caribbean, Sri Lanka and Afghanistan, where they have provided free medical care and built homes and community centers.

The foundation in the U.S. has an annual revenue of $15–20 million, with more raised by special appeals in the event of a major disaster. Many volunteers were not born in the U.S. and emigrated there from Taiwan, China and Southeast Asia. They take part in Tzu Chi activities because they wish to give something back to the country that has accepted them. They are acting in response to Cheng Yen's call to her members to contribute to their communities wherever they are and regardless of race, religion or ethnicity. Initially, most recipients of their aid were ethnic Chinese, whose needs the volunteers knew most clearly. Two decades later, the recipients include people of all colors and backgrounds. The recipients of the free meals in Los Angeles include blacks, whites, Chinese and Hispanics, just as the volunteers include people of all races living in the city.

Together with China, the U.S. is the most important foreign country for the foundation's future. Thanks to the substantial and thriving Taiwanese-American community, it has established a large and well-motivated membership, the largest outside Taiwan. It aims to expand this membership and develop the same missions as in Taiwan—medicine, education, charity, culture and environmental protection. Like China, wealth is divided unequally, and provision of social welfare is uneven. Millions of people are at the lower end of society who need help and support, leaving enormous space for the work of non-government charities.

Over the next 10 years, Tzu Chi's objective in the U.S. is to become as well known as the Red Cross. "Over the next five years, we aim to double the number of donors and triple the number of commissioners," said William Keh, a former medical doctor and businessman who is Tzu Chi's chief executive in the U.S.

"We must Americanize and join the mainstream. We must attract mainstream Americans to join. The U.S. is an important international platform, which gives us a very great opportunity to spread the philosophy, wisdom and spirit of Master Cheng Yen in the international society. I hope that, within 10 years, there will be an American sitting in my chair."

That means reaching out beyond the ethnic Chinese community, who currently account for 95 percent of the commissioners and 75 percent of the donors. Many of the non-Chinese volunteers are spouses of Chinese members.

Keh is keen to recruit people outside the Chinese community, including whites, blacks and Hispanics, but admits the difficulties ahead. "Many Chinese have done well in the United States. Almost everyone is willing to donate and many are willing to volunteer. But it is hard to recruit whites, because of the culture and language gap. They can understand the theory but it is hard to put it into daily practice. Time is needed to persuade them. In some cities, like Phoenix and Orlando, we have whites who are devoted members. We need more white members and more material in English. We must do more."

The foundation has made its biggest contributions during major disasters, such as the 1992 Los Angeles riots, the 1994 earthquake in Northridge, California, the attacks on the World Trade Center in New York on September 11, 2001, the serious wildfires in Southern California in 2003 and 2007 and the major hurricanes that struck the South coast from 2003 to 2005, notably Katrina in 2005. But it was often unable to play a central role in disaster relief because it was not well known enough to the national agencies. After Katrina, for example, it took five days before federal authorities would allow Tzu Chi volunteers to begin their work. Only in 2006 was it admitted to the National Voluntary Organizations Active in Disaster (NVOAD), a group of non-government agencies. Joining the mainstream charity organizations in the U.S. means that in the future it will play a larger role. And membership also means that it is informed immediately of disasters and allowed to take part in frontline relief operations.

The U.S. branch aims to follow the mother charity in Taiwan, by operating its own hospitals and building an educational network, from the elementary to the university level. A Tzu Chi hospital would greatly raise the profile of the foundation, like the Hualien facility in Taiwan, a vivid illustration to Americans of Buddhism in action. It would be the best advertisement for its philosophy and a magnet for donations and volunteers.

History

Tzu Chi began life in the United States in 1984, when a Taiwanese couple registered the foundation in Sacramento, capital of California. It developed slowly until Stephen Huang, an entrepreneur in real estate, clothing and banking in California, sold his businesses and joined the foundation full-time. Cheng Yen asked him to develop it in the U.S. but gave him no money or staff to do the job. Using his own money, he purchased the office of an insurance company in Alhambra, a suburb of Los Angeles with a large Chinese population, and donated it as the first branch in December 1989. In 1993, the foundation bought a church in Monrovia, in another section of Los Angeles, and converted the Alhambra office into a free clinic, which opened in November that year. Since then, the clinic has served patients on low incomes, including illegal immigrants, both Chinese and Hispanic, who cannot go to a government hospital because they have no identity documents.

California was the obvious area to begin the growth of Tzu Chi because it has the largest number of Taiwan immigrants, about 600,000, most living in the South of the state. They have provided the majority of donors and volunteers in the U.S. In his new mission, Huang used the same drive and organization which he had thrown into his business, flying across the U.S. to address meetings, explain Tzu Chi's philosophy and projects and recruit members. He played a major role in increasing the membership, especially in New York, Houston, Chicago, Hawaii and San Jose, cities with substantial numbers of Taiwan migrants.

In 1997, Huang moved to Taiwan, to take on a senior post at the headquarters, and was replaced by a collective leadership. Without such a charismatic figure, the growth slowed down and each branch developed on its own. In 2000, the foundation decided to return to a centralized leadership. Cheng Yen picked Southern California as the headquarters and named a retired computer engineer from Northern California, Austin Tsao, as the chief executive. The new leadership was in place to react quickly to the September 11 attacks.

As the activities increased, the foundation purchased a Bible college on 90.5 acres of rolling land in San Dimas, Los Angeles County, as its new headquarters. The site has more than 20 buildings in the style of the Spanish missions in the early years of California, white with red tiles. It includes offices, meeting rooms, a restaurant, dormitories, a Buddhist temple, a bookshop, a small lake and an auditorium that can hold 1,000 people. The staff includes salaried employees and volunteers who receive no pay. Tzu Chi turned the office in Monrovia into the foundation's first U.S. kindergarten, while the original Alhambra office remains its first free clinic.

In the history of Chinese migrants to the United States, Tzu Chi has played a significant role. It is changing the perception of Chinese toward American society and vice versa. Traditionally, the Chinese community in the U.S. kept to itself and looked after its own, staying out of politics and civic life. This was a reaction to legal discrimination from 1882 to 1943, which barred most Chinese immigrants from entering the U.S. and those who were there from naturalizing as citizens. They were also banned from living in the better areas of major cities. So they set up Chinatowns in which they felt safe and secure among their own community. Americans saw Chinese as diligent, studious and frugal but insular and unconcerned with the issues of the wider society. If a disaster befell Chinatown, the Chinese would rally round to help the victims. But, if it hit another part of town, it was none of their business.

The Taiwan migrants who began to arrive from the 1960s were better educated, more self-confident and spoke better English than the Chinese who had come before. They did not live in Chinatowns but bought homes in the white communities in middle-class areas. The Tzu Chi ethos asks its members to repay the society in which they live. So the volunteers aimed their charity at all races in society, not only Chinese. Its free and low-cost clinics initially attracted mainly Chinese patients but this soon broadened to all races. Its work in Southern California also includes providing aid to the poor, hot meals to the homeless, disaster relief work and schoolbooks and scholarships to low-income students. A majority of the recipients are not Chinese—but migrants from Mexico and Central America, legal and illegal, the poor, street people, alcoholics, drug addicts and new arrivals to the country. These activities have pushed volunteers out of their community, giving them new networks and connections and a channel into mainstream society. At the same time, the projects have presented to the American public a new face of their Chinese neighbor—not only restaurateur, grocery owner, real estate agent and doctor, but someone doing charity work and involved in their community.

Medicine

Since 1993, Tzu Chi has established seven clinics in the United States and is seeking to operate its own hospital, ideally by acquiring an existing one. It runs free outreach clinics in rural areas, and the foundation's medical personnel also take part in overseas medical missions. These services rely entirely on good will—doctors, dentists, nurses and volunteers who give their time for no financial reward. In recognition of its achievements, Tzu Chi received an award in January 1998 from the San Gabriel Valley Medical Centre Foundation in California for its work in helping the poor.

The free clinic in Alhambra, which has served more than 150,000 patients since its opening in 1993, is aimed at those on low incomes and without medical insurance, including illegal immigrants. "Great mercy even to strangers and great compassion for all," reads a calligraphy by Cheng Yen which hangs on the wall of the clinic.

The foundation has also opened free clinics in Hawaii and El Monte, also in East Los Angeles, and a Chinese medicine clinic in Alhambra; all charge a flat rate of $20, medicines are free, and if patients need a specialist they are referred for one consultation. In addition, Tzu Chi operates a family health clinic jointly with the Amhurst hospital in Flushing, New York. It has two mobile dental clinics, is building a third and runs support groups for cancer and diabetes patients. Its long-term goal is to continue expanding its network of low-cost clinics for the poor, and build up its medical team, with the aim of opening its own hospital. The target group for these services is the 45 million Americans who have no health insurance, an astonishing figure in the country with the greatest wealth and most advanced medicine in the world.

"Many illegal immigrants do not qualify for state medical insurance, yet they are the most impoverished members of society," said Hsu Ming-chang (許明彰), a doctor who has worked at the Alhambra clinic since it opened. "Many Chinese work and receive a mediocre income. Once they pay the rent and the car loan, they have no extra cash to pay for doctors. They do not qualify as low-income families. It is such people the free clinic aims to serve."

Applicants must show that they have no public or private health insurance and have a low income and limited financial resources. They use social security cards, pay slips and bank statements. Each year, the clinic sees more than 10,000 patients and costs $1 million to $1.3 million to run: all the money comes from donations.

One evening in 2006, the foundation raised $2.5 million at a fundraiser, mostly from Chinese, with one donor agreeing to match whatever the others gave—he gave $1.25 million.

The Alhambra clinic has three dental rooms, with 20 dentists coming part-time on a volunteer basis. Hsu attends the clinic three days a week as well as one day at the El Monteclinic. "I have almost closed my own clinic and just kept the old patients," he explains of his busy schedule. In the early days, Hsu was the only doctor who served regularly at the free clinic. When it failed to find other doctors, it called him and he never hesitated to close his own clinic and come to help. He also sets aside time on Sundays to treat Tzu Chi members.

In the beginning, few doctors were willing to work there. But, as its reputation spread, more offered their time, enabling the clinic to offer more services, and hospitals and institutions donated equipment to the new facility. It now provides outpatient services, including gynecology, pediatrics, minor surgery, psychiatry, dentistry, herbal medicine and acupuncture. The dental practice includes full dentures for patients whose missing teeth severely impair their appearance or otherwise affect their health. In a commercial practice, a false tooth costs $200 and a root canal treatment $500–800. Since a missing tooth is not considered an urgent illness, most charity medical clinics do not offer the provision of new dentures.

It remains a battle to find volunteer doctors, however, in a medical culture that is money-driven and litigious. "They are busy and there are issues of malpractice and liability," said Hsu. "What if you are here once a week, for example, and others do tests for you?" Tzu Chi can call on the services of 20 Western and 10 Chinese doctors. The clinic has a small number of paid staff, including nurses and medical assistants, but relies heavily on volunteers, many former patients, to support the doctors and give a personalized service to the clients.

In 2006, Tzu Chi was offered the opportunity to buy the El Monte hospital, next door to its clinic, at a cost of $1.35 million. Buying an existing hospital is more economical than building a greenfield one (U.S. regulations and standards mean that a new one would cost $1 million a bed) and such a purchase would have helped the foundation realize its dream of operating a Tzu Chi hospital in the United States. However,

Tzu Chi declined the offer because it did not have the medical personnel to operate it. In the end, a group of Taiwan investors, unaffiliated with Tzu Chi bought the facility, one of six in the area they purchased.

Education

In a converted church in a prosperous suburb of Los Angeles, young children sit around a table as two teachers instruct them how to count. "One-two-three," says one teacher and the young ones repeat after her. "Yi-er-san," says the other, and the children repeat this too.

Welcome to Tzu Chi's bilingual kindergarten, the first of what it hopes will be dozens of such schools across the United States, and an important part of its strategy to enter mainstream society.

The school opened in September 2006 in Monrovia, where it sits in a row of well-kept houses, surrounded by grass and flowers. It has 10 teachers and 48 students, between the ages of 2.9 years and six, with 53 on the waiting list. Of the students, 60 percent are Chinese and the rest Caucasian, Indian and Hispanics. Several features distinguish it from other kindergartens. One is that every class is bilingual, in English and Mandarin, with one English-speaking and one Mandarin-speaking teacher in each class.

Another is that it is vegetarian, with a dedicated cook in a large kitchen preparing a wide range of dishes. A third is that the students are taught the values of Tzu Chi—kindness, responsibility, self-esteem and a moral character. The teachers take them to visit the city's homeless and teach them about recycling. There is no class in Buddhism, but the teachers follow the education philosophy of Tzu Chi, which places equal emphasis on the cultivation of morality and discipline as on academic achievement.

The principal of the school is not a Chinese but an American of Sri Lankan origin, Keshini Wijegoonaratna, a resident of the U.S. for 33 years, who has worked in education for 23 years, in both the U.K. and the U.S. She was born in Britain, where her father was Sri Lanka's ambassador, and moved to the United States in 1974, taking a bachelor's degree in child psychology.

In 2006, Tzu Chi invited her to become principal, after she had retired from 15 years as a director of Knowledge Learning Corporation (KLC), the largest private provider of early childhood and school-age care and education in the U.S. "When I received the offer, I was uneasy because I did not know Chinese. In May 2006, I went to Hualien, met the Master and was very impressed. I felt connected and had an immediate rapport with her. I shared her goals." It was also an important moment in her life, because her mother had passed away two months before. She accepted the post, which carries a salary similar to that of the head of comparable government schools. The school, which has a lower student–teacher ratio than a public school, where the proportion could be 30–1, is part of the foundation's plan to attract people from the mainstream. Fees are $640–$690 a month for pre-school and $720–$740 for kindergarten. "It will be in profit this year but that is not an issue for Tzu Chi," Wijegoonaratna said. "Master Cheng Yen wants to provide the best quality education for the children." Tzu Chi plans to spend $5 million on building an elementary school on the Monrovia site. It opened a second kindergarten in Richardson, a suburb of Dallas, in August 2007, and plans to open others in Hawaii, New York and Washington and eventually all over the nation. Over the long term, it wants to follow the model in Taiwan and build primary and secondary schools and a university. The sprawling site at San Dimas, with rolling hills and large tree cover, would be ideal as a university campus.

Another part of the education mission is to help disadvantaged students, through scholarships and teaching by Tzu Chi members. Beginning in 1991, it has targeted talented children in secondary schools who have the ability to reach university but are unable to because of a lack of money.

This scholarship program extends to California, Hawaii, Chicago, New Jersey, Washington DC, New York and Texas, and to students in Mexicali and Tijuana in Mexico. In 2005, the foundation gave 182 high school students $1,000 each in such scholarships.

It also runs a Gift of Books program, to children of inner-city schools whose families cannot afford to buy books. Since 2000, it has donated more than 400,000 books in Los Angeles, San Francisco, Dallas and Chicago. In 2005, the foundation gave new books worth $230,000 to public schools in California.

Charity

Every Friday afternoon, volunteers from the foundation's San Francisco branch arrive at the John Muir Elementary School. Its 280 pupils are among the poorest in the city, 70 percent Hispanic and 95 percent eligible for free lunch programs the government offers to the poor. At the same time, a truck arrives from the Food Bank, which the volunteers visited the day before to buy 350 pounds of food. They unload the items and lay them on tables in one of the classrooms, like a supermarket.

It is enough to feed 60 families for a week. In mid-afternoon, the parents arrive and walk with their children around the room, picking up items they need, at no charge. The volunteers give them a recycled bag to carry the food. Without it, many of the children would have little or nothing to eat at home. Such poverty is shocking in one of the world's richest cities.

Charity plays an important role in Tzu Chi's work in the U.S. The largest projects involve help to victims of natural disasters, like earthquakes, floods, hurricanes and terrorist attacks. Since 1989, it has helped more than 13,000 individual families, some for more than 10 years. Volunteers also provide hot meals on a regular basis to the homeless in 12 cities, visit old people's and convalescent homes and during winter provide gift baskets, blankets and other necessities to individuals, families and old people living on their own. They provide financial help and backpacks, shoes and uniforms to neighborhood schools and local organizations to families who cannot afford these basics.

Since 1994, volunteers from the U.S. have played a prominent role in international relief missions to Latin America, providing aid and medical services in Mexico, Honduras, Dominican Republic, Guatemala, El Salvador, Haiti, Colombia and Peru as well as Afghanistan. In 2003, the U.S. foundation completed a housing project in El Salvador costing $6.5 million, to rebuild homes destroyed by earthquakes in 2001. Located into the two villages of Sacacoyo and Chaminco, the projects included 1,175 homes, two schools, two community centers and two clinics.

September 11, 2001

After the attacks on the World Trade Center, Tzu Chi volunteers were invited to the New York City Family Assistance Centre at Pier 94, where they helped those who had lost loved ones. They offered psychological counseling and assisted them in applying for financial aid for medical costs, insurance applications, DNA collection and applications for death certificates. Many people could not get any immediate help from government organizations. The foundation handed out cash to people in need, $100 or $200, which could buy milk for their children, clothes or enable them to travel back home. The foundation received referrals from the Red Cross, the Salvation Army and the city government. The foundation also had a booth at the victim relief center in New Jersey and a service station in Chinatown, to help Chinese speakers who had survived the attack. The volunteers provided psychiatric therapy, interpretation and translation and food assistance for workers and the families of victims.

At the booths, they heard heart-rending cases of those who had lost husbands, colleagues and friends in the disaster. They did their best to offer comfort and psychological support to those who had survived. A woman brought a child, explaining that his father had been a passenger on one of the hijacked planes and his mother was one of the people reported missing. None of the volunteers could find the words to say. They gave $1,000 in emergency aid to the surviving relatives and added them to their long-term care list.

By September 26, the foundation had processed 289 cases of emergency aid, of whom 247 received emergency funds. Most of the recipients were families from Taiwan and the U.S., with a maximum of $1,000. In total, Tzu Chi gave $2 million to 3,164 families.

Hurricane Katrina

Hurricane Katrina, the worst natural disaster to hit the United States for decades, was a milestone for the foundation, causing its largest mobilization of volunteers and distribution of aid in the U.S. The disaster was also a milestone in U.S. history, showing the inability of the world's richest and most powerful government to deal promptly and efficiently with a disaster and its aftermath. Tzu Chi was one of dozens of civil organizations who played an essential role in helping the victims and doing what the government failed to do.

In the early morning of August 29, 2005, the hurricane, a category 5 storm, moved through the Gulf of Mexico and made its first landfall East of New Orleans, with wind speeds exceeding 144 miles per hour. The torrential rain and winds brought by the hurricane ravaged the city, forcing millions of people to evacuate. About 80 percent of the city was submerged when water poured in through levees that had been breached, with the floodwaters reaching 18 feet in some areas. It devastated the coastal areas of three states—Mississippi, Louisiana and Texas—caused more than 2,000 deaths and destroyed 300,000 homes, leaving damage estimated at $120 billion.

In response, Cheng Yen appealed through her Great Love Television channel on September 1 for members around the world to help the victims. On September 3, 4 and 5, volunteers in Dallas and California went on the streets to raise funds, in front of supermarkets and restaurants. The foundation raised funds in 30 countries around the world. Among the collectors were students from the foundation's secondary school in Chiang Mai, Northern Thailand, who went to a local market and received donations from shoppers—and even beggars, the poorest people in the society, who wanted to make their modest contribution to a disaster on the other side of the world.

The foundation set up a disaster relief center in Houston, led by Stephen Huang, head of its international affairs division, and Austin Tsao, then chief executive of the foundation in the U.S. The head office in Hualien sent volunteers and $5 million, volunteers came from the Canadian branch bringing $1 million, joining those from California, Texas and Atlanta. In total, Tzu Chi volunteers came from 30 countries around the world. For its part, the Taiwan government promised $2 million in aid to the victims.

On September 1, Tzu Chi volunteers were at work, in Mesquite city, Texas, a rest stop for New Orleans' evacuees. At the invitation of the city's social welfare department, they provided meals for its staff as well as paper napkins, anti-sweat towels and mineral water for the evacuees.

But not all U.S. officials were so cooperative, because many were unfamiliar with Tzu Chi. On September 1, two members went to the Emergency Operations Center (EOC) in Dallas, with $2 million in hand, but were told the officials were too busy to see them. Only after protesting that they had a substantial amount of money to offer were they allowed in: the officials invited them to help in the relief effort. On September 3, they started work at the Ford Park Gymnasium in Beaumont, Texas, where 6,000 people had been evacuated. The members gave out $200–$300 to each evacuee and were among the first charity organizations to provide such aid. They decided to give the money not in cash but in Wal-Mart cash-value cards, which the recipients could spend at the giant retailer. They also gave out telephone cards worth $50–$100, to enable the victims to contact their family and friends. In addition, they gave out rice and 10,818 medical packages, assembled in Taiwan and flown free of charge to the United States by Taiwan's national carrier, China Airlines, with more than 30 items, including U.S.-made flu vaccines, fever and headache medicines, thermometers and small surgical knives. Over the next 12 days, the foundation distributed in Beaumont nearly $500,000 to 2,657 families, a total of 6,356 people: its mobile clinic provided emergency dental treatment to 157 people. The volunteers went on to extend aid to half a dozen other shelters in the greater Houston area.

The state of Texas offered 130 public shelters and took in 140,000 people, of whom the largest number were held in the Astrodome, Houston's largest sports arena and home of the city's baseball team, with a capacity of 55,000 spectators. It sheltered nearly 25,000 people. Dazed and disoriented, the evacuees arrived at the shelter, had their baggage searched and were directed to different areas, based on their gender, marital status and whether they had children. Even pets had their own section. Thanks to the generosity of Texas people, there was an abundance of food, drinks, clothes, telephones, internet services and information on services available to them. Evacuees went from booth to booth to pick up food, drinks and daily necessities. There were playpens for children and the elevators, stairs, washrooms and makeshift showers were in use 24 hours a day. Tzu Chi members were among thousands of volunteers in the Astrodome. Many evacuees had lost all their possessions in the disaster, as well as loved ones, so volunteers needed to give not only material help but also warmth and psychological support.

In its first nine days of operations at shelters in Houston, Tzu Chi distributed about $650,000 to 2,600 families. When the government announced a policy of evacuating the victims to different parts of the country, the foundation provided many with $200, toward the cost of a plane ticket. It also extended aid to evacuees after they had moved to other parts of the country, such as Kansas, New York, Phoenix and Northern California.

Its relief gave Tzu Chi a higher profile than it had hitherto enjoyed in the U.S. Hurricane Katrina and its aftermath were the top news story in every television station and newspaper in the country, which were covering the relief effort in great detail. Working with the Federal Management Emergency Agency (FEMA) and the Red Cross, the foundation was the object of media attention. Its active participation also gave it access to the governors and mayors of the affected area, as well as to senators and officials from the central government. For the first time, the American public saw volunteers with white trousers, blue shirts and white caps, working for a Buddhist charity from distant Taiwan.

For the Tzu Chi volunteers who took part in the aid operation, it was an experience that was both humbling and inspiring. "The devastation brought by Hurricane Katrina transformed three states in the Southern U.S. into flooded towns, which shocked and saddened all of us," said Austin Tsao. "Tzu Chi volunteers gratefully distributed the aid and with utmost respect for the hurricane victims. Many people embraced the volunteers and both were in tears. In comforting the evacuees and helping them settle their minds and bodies, our volunteers felt a deep happiness. This warmth and outpouring of the human spirit moved people and opened their hearts, giving them a source of strength to rise above their difficulties."

For the older volunteers, the aid effort was also a reversal of history. In the 1950s and 1960s, Taiwan was a poor country that depended heavily on American aid, including food and medicine. Many children grew up drinking American milk. Their mothers used flour sacks printed with Chinese or American flags to make underwear for their children, so it was a common sight to see children with underpants carrying the Chinese flag on the front and the American flag on the back. Katrina was an opportunity for the people of Taiwan to repay the United States for its aid 50 years earlier.

Stephen Huang saw in the disaster a deeper significance. "With my own eyes, I witnessed human tragedy, death and illness. This made me realize that nothing is immune from change in this world. I also realized that natural disasters are rooted in human mistakes. Observing events from the recent centuries, the Industrial Revolution brought civilization to the human race, yet it accelerated the deterioration of earth and 'nurtures' major disasters, which impact the planet. Hurricane Katrina was the worst disaster to hit the United States in recent history; it was actually a response to our neglect to preserve the earth, to control air pollution and to value energy resources."

PART THREE

CARE FOR THE MIND, CARE FOR THE EARTH

II

EDUCATION

"The world has advanced in material technology but human civilization is regressing. Human nature is no longer honest and unsophisticated as before. How we return to the source of ethics and morality is a very important issue.
In our education, we must retain the traditional rules and ethics. We must instill in everyone a sense of goodness and only then will society be blessed. If we speak only of freedom and openness, it will lead to chaos and disorder, which would be a dangerous thing."

—Cheng Yen

EACH MONTH STUDENTS OF TZU CHI primary and middle school in Chiang Mai, North Thailand, are taken by their teachers to visit the homes of poor people and those living alone, bringing daily necessities. The students kneel before their hosts and hand the gifts up to them, to show their respect.

At a Tzu Chi kindergarten in Penang, Malaysia, the teachers regularly organize a ceremony, at which the students wash the feet of their parents, to thank them for their love and care.

Cheng Yen holds strong convictions about education and the inadequacies of mainstream schools. These convictions persuaded her to make education the third of Tzu Chi's four missions and set up its own network, from kindergarten to doctorate level. This network has grown rapidly over the last 15 years. In Taiwan, the foundation has built a university, college of technology and eight kindergartens and primary and secondary schools. It rebuilt 52 schools in the area affected by the 1999 earthquake within three years and gave them, at no charge, to the local authorities. It has also built seven centers of continuing education, aimed at adults. Abroad, it has constructed 84 schools, in South Africa, Iran, Indonesia, Thailand, Sri Lanka, China, Mexico, Paraguay, El Salvador and the Dominican Republic and given them to the local governments. It has also set up over 50 of its own schools and kindergartens abroad, in Malaysia, Australia, Canada, the United States, Indonesia and Thailand.

This represents an enormous investment of capital, building, recruitment and training, not to speak of the bureaucratic obstacles for a Buddhist charity to obtain approvals in Christian and Islamic countries. Driving this is Cheng Yen's conviction that education is as important for a child's future as a well-built home, healthy diet and a warm and united family. "Education is hope. A life without education is a life without hope," she often says.

Most of the schools Tzu Chi has constructed overseas and those it rebuilt in Taiwan after the 1999 earthquake are gifts to the local community. While they bear the foundation's name and its volunteers visit them regularly to offer scholarships and material help, it is the local authorities who decide the content of the education. The rest are schools managed by Tzu Chi itself and which implement the educational ideas of Cheng Yen.

She believes schools must provide both specialist knowledge and physical education and also a strong sense of morality and manners. She set out her objectives in a book *Liyi Zhimei* (The Beauty of Manners), published in 2006.

During the six years of primary school, the teachers must teach the students ethics and moral principles and the rules of living, so that they implement them in their daily life. In middle school, the teachers must do a good job of caring for the heart and aspirations of the students and open to them a path for life. . . When they enter university, does it mean that the basic education is completed? No, because the students there also need enlightenment. As an adult, he must start to study the ethics and morality of adults, including how to interact with society. This enlightenment at university is especially important. Without a sense of morality and humanist spirit, a person can, as his level of knowledge increases, commit bigger and bigger mistakes, with serious consequences. So, to build a correct path for life is extremely important. . . From kindergarten to primary and secondary school and university, love and ethics are essential to education. These two must be continued.

Driving the mission is her belief that human society has taken a wrong turning. She sees mainstream culture and education as self-centered and materialist.

Modern science is very developed, the ideals of modern man and the level of scholarship have greatly advanced and are rising all the time. But, sadly, the morality of man is deteriorating. Everyone must work earnestly, from all aspects and at different levels, to improve human morality. The thinking of modern man has gone off the rails and regards too lightly the phenomenon of life. This makes people worry. How can we help the young generation turn from their confusion into the correct way of thinking and study how to manage life? The key is education in living. Through exchanges between one life and another, people will see suffering and their compassion will be awakened and the seeds of wisdom will begin to sprout. Using stories from real life—that is the real education for life.

For Cheng Yen, morality and manners are as important as academic lessons to enable the student to lead a balanced and happy life in which he will love and respect his fellow human beings and in turn be loved and respected by them. Wisdom about how to live is more precious than intelligence: an advanced level of education is no guarantee of moral behavior.

Tzu Chi instills these values through words and deeds, in its schools, in Penang, Chiang Mai or Hualien. Teachers take students to visit the sick in hospital and the poor and elderly, so that they appreciate better the blessings they have. They do menial tasks in the school, like cleaning floors and washing toilets, to learn humility. They are taught the proper way to hold a rice bowl and use chopsticks. The schools and university have a code of uniform that is strictly enforced, with the emphasis on neatness and frugality. Students wear short, combed hair.

For Cheng Yen, community work is as important as lessons in the classroom: "We not only impart knowledge to the students, we also try to cultivate their wisdom and teach the correct way of living, including the proper way to dress, eat, live and behave. . . How do people judge your character? They start by judging the way you dress, eat, live and behave. Thus, our teachers mindfully teach our students to behave and remind them to fine-tune their manners and hearts to display the demeanor of decent people at all times. Such is the genuine function of education."

Such manners do not depend on wealth and comfort. "Guizhou is one of the poorest provinces in China. Its children are poor in material goods but are very able to accept the education of life. Their homes are old and decrepit, some have no roofs and the walls have holes but the children arrange their lives in an orderly way. Their cotton quilt is old and torn but they fold it with neatness and care. The scope of ethics is not only interaction with other people but how you arrange the living space around you. A successful education is in implementing manners and etiquette in daily life."

A landlocked and mountainous province in Southwest China, Guizhou is one of the most backward regions of the country, where Tzu Chi has been active in building schools and providing scholarships to poor children. Volunteers compare the diligence and simplicity of Guizhou children to the idleness and self-indulgence of students in Taiwan—their own children—who enjoy a far higher level of material comfort and conditions for learning but do not appreciate them.

Students at Tzu Chi's educational institutions follow both the academic and sports courses of the national curriculum and in addition do voluntary work at hospitals and old people's homes and courses in flower arrangement, tea ceremony, Zen meditation, calligraphy, performing arts and sign language. Flower arrangement aims to teach students to appreciate beauty and show the relation between man and nature; tea ceremony to treat guests courteously and to follow etiquette and Zen to promote self-reflection. Classes in these subjects at Tzu Chi's university in Hualien are given in classrooms designed in the style of the Tang dynasty, with wood and bamboo and with a miniature garden.

Steve J. Lin, director of the humanities department, said that theirs was the only university in Taiwan with such a humanities course. "We teach students to relax, to focus and how to treat others. The flower is like the love of the parents for their children. The farmer nurtures the flower until it blooms. Musicians play the *guqin* (a classical Chinese string instrument) at the tea ceremony."

Cheng Yen's philosophy combines Buddhism and Confucianism. Like Confucius, she believes in the importance of filial piety and that correct moral behavior of an individual leads to the health of the family, the society and the nation. She also follows Confucius in believing that solving the ills of society begins with the personal cultivation of the individual. The moral cultivation of the individual is the key to a productive life and a healthy and peaceful society. In this, education plays a critical role.

Math and morals

In September 2000, Tzu Chi opened its first secondary school and primary school, with a nursery school the next year, on a site in Hualien close to the hospital.

The primary school has two- and three-story buildings, in gray and white, with wide corridors, around a lawn in the center. The design is simple, natural and low-key—the Tzu Chi style. In a room with a *tatami* floor and an image of the Buddha, they learn "humanities"—classes in tea ceremony, clothes making, etiquette and manners.

Non-profit-making, the primary school charges NT$26,000 ($800) a term, which is low for a private school in Taiwan.

The primary and secondary schools follow the same curriculum as a state institution, with the addition of the humanities courses. Students also learn manners and deportment and study *Jing Si* (Still Thoughts) *Aphorisms*, the sayings of Cheng Yen. There is no class on religion or Buddhism.

Students are encouraged to do community service. For those applying for a scholarship in the middle school, a minimum of 18 hours per semester of such service is a requirement.

The foundation plans to expand its network of schools. In 2007, it opened a primary and secondary school in Tainan, in the Southwest of Taiwan, with 96 classes from elementary to senior middle level and six percent of places reserved for children of poor families and the handicapped.

It has built centers of continuing education for adults, managed by Tzu Chi University (慈濟大學), in seven cities in Taiwan and is building four more. These offer a wide range of fee-paying courses, including flower arrangement, tea ceremony, environmental protection, computing and English.

Among the students are some of the 350,000 foreign brides of Taiwanese men, from Vietnam, the Philippines and other countries, who take classes in Mandarin and on how to adapt to the rules and customs of their new society (including how to live in harmony with their mother-in-law!).

Over the last 10 years, more than 23,000 teachers have joined the Tzu Chi Teachers Association and use *Jing Si Aphorisms* as a textbook in their classes. The foundation also runs an association of college students.

"The purpose of Tzu Chi's education cannot be separated from love," said Cheng Yen. "Teachers must first sincerely express their love for students to be moved by it. If only one farmer works a large field, he becomes exhausted. It requires the efforts of many farmers to work together and produce a good crop."

In October 2004, the foundation held a Tzu Chi world education fair in Hualien and invited students from their foreign schools to attend. They included 16 students from six schools it has funded in Ladysmith, South Africa. Wearing striking black and white outfits made by women at the foundation's training classes in South Africa, they performed songs and danced in front of thousands at the Hall of Still Thoughts.

They also sang songs in Mandarin and Taiwanese. A boy and a girl named Tobes and Lungelo brought the house down with a popular song in Taiwanese. Few could control their tears as they saw and heard this expression of gratitude from two children from the other side of the world.

The Forgotten Army

In May 2005, on the side of a mountain in North Thailand, a school opened to serve a community that had been without education for 50 years.

The Tzu Chi elementary and middle school is in the village of Amphur Fang, 150 kilometers from Chiang Mai, and offers lessons in both Thai and Chinese. Its students are Thais, minority people, and the descendants of Chinese soldiers who have been living in the region, stateless, since 1949. It offers them the hope, for the first time, to escape from the poverty and isolation of their parents and grandparents.

What brought the foundation to this isolated region was the plight of the abandoned soldiers.

In 1949, after the Communists won the civil war in China, a division of the defeated Nationalist army escaped from the Southwest province of Yunnan into neighboring Burma. Some were evacuated to Taiwan, but the rest were ordered by President Chiang Kai-shek to remain to prepare for his planned recapture of the mainland.

They fought 10 years of guerilla warfare with the Burmese army, before retreating to the remote mountains of Northern Thailand, where they settled in 64 refugee villages. The government allowed them to stay in exchange for fighting Communist insurgents in the area and gave them refugee status but no citizenship. By 2000, the number of these soldiers and their descendants had reached 60,000, citizens neither of China nor Taiwan or Thailand.

Chiang Kai-shek never tried to recapture the mainland and gradually abandoned his former soldiers. They eked out a living from farming but were barred from most careers because of their refugee status: they were supported by the Taiwan government and private charities, which installed water and electricity in their homes, trained teachers and gave scholarships.

In 1994, John Chiang, chairman of the Overseas Chinese Affairs Commission of the Taiwan government—and a grandson of President Chiang—went to Hualien to ask Tzu Chi to help reconstruct the villages of the refugees. The government had decided to discontinue its annual subsidy of $800,000 to the refugees and asked Cheng Yen to take over.

After an evaluation, Tzu Chi launched a three-year program that included construction of homes, advice on agriculture and care for the soldiers who had retired.

The foundation built more than 120 homes in four villages, two nursing homes and a 1.3-kilometer road to connect a village that did not have one: it provided expertise to grow tea and fruit.

Chinese merchants in Bangkok read of the project and came forward with donations of blankets and winter clothes, setting up the first Tzu Chi branch in Thailand in June 1995.

In 1997, when the three-year program ended, the foundation decided that, since education was the only way to end poverty and enable the young people to enter mainstream Thai society, it should build a school. That year the government lifted a ban of more than 30 years on teaching Chinese.

There were many obstacles, including the location of a suitable site, the ambiguous status of the refugees and government indecision. Finally, the foundation found a site of 19.4 hectares in Amphur Fang.

The principal is Chen Lan-ying, a Thai of Chinese ancestry who studied in Taiwan for 10 years. After meeting Cheng Yen in 1999 and finding they shared the same ideals for education, she accepted the post of principal and was certified as a Tzu Chi commissioner in 2001.

Both Thai- and Chinese-language teachers received six months of training at the foundation's schools in Hualien, including community service, which they practice in the new school. *Jing Si Aphorisms* is part of the curriculum.

At the opening ceremony, there were 59 students together with seven Thai and three Taiwanese teachers. The flags of Thailand, Buddhism and the school were raised at the event.

The school follows the model of Tzu Chi schools in Taiwan—the national curriculum, with the addition of humanities classes and voluntary work in the community. It aims to give the students the opportunity in life, which their parents and grandparents never had.

Seeking nurses

The idea for the education mission came after the Hualien hospital opened in July 1986. Cheng Yen quickly discovered that it was difficult to recruit nurses as well as doctors to work there. Few wanted to exchange a bustling city for a poor, remote town with few amenities and poor transport links to the rest of the island. So she decided to open her own college to train nurses for the hospital. In 1988, the foundation received approval from the Ministry of Education to establish Taiwan's first private nursing college. The new campus opened in September 1989, with an initial enrolment of 107 students and an investment of NT$2.2 billion ($65 million), most from the foundation. It offered scholarships to students in financial need.

The college first offered a two-year nursing course and added a five-year nursing course the following year. It later added courses in physical therapy, early childhood care and education, health education and radiology.

Cheng Yen introduced the elements that have become common to all Tzu Chi educational institutions. First, the college offered classes in humanities, including tea ceremony, flower arrangement and meditation, as well as in music, dance, theatre, sign language performance and Chinese painting. Second, students had to wear a uniform, and only vegetarian food was served on campus. Third, the students were expected to take part in volunteer activities. Fourth was the introduction of "life coaches"—middle-aged Tzu Chi commissioners, who helped the students, living away from home for the first time, with their personal and academic life. There were one of these "mothers" and "fathers" for every three students.

The college aimed to recruit students from among Taiwan's indigenous Aboriginals, the poorest people in Taiwan, many living in remote mountain villages and with a poor command of Mandarin and Taiwanese. To support their families, some Aboriginal girls have been forced into prostitution. Since 1996, the college has offered 50 free places to Aboriginals, who take a separate entrance exam from other students. Aboriginal nurses trained at the college can work in Tzu Chi's hospitals or return to clinics in their hometowns and villages, which are short of good medical care.

Over two decades, the college has been partially successful in helping Tzu Chi General Hospital, the mother hospital—it graduates 300 nurses a year, of whom 80 percent leave to work in areas near home, and 20 percent who stay in Hualien.

In 1999, the college was upgraded into the Tzu Chi College of Technology (慈濟技術學院) and now has six departments—nursing, physical therapy, early childcare and education, radiological technology, health administration, accounting and information engineering.

It has 2,300 students a year and needs an annual subsidy of NT$100 million ($3 million) from the foundation. The fees for a one-year nursing diploma are NT$86,000 ($2,500). If a student agrees to work in Tzu Chi hospitals, she pays no fees. However, Taiwan's declining birthrate, according to Horng Dang-Ming (洪當明), president of the college, means that it is difficult to recruit enough students to meet its funding requirements.

Doctors for the hospital

The same need for qualified staff persuaded Cheng Yen to set a more ambitious target: a medical school. Initially, the Ministry of Education refused her application since its forecasts showed a surfeit of doctors by 2000, due to an increasing number of graduates and a declining population. The foundation argued, however, that it was a special case, since the school would provide doctors for the first major hospital in East Taiwan and that, without them, it would be unable to function. This lobbying convinced the ministry to give its approval in July 1990. To build the school, she selected a large site adjacent to the hospital and the Hall of Still Thoughts.

The new facility became the first medical school in East Taiwan and the first Buddhist medical school in China. It included a doping control center, a gymnasium with an Olympic-size swimming pool and a jogging track made of recycled tires. On October 16, 1994, the foundation held the ceremony to open the medical school, attended by 12,000 people, including senior Buddhist monks and political leaders. In its first year, the college had 150 students and three faculties—medicine, medical technology and public health.

In August 2000, the school was renamed Tzu Chi University, with the addition of three more colleges. It now has 22 departments and 17 research institutes, in addition to colleges of medicine, life sciences, humanities and social science, and education and communication. Its tuition fees are higher than those in public universities but lower than those of other private institutions. The fees cover 28 percent of the costs of the university, funds from the foundation about 50 percent and the rest comes from the Ministry of Education. It has a student body of about 2,000 that live four to one large room, and a low teacher-student ratio, with one to three in the medical department and one to four overall. In 1996, it started a two-year nursing degree, with 50 places. In 1997, it set up Taiwan's first doping control centre and, two years later, research centers for molecular and cell biology, human genetics and neurology. It aims to become a centre for advanced research as well as a university.

The university follows the practices of the nursing college. Its cafeteria provides cheap vegetarian meals; students must bring their own utensils. Alcohol and tobacco are banned on campus, although the college cannot prevent students consuming them in the town. Hair is worn short and well-combed. Students must wear uniforms on campus, in white, gray and dark blue, and take classes in humanities. Freshmen are required to perform at least 10 hours of community service. The university also provides "life coaches"—10–12 students have one "father" and two "mothers," Tzu Chi commissioners, to help them in their work and personal life.

Although the university is Buddhist, it does not have a specific course on Buddhism but includes it in its religion classes.

"What distinguishes us from other universities is our education in morals and manners," said president Wang Pen-jung (王本榮), also a professor in the department of pediatrics. "Our students have a close relation with their teachers and are gentler than those elsewhere. Students in Taiwan are too free and individualist. The Master fears for this. The role of our university is to develop knowledge and train skilled personnel," he said.

In his early years at the then medical school, Wang used to travel once a week from Taipei to Hualien from 1987 to 1998, to hold a clinic at the hospital. During this time, the hospital kept asking him to work full-time, but he was unwilling to leave his patients and students in Taipei. Finally, in 1998, when the first graduates of the medical school needed a good professor to guide them through their internships at the hospital, Wang agreed to work there full-time. He continues to do teaching and clinical work one day a week in Taipei. His wife, a Tzu Chi commissioner and teacher of tea ceremony, divides her time between Hualien and Taipei, where their children live.

Because of its location, as in other Tzu Chi institutions in Hualien the university found it difficult to attract students and teachers. The big teaching hospitals in Taipei and Kaohsiung offered money, prestige and international exchanges, and students generally chose a university in a big city or to study abroad, including an increasing number to mainland China.

Cheng Yen remained confident that, despite these difficulties, the growing numbers and strength of her foundation would attract sufficient students and teachers. She believed that, once they had trained in Hualien, close to the hospital and in daily contact with Tzu Chi people, students would be more likely to stay in the town and work there. In turn, the corps of doctors would grow, creating a medical community others would be keen to join.

Chang Yu-shun, a native of Taipei, was among the first group of medical students who chose Tzu Chi University specifically. "My exams qualified me for a medical school in Taipei, but I came to Hualien. As a child, I went to a Buddhist nursery in Taipei and my mother is a Tzu Chi commissioner. Compared to Taipei, Hualien is quiet and does not have so many places of entertainment."

Chang studied pediatrics. "Since ours was the first year, Cheng Yen chose very good people as our 'fathers' and 'mothers' (life coaches). They used to invite us for meals and take us to do community service with them. We were very moved. Of the 47 students in my graduating class, 20 chose to work at the Hualien hospital. I want to pay back those who helped me. I plan to stay a long time. If I wanted to make money and be famous, I would not stay here."

Overseas Taiwanese are also now finding satisfaction with the university. According to Hung Su-chen, secretary-general of the university, the Taiwanese she had met in the United States could not enter mainstream society. "Tzu Chi gives them a sense of home, a belief and a purpose. They attend these humanities classes on weekends with volunteers and children. It is a chance to meet and eat together. They send their children to Taiwan to study, so that they can have access to both cultures and keep in touch with their ancestry. You can emigrate but cannot change your DNA."

Because the university was founded as a medical college, it remains strongest in medicine. In 2003–2005, the pass rate of its students in Taiwan's national medical exam was 100, 90 and 92 percent respectively. "Specialist knowledge is not the only factor in being competitive," Wang said. "Ability to mix well and work in a team, and morality and ethics are also essential for competitiveness. I hope that the students we train here win the trust of people through their specialist ability and their moral quality. When they first enter society, our graduates may feel less sophisticated than other people. But, over the long term, their good behavior will be an excellent asset. People who are soft and sincere and take the interests of others into account will be appreciated by other people and they will have a longer, smoother future."

Wang is also proud of a program that has given his students the best anatomy classes in the Chinese world. After an appeal by Cheng Yen, more than 17,000 members of the foundation have, since 1995, agreed to donate their bodies after death to the medical school. She calls them "Great Teachers of the Body." To date, the university has accepted more than 240, giving its students more opportunities to study anatomy than any other medical school in the Chinese-speaking world.

Great Teachers of the Body (大體老師)

The roadway leading to Tzu Chi University was lined with people, hands clasped in prayer and heads bowed in mourning. A van arrives at the entrance and drives slowly down the roadway. As it passes, the onlookers close their eyes in deep sadness.

The van is bringing a veteran volunteer, named Huang, who had died suddenly the night before in Tainan, Southwest Taiwan, and had requested that his body be brought to Hualien, his spiritual home, for his final journey.

Huang is one of more than 17,000 people who answered the appeal of Cheng Yen to donate their organs to the medical school after their death and become a *Dati Laoshi* (Great Teacher of the Body), as she poetically calls such donors.

Donations of this scale are unprecedented in the world's Chinese community, which has for centuries regarded the body as a gift from the parents that must be left intact after death. To change this mentality required an enormous feat of persuasion, of which perhaps only someone of the stature of Cheng Yen was capable.

The van drives to a door in the university and Huang's coffin is carried into a well-lit room for the funeral service, accompanied by his widow and three sons, their faces frozen in grief.

The mourners, relatives and friends of the dead man, and nuns in grey robes chant Buddhist sutras for the dead, the air thick with incense. Huang's body lies on a bed, covered by a white sheet, with his shoes and socks sticking out.

Cheng Yen enters from a side door and walks to the coffin where she speaks to "Brother" Huang. She praises him for his work in Tzu Chi, saying that he had made a great contribution to the foundation and that he would return soon. She comforts his family members.

Mourners then carry the coffin out of the room to the second floor of the building where it will be treated, frozen and kept in readiness for the school's medical classes.

Wang Pen-jung is very proud of this program and sees it as a pioneer in the Chinese world.

It was in 1994 that Cheng Yen began to encourage her members to donate their bodies for medical research, flying in the face of Chinese tradition that demands that the body in the coffin enter the earth untouched.

The Buddha himself said nothing against the use of a cadaver for medical purposes but it became the custom to leave the body untouched. In rural China, people buried their relatives close to home, so that they could stay close to them, visit their graves and show respect to their memory.

But Cheng Yen argued that we possess "the right of use" but not "ownership" of our bodies and that offering them for medical research gives students an invaluable opportunity to study the complexity of the human body and the donor an opportunity to make an extraordinary gift to society. It was an idea many people could not and cannot accept. Opposition to the idea remains strong, with a person wishing to sign the consent form often denied the opportunity by members of his own family.

Chinese have a great fear of the dead. People do not like to live near cemeteries and properties close to them are cheaper than others. When President Wang was a medical student, anatomy classrooms were dark and stank of formalin and other chemicals. "No doctor, including me, wants to look back or remember the anatomy classes of that time."

In February 1995, a woman named Lin became the first person to donate her body to the medical school. Since then, the school has received 241 bodies, aged between 16 and 93, and transferred another 286 to other universities, while 17,600 people, over half of them Tzu Chi members, have signed consent forms.

Cheng Yen changed tradition by appealing to the charity of donors and showing painstaking respect for the donor. The students visit the families of the donor in order to know him or her as a person and, in some cases, meet the donor in his final days. In this way, the students develop their own compassion and help the family deal with its grief.

The medical school arranges the procedure with great care. It invites Buddhist monks or nuns or Christian priests to conduct a memorial service, according to the faith of the deceased. Before the class begins, the students meet the family members who speak of their loved ones, read stories about them and show photographs.

The purpose is to make the students regard the body as a person and not an object. At the end of the class, the students sew back the pieces they have cut and cover the bodies in a white robe designed by Cheng Yen. Into the coffin, they place flowers and letters of thanks, before carrying them to the crematorium. The ashes are then placed in crystal urns and kept in a hall of remembrance, which relatives can visit at any time. The school is building a hall with space for 10,000 urns.

The procedure has become not only a matter of medicine and science but an education in life and death, for the students and Tzu Chi nuns and volunteers who take part.

President Wang said the program is the envy of other medical schools in Taiwan and the mainland, providing one body for every four students–who have also come from Beijing and Indonesia to take part in the program—compared to a national average of 40 students and up to 200 in some schools. "The anatomy class offers medical students their first glimpse into the wonders of modern medical science."

He said that his university has too many bodies and is happy to donate them to other medical schools, provided that they follow the same procedures toward the families of the donor and respect the body.

This availability has, since 2002, allowed sixth year medical students to hold practice operations in a fully equipped theatre, to prepare for diseases they will encounter in the future.

Before one class, a widow said she would rather the students make many wrong cuts and mistakes on her husband's body than a single false one on a live patient.

12

BONE MARROW

"Life is not about longevity. It is important to live for a worthy cause. I returned to save our fellow Taiwanese."

—Wen Wen-ling, a student whose leukemia led to the foundation of Tzu Chi's bone marrow bank.

WEN WEN-LING (溫文玲) WAS BEAUTIFUL, intelligent and about to earn a PhD in business from a large U.S. university. The world was her oyster. Then she was diagnosed with leukemia, cancer of the blood or blood marrow.

Wen discovered that her only hope was a bone marrow transplant. She searched in vain for a donor in the U.S. and, in desperation, returned home and asked Cheng Yen to help. Moved by her request and the blessing that a person could receive by giving a part of herself to save the life of another, Cheng Yen established the Tzu Chi Bone Marrow Bank in October 1993. It is now called the Tzu Chi Stem Cells Center.

As of the end of 2007, the bank had saved the lives of 1,476 people, 437 in Taiwan and 1,039 abroad in 25 countries, and built a donor base of 307,506, the largest in Asia and the fifth largest in the world. It accounts for 10 percent of the world bone marrow types, the highest such ratio among the world's data banks. It is the most important bank for Chinese, who account for one fifth of humanity. An agreement signed in December 2006 with the world's two biggest banks, in the United States and Germany, means that patients now have access to a base of 10 million donors.

The bank is a poignant symbol of the foundation's ideals of unselfish love across national, racial and religious boundaries.

The person who donates his or her marrow asks for nothing in return but the joy of making the gift, a piece of himself to save the life of another. Tzu Chi believes that a gift brings blessing to the donor as well as to the receiver. As the new marrow can save a life, many donors consider their gift the most important thing they have ever done. Some overcame strong opposition from their family—sometimes they deceived them. A Taiwan nurse has given marrow twice, to a patient in Japan and to one in the United States; a Taiwan couple also both donated marrow. Leukemia patients around the world—in Norway, Denmark, Holland, Israel, South Africa, Thailand, Australia and New Zealand—are alive today because of donations from the bank. It has earned Taiwan the respect of the medical profession around the world.

The bank is a costly and complicated operation. Each transplant costs $45,000 and requires state-of-the-art medical technology. The chance of finding a successful match is one in 100,000. Maintaining the bank means maintaining a giant database, with tens of thousands of names and detailed medical information and constantly updating them, so potential donors can be found and invited to give their marrow when a match is found.

At the time Wen Wen-ling was diagnosed with leukemia, in 1992, there were few options available to her. She could not find a match among her family members, nor was the U.S. bank, which consists of bone marrow predominantly from Caucasians, able to help her. Tzu Chi members held a blood test drive, but they too could not find a match. Back then, Japan was the only Asian country to operate bone marrow bank for Asians, with a membership a fraction of those in the United States and Germany. This was largely because the vast majority of Chinese, and East Asians in general, oppose donating parts of their body: they believed the words of Confucius who said it is a gift from their parents which they should not damage.

Back in Taiwan, Wen approached Chen Yao-chang, a surgeon at the medical school of National Taiwan University (NTU), the island's top university. He told her that, to prevent a black market in organs, Taiwan law only allowed transplants between members of the same family: it would be necessary to change the law to allow her to receive marrow from someone who was not a relative.

In early 1993, accompanied by Professor Chen, Wen went to Hualien to explain her predicament to Cheng Yen. She said Tzu Chi was the only institution in Taiwan with the public trust and mass membership that could set up a bone marrow bank and attract thousands of donors. It had an excellent fund-raising network, vital to raise the money needed. Doing the necessary analysis of HLA (human leukocyte antigens) for a single potential donor costs more than NT$4,000 ($150). Cheng Yen sympathized with Wen and understood the need for such a bank: but she was unsure if a transplant would harm the donor or cause side effects. If it did, the project would not be a good one. She was also uncertain of public acceptance: she began a lengthy process of study and deliberation.

In the meantime, Professor Chen successfully lobbied the national parliament to amend the law, in May 1993, to allow transplants between people who were not related. In August, NTU launched its own bone marrow donation scheme, attracting nearly 3,000 donors. But the number was too small to help Wen: NTU did not have the funds to build its donor base further.

In October 1993, after 10 months of study and satisfied that a transplant would not harm the health of the donor, Cheng Yen announced in a public lecture in Changhwa that Tzu Chi would establish the first bone marrow bank in the Chinese world. "The sutras tell us that, to be the Buddha's disciple and implement the ways of the bodhisattva, we need to possess the Great Love of 'donating head, eyes, marrow and brain to those in need,'" she said. She emphasized her principle that Tzu Chi would never harm a person's health for the benefit of another. "Our modern technologies, medicine and science have been very advanced. Suppose we have a patient with malignant leukemia and suppose we are willing to donate our matching bone marrows to her. Such a match, perhaps only one in every 20,000, is a unique affinity."

It was not an easy decision, given the traditional beliefs among the Chinese, who also believed that making such a gift would permanently harm the health of the donor. To set up a bone marrow bank meant persuading thousands of people to change their beliefs and register as donors.

In addition, the chance of finding a successful match is only one in 100,000. This makes the establishment and maintenance of such a bank a high-cost operation. Once a match is found, the bone marrow must be delivered to the recipient within 24 hours, making transnational donations a major operation, with a delay due to bad weather, a canceled flight or a traffic jam able to render the operation impossible. Recipients must undergo radiation treatment to kill their own diseased marrow. If the marrow is not delivered on time, the patient dies. A third negative factor is that the success rate of such transplants is about 50 percent, with half of the patients dying because their bodies reject the new cells or for other reasons. Was such a bank a good way to spend Tzu Chi's money?

Miss Wen proved right. The moral authority of Cheng Yen and her members' faith in her persuaded thousands of them to launch a nation-wide drive for donors, even though many knew little of the medical details or where bone marrow came from. More than 50,000 volunteers took to the streets, in Taiwan, elsewhere in Asia and the United States, to persuade people to register and take a blood test. They used the slogan: "It never hurts to save a life." The first success came in the Southwest city of Changhua, where 800 people signed up as donors.

The volunteers encountered strong opposition from the public, who said that a transplant would inflict long-term damage on the donor by removing a piece of his spine. Volunteers were abused and shouted at and their pamphlets thrown away. In fact, the tissue comes from the ilium, either side of the hip, and grows back after surgery, so that there is no risk to the donor and no damage to the central nervous system. Donation requires transferring five percent of the hibernating marrow cells from the donor to the patient. Because marrow consists of cells that can divide and reproduce, the extracted amount can be replaced within about 10 days.

Despite the opposition, the authority of Cheng Yen and the dedication of her members got the project off the ground. By July 1995, the number of donors had exceeded 100,000 and the bank had arranged 28 transplants involving non-family members, including three transnational ones. Within two years, it had become one of the top five bone marrow banks in the world. Hong Kong film star Jackie Chan made a free advertisement: "Tzu Chi and I are looking for someone and that person could be you."

But the bank came too late to save Wen Wen-ling. She could not wait and found a match in Hong Kong, where she went for an operation. Six months later, she caught a high fever, was diagnosed with a lung infection and passed away two weeks later. She lost her own life but the marrow bank she helped to found has saved more than 1,200 others. Before she died, she told her mother: "Life is not about longevity. It is important to live for a worthy cause. I returned to save our fellow Taiwanese."

Cheng Yen persuaded a Taiwan-American specialist, Lee Cheng-dao, director of the Immune Genetics Laboratory in New York, to run the bank. He had supported and admired Tzu Chi's philosophy of compassion and respect for all. As a doctor in the U.S., he had been unable to help Chinese-American leukemia patients because the donors were mostly Caucasian. "Now that I had a chance to help more patients, I had fulfilled my life-long dream. The happiness and excitement I feel each time a patient is saved by a bone marrow donation is indescribable," he said.

Leukemia is cancer of the blood or bone marrow and its causes are unknown. It can strike people of any age and race. Each year, over 600,000 people in the world develop the disease—in the United States the rate is seven out of 100,000 people and in developing countries the proportion is higher. To treat it, doctors use intensive chemotherapy and radiotherapy, which is very painful and causes loss of hair and appetite. When this treatment does not work or destroys essential bone marrow, a transplant is the only hope of recovery. This infuses healthy bone marrow into the blood stream, which will, if accepted, produce normal, healthy blood cells. The best donor is a member of the patient's own family but fewer than 30 percent of patients can find such a donor. It was for this reason that doctors, from the 1950s, began researching the transplant of bone marrow from one human to another.

History of transplants

The first successful bone marrow transplant, on twins, was performed in 1958 by an American surgeon, Dr. Edward Thomas. Since then, he has carried out more than 20,000 successful transplants, for which he was awarded the Nobel Prize in medicine in 1990. He has saved the lives of more than 10,000 leukemia patients.

The bone marrow cells—called hematopoietic stem cells (HSC)—are removed from a large bone of the donor, typically the pelvis, through a large needle that reaches the centre of the bone. It is performed under general anesthesia because hundreds of insertions of the needle are required to obtain sufficient material. The HSC are infused into the blood stream of the recipient through an intravenous catheter. A difficult procedure, the operation is reserved for patients with life-threatening diseases: it remains the best hope for leukemia patients. The success rate is about 50 percent, because the recipient's immune system may reject the foreign bone marrow.

Over the last 20 years, medical technology has advanced to include two other kinds of transplants for leukemia-peripheral blood stem cells (PBSC) and umbilical cord blood (UCB). The first requires five days of preparation, during which doctors stimulate the growth of a donor's stem cells around his peripheral blood vessels. He gives blood without having to go under anesthetic. The second takes blood from the cord between the mother and newborn child. Like other banks around the world, the Tzu Chi center offers all three kinds of transplants.

The first bone marrow bank, the Anthony Nolan Trust, was set up in the United Kingdom in 1974, by Shirley Nolan in honor of her son Anthony, who was born in 1971 with the rare disease Wiscot Aldrich Syndrome, and whose only hope of a cure was a bone marrow transplant. She was unable to find one and Anthony died in 1979. Since it began, the trust has saved the lives of more than 7,000 patients and built a register of 360,000 British residents who have volunteered to donate bone marrow.

In July 1986, the National Bone Marrow Donor Registry was set up in the U.S.: in June 1988 it changed its name to the National Marrow Donor Program (NMDP). Since 1987, it has facilitated more than 25,000 transplants, with an average of 220 patients per month, and has a register of more than six million volunteer donors, the largest in the world. Globally, of those who receive a transplant, 40 percent are from the United States. Since the U.S. contains so many racial types, 30 percent of cases handled by the NMDP involve an international donor or recipient. The second largest bank is the German Bone Marrow Donor Center, established in 1991, with 1.8 million donors. Worldwide, there are 62 bone marrow data banks, with the total number of donors exceeding 10 million for the first time in November 2005.

In 2004, 4,961 transplants were performed around the world, of which 2,754 used stem cells from outside their own countries—or 55 percent. Cross-border donations are becoming increasingly popular and important. Of the 62 banks, only a few focus on exporting stem cells abroad, of which the Tzu Chi bank is one. As of August 2005, the bank had accepted 8,000 applications from foreign countries.

The first bank in Asia was the Japan Marrow Donor Program, set up in December 1991, which has 220,000 registered donors. The average number of transplants in Japan is more than 700 a year. A similar bank was established in South Korea in 1994 and has 90,000 donors.

Because a patient's genetic make-up is inherited, he is most likely to find a matching donor from his own racial or ethnic group. Yet despite the Japan and South Korea banks, and Tzu Chi's efforts, people of Asian origin are still greatly under-represented in the global database, as are donors of all ethnic groups other than those of Northwest European origin. In Asia, the establishment of such banks has been held back by the cost and complexity of bone marrow transplants, lack of medical expertise, legal and regulatory factors and resistance on cultural and religious grounds.

The incidence of leukemia in the Chinese world is the same as else-where, which means 40,000 new leukemia cases a year in mainland China, where there exists around four million leukemia patients, of whom one million need transplants. Most will die because they cannot find a match. The one-child policy, in force since 1980, means that millions have no brothers and sisters who would provide the closest match. In 2001, the Chinese Red Cross established the Chinese Bone Marrow Bank in Beijing and announced 500,000 registered donors by the end of 2006. However, it does not have a central headquarters able to match donor and recipient. Many who register are unwilling to give when asked, because they did not understand the implications of what they agreed to. So China still has to rely heavily on donations from Taiwan.

This makes the Tzu Chi bank the principal reserve for the 20 percent of the world's population who are Chinese. Patients from the mainland rank first, accounting for about 40 percent of all recipients from the Tzu Chi bank, whose reach is wider than the bank in Japan, where the gene pool is narrower. Taiwan's genetic mix is more varied than Japan's, since the population includes people from all over China and overseas Chinese. The bank is also a source for the overseas Chinese diaspora, who number 60–70 million around the world.

Blood stem cells

With the addition of the two new kinds of transplant—peripheral blood stem cell (PBSC) and umbilical cord blood (UCB) transplant—the hopes of leukemia patients are improving. Procurement of PBSC is easier and less traumatic than collecting bone marrow and does not require anesthesia. In Germany, most donors prefer giving PBSC to bone marrow. The second alternative is UCB, using the blood that joins mothers with their new babies. The first successful cord blood operation was performed in Paris in 1988, on a boy with a lethal type of anemia, who is alive and well today. Since then, more than 6,000 such transplants from unrelated donors and several hundred from sibling donors have been performed worldwide.

According to figures from the NMDP, cord blood operations in the United States account for 10 percent of transplants, bone marrow 30 percent and peripheral blood stem cells 60 percent. It estimates that, by 2011, cord blood will account for over half of all transplants.

In 1999, Tzu Chi set up a bank for umbilical cords and by the end of 2005 had stored 13,000 samples. Keeping them accounts for 50 percent of the annual costs of the stem cell registry. As of the end of November 2006, the Hualien hospital had performed 24 cord blood operations for patients in seven countries. Doctors in Japan, China and Taiwan hope to set up an Asian UCB HLA database, to which patients all over Asia will have access.

Chen Nai-yu (陳乃裕) said Tzu Chi's bank was small compared to those in the United States and Germany but that it performed its work with thoroughness and diligence. "Donations by the bank have brought Taiwan to the attention of the world. Many banks and individuals in the world have received our donations, have been moved and given us respect. Many countries want to put on international symposia on bone marrow and we organize two a year. Our bank is the reason.

"If it is a good fortune to be a member of Tzu Chi, then to promote a bone marrow transplant is the most fortunate of all. Each case is a dialogue with life. When you see how difficult it is for a person to hang on to life, then you understand its significance and how this desire must be respected."

Work in Taiwan

Since 1993, Tzu Chi volunteers have added 15,000–20,000 new donors per year, to replace those who have become too old, changed their mind or become untraceable. In per capita terms, that is the highest for any Asian country, at 1.3 percent of the population, but less than Germany, which ranks first in the world, with 2.5 percent.

Chen Nai-yu, head of the bank, said that the mass mobilization of Tzu Chi volunteers since 1993 had changed the consensus in Taiwan, by explaining to the public that giving bone marrow did not damage the health of the donor and that the body naturally regenerates the tissue that was lost. "In the early years, there was strong opposition and we had to do our work discreetly," he said. "But now there is widespread support and fewer and fewer people oppose a transplant." While the foundation wants the family of the donor to agree, it leaves the final decision to him or her. In some cases, the donor deceived their family because they could not overcome their opposition.

Sometimes, volunteers seeking to reach a donor are abused and shouted at by family members and refused entry to the home. They may wait for hours in the evening, in the hope of catching the donor on their way home from work. In one case, a man was contacted several years after registering. He had changed his mind but could not bring himself to say it directly and made appointments, which he never kept. One day he agreed to meet a volunteer at Sogo, one of Taipei's biggest department stores. He arrived four hours late, thinking that she would be long gone—only to find her still waiting. He was shamed into agreeing!

A transplant requires not only a skilled medical team of surgeons and nurses, but teams of wise and experienced volunteers to work with the two families. The foundation has created care groups of volunteers, who number over 5,000 and look after both donor and recipient. No other bone marrow bank has such a large team of full-time volunteers.

When the bank finds a match, volunteers must locate the donor, who may have moved house or emigrated abroad. They must ascertain if he or she is still willing to give. The donor may now be older than 55, may have changed their mind, or personal or family circumstances may have altered. Volunteers work with the donor and their family, to ensure they understand the process and accompany them through the surgery and afterwards. They cook for the family, clean their home, look after their children and provide financial aid. Volunteers must explain the surgery and risks to the recipient's family and accompany them throughout the recovery process. If the transplant is not successful and the patient dies, they must guide the family through its grief.

Song Hsiu-duan is a middle-aged woman who has been working in such a care group in Taipei since 1997. "The period before the operation is an anxious time for the recipient and his family. They want the transplant but fear that the other side will change its mind. We must give all the encouragement we can. Then, after the operation, the patient must stay in hospital, for one, two or even three months. We must always be positive and not show a negative face. We go to the hospital two to three times a week. We must treat them like members of our own family."

Most difficult is the time after the death of a patient. At 3.45 one morning, Song received a call from a man whose wife had just died after the transplant had failed. "She was a woman in her 40s with children and had accepted the fact of her own death. By 6 AM, we had reached their home and accompanied her husband to the funeral home. We teach the family to come to terms with the loss. We must be available at any time of the day or night."

The foundation is eager to export this system of care groups to other countries, such as China, Thailand, the United States, Australia and Hong Kong, where it has members.

The costs are substantial. The registry requires NT$100 million ($3 million), of which the foundation contributes around $1 million and patients pay the rest. The government has declined the foundation's request for financial aid. Transplants to Taiwan recipients are done at the Hualien hospital, while foreign recipients send representatives to pick up the bone marrow at the hospital. The biggest expense is providing the marrow to mainland recipients: Tzu Chi members take it in person to the hospital involved. The patients are usually too poor to pay, so that the foundation and its members in the mainland, mostly Taiwan businessmen, cover the high costs of the treatment.

The banks in the U.S., Germany and Japan receive government subsidies but the Anthony Nolan Trust and the Tzu Chi bank rely entirely on private funding. The basic cost of a match is NT$1.5 million ($45,000), of which Tzu Chi charges the patient NT$113,000 ($3,500) and pays the rest itself: it is the cheapest of any major bank. If a patient is too poor, the foundation will evaluate his financial situation and, if necessary, offer a gift of NT$50,000 ($1,500) or NT$100,000 ($3,000). In 2006, it gave NT$2 million ($60,000) in such payments.

The bank's first non-related transplant was in June 1994. The donor was a 21-year-old woman, a law student at NTU, and the recipient a 15-year-old boy. "I experienced opposition from those around me," said the student Yeh Meei-jing. "However much you say, people do not listen."

Chen Nai-yu was involved in the first overseas transplant, to a 16-year-old girl in Singapore. He was responsible for delivering the marrow. To ensure it did not coagulate in its cold storage box, he shook it throughout the flight. When he walked through the arrival door, he saw the family of the sick girl waiting, their eyes glued to the box in his hand, the worry etched on their faces.

The bank made its first donation to Germany in 1997 and to France in 2005.

The biggest beneficiaries have been patients from mainland China, who have a genetic make-up similar to people in Taiwan and accounted for 415 of the 1,476 recipients, as of the end of 2007. These exchanges across the Taiwan Strait have been especially poignant. With no direct flights between Taiwan and the mainland until 2008, delivering bone marrow was a major logistical problem. The marrow must be put into the body of the recipient within 24 hours, after which it will not survive. Before the operation, the patient undergoes radiation to kill his diseased marrow and, if the new tissue does not arrive in time, he will die.

In 2001, a severe storm closed Taipei's domestic airport. So the volunteers carrying the marrow had to take the train to Taipei, a journey of three hours. On arrival, a car from the association of Tzu Chi members in the police force drove them to the international airport, which fortunately was not closed. There they took a flight to Hong Kong and switched planes to Hangzhou. They arrived with a few minutes to spare at the hospital, where the family members of the patient and the medical staff were waiting anxiously. The operation was carried out at the hospital of Zhejiang University, which since 1998 has done more than 50 such transplants, the most of any hospital in the mainland.

13

EARTHQUAKE

PROJECT HOPE AND THE 1999 EARTHQUAKE

*"May the love in each of us converge into a vast ocean of love,
which can then be given to everyone in the world without end."*

—Cheng Yen

THE DEVASTATING EARTHQUAKE that struck Central Taiwan in September 1999 was a milestone in the history of Tzu Chi. The speed and efficiency of its mobilization, fund-raising efforts and construction of 52 schools and nearly 2,000 homes made a deep impression on the Taiwanese public and helped to recruit thousands more members. It showed vividly "Buddhism in action." This response was a result of years of practice in disaster relief, at home and abroad, and training of its members, who took the initiative within minutes of the quake, without orders from Hualien.

The earthquake measuring 7.6 on the Richter scale struck at 1.47 AM on September 21, with its epicenter on land close to the city of Taichung. It damaged buildings all over the island, including a 12-story apartment block in Taipei 140 kilometers away. It killed 2,300 people, injured 8,700, destroyed 13,000 high-rise apartment blocks in Central Taiwan and left 100,000 homeless. It was the worst earthquake to hit the island since a tremor in 1935, which killed 3,000 people. It ruptured power and telephone lines, cut roads and brought down trees. Worst affected was the town of Tungshih, where virtually every building was damaged and residents were left without electricity, water or telephones. In some places, the land slipped up to 26 feet, new hills were formed and waterfalls erupted. In the months after the quake, the island recorded 8,000 aftershocks.

Within minutes of the earthquake, Tzu Chi members sprung into action. By 2 AM, two members had reached the site of the Tung Hsing Building, the 12-story apartment block in Taipei that collapsed, killing 87 of its residents, injuring 138 and leaving more than 250 homeless. Heavy smoke was rising from the rubble, caused by a gas leak: it would take five days to seal. Before 5 AM, several hundred volunteers had gathered at the scene.

A member had ridden on his motorcycle to the foundation's branch in Taichung. In Puli, one of the worst hit towns, a member rushed to the local Protestant hospital and climbed to the seventh floor, from where he carried out the patients to safety on the ground. Hundreds of other members in Central Taiwan walked or hitchhiked through the night to the disaster area.

Asleep in her small room in the Abode, Cheng Yen was awoken by the tremors, turned on her emergency light and switched on the radio. As she realized the extent of the disaster, she leapt out of bed, rushed to her office and asked her staff to call Tzu Chi hospitals and commissioners around the island to assess the damage. Many lines were dead—everyone realized that something catastrophic had happened. She instructed staff to withdraw money from banks as soon as they opened, for distribution to the victims. She told them to withdraw NT$20 million ($600,000) from a bank in Hualien and to withdraw similar amounts from banks in Taipei and Taichung. She said relief payments must be distributed at once, because all the victims possessed was in their homes, which had collapsed. But, because of power cuts, in the earthquake-hit cities, banks were not open and computers not functioning. Using money from banks that were open, or from their own funds, Tzu Chi gave out NT$160 million ($4.5 million) in relief payments in the first three days—NT$5,000 ($150) to each household in the disaster area and NT$50,000 ($1,500) for each deceased person.

Despite the darkness and lack of telephone contact, the disciples knew what to do. Their training had prepared them and, by the time the sun rose, they had established 30 emergency centers in the worst-hit areas, providing food, shelter and counseling. By car, van and lorry, they brought in vast quantities of relief supplies.

Asked how Tzu Chi had mobilized so many people in such a short time, Cheng Yen replied that it was not due to any plan but the love in the hearts of her members. At the Tung Hsing building, the members organized three eight-hour shifts, providing cooked food, comforting the families of the victims and helping the rescue workers. For the families, it was an agonizing ordeal, with more than 50 people trapped inside the building three days after the quake. It was a nightmare for the fire service because the building was leaning sideways and kept slipping because of aftershocks. The rescuers had to penetrate the floors one by one. Two brothers, playing bridge that night on the third floor, emerged from the wreckage after being trapped for 130 hours. They survived by talking to each other and drinking water, which seeped through the walls. On the sixth day, they were preparing to die when one had a dream in which a person told him there was a hole behind the refrigerator. They found the hole and dug themselves out.

On the afternoon of September 21, a team of 12 doctors and 28 nurses led by the deputy chief of the Tzu Chi hospital in Hualien, left for Taichung taking equipment and medicines. They began providing medical aid that day. The foundation set up medical stations in seven of the worst hit districts, working mainly in the open air, in fields and sports stadia and with inadequate equipment. Transport was severely disrupted and electricity and telephone services intermittent. Sanitary conditions were poor, due to an inadequate supply of water. Thousands had to sleep in the open, many without tents, with a wide difference in temperature between night and day that could cause illness. Many suffered from severe trauma, having seen their homes and belongings vanish in a few seconds and having lost family and friends. Tzu Chi members worked to sterilize the affected areas to prevent epidemics and install water supply systems and drainage equipment.

During these first days, the volunteers worked with thousands from the government and civil society, to provide the victims with clothing, tents, blankets, hot food and daily essentials. They organized cooking teams in the disaster area, with 30–40 members working in each shift to provide meals for quake survivors and rescue workers. They brought everything with them, from cooking utensils and groceries to scrub brushes and clothes hangers. Some victims received a hot breakfast—a vegetarian one—early on the morning of the quake. The volunteer cooks slept where they worked, covered with newspaper or cardboard.

Not everything went smoothly. For the first two days, telecommunications in the disaster areas were down, including mobile telephones. Emergency goods piled up, container trucks arrived and created traffic jams and many good-hearted people delivered food and mineral water in their own private cars and trucks. By the second night, there was no bottled mineral water in the shops of Taichung, but a surplus of it in the earthquake zone. With so many organizations involved, there was a lack of coordination. Tzu Chi members were fortunate to meet a group of jeep enthusiasts, called "the Camel Jeep Troop" who had earlier met the foundation when it conducted free clinics in remote mountain villages. Eager to repay the favor, they put at their disposal their own excellent telecom equipment. In this way, the volunteers collected information on the stricken areas and contacted people coming from Taipei and other places to tell them what items to bring and where they should go.

On September 22, as the extent of the damage became apparent, Cheng Yen drew up plans for temporary homes and the materials to build them. She ordered a halt to existing work on Tzu Chi schools, so that all the funds could be concentrated in the quake area. After a few days, she went to the worst-hit areas to take personal charge of the rescue effort. Her first instruction to members was not to take personal risk, such as going to areas that were cut off. Each evening, group leaders would call members of their team to ensure each had arrived home safely. During the relief effort, none of the 100,000 Tzu Chi members mobilized was killed or injured. Cheng Yen stayed in the Taichung area for two months, working the same high-speed, 18-hour day as at home. During the day, she inspected disaster and reconstruction sites and listened to reports late into the evening.

The foundation launched a giant fundraising campaign at home and abroad. Within two days, volunteers around the island had raised NT$150 million ($4 million) and, by the end of the month, NT$2.53 billion ($78 million) worldwide, a record amount in such a short time. In the first week after the quake, 500,000 people visited the website of the Tzu Chi office in San Jose, California. Within three days, money, power generators, body bags, tents, sleeping bags and other relief goods, as well as volunteers, were pouring into Taiwan, from many countries. This was a testimony to the foundation's organization and good reputation and the generosity of the donors. Doctors, rescue teams and volunteers came from the U.S., Mexico, Russia, Japan, South Korea, Singapore, Turkey, Britain and Switzerland. The team from Turkey was a gesture of thanks for a team Tzu Chi had sent to that country a month earlier to help victims of an earthquake in Izmit, 80 kilometers Southeast of Istanbul, which had killed 2,000 people and injured 10,000.

After the immediate needs of the victims were met, the next challenge was to rehouse them. The government offered a monthly allowance of NT$3,000 ($90) to people to find their own housing or a temporary home to be built by it or a non-government organization on land provided by the government. Cheng Yen decided that the foundation would play a major role in this. She set several criteria: the structures must be close to the original homes of the victims and contain three rooms with a floor area of 40 square meters, including a bathroom. This was 50 percent larger than the government minimum, the standard used for temporary homes built in Kobe after its earthquake in January 1995. Further, Cheng Yen said the homes must be able to resist typhoons and earthquakes and have open space between the floor and the ground, allowing it to breathe and to reduce dampness. Each community would include a police station, fire brigade, guardhouse, library and activity center. The foundation started construction on October 1, with the first batch of 118 completed by November 1. In all, by November 15, it had built 1,882 pre-fabricated homes in 18 locations, including a "village" of 320 units in Puli.

The foundation mobilized 200,000 volunteers, including some from foreign countries, for the housebuilding. They included office workers, shopkeepers, company directors and members from overseas. Each member utilized their skills—those in construction and engineering offered these services, those who ran hardware stores installed water and electricity and carpenters did interior decoration. The foundation in Taipei provided a two-day intensive training course to more than 800 members, so that they could work on the construction sites. Others were amateurs who assisted however they could, laying bricks and tiles, building walls and cleaning. The volunteers helped the residents to move in and donated domestic appliances such as water heaters, curtains, blankets and cotton quilts.

This mobilization was unprecedented for the foundation, involving people from chief executive to street hawker. Cheng Yen described it in this way: "When a drop of water falls in the middle of a desert, it quickly evaporates without a trace. However, if it falls into an ocean, that same drop of life will never dry up. May the love in each of us converge into a vast ocean of love, which can then be given to everyone in the world without end."

For many, Tzu Chi responded to the disaster more quickly and efficiently than the government. This was due in part to the mutual trust and confidence between members, enabling them to act without going through administrative and financial procedures normally required by a government. Another factor was the internal reorganization Cheng Yen had carried out in 1996. Then, she had made the foundation's basic unit a neighborhood, instead of one based on a network of people known to individual commissioners, who could live in different areas. This made it possible to respond more quickly, since members of one unit lived in the same area.

The government faced an unprecedented disaster and was criticized for poor coordination of the relief effort and inadequate high-tech search and rescue equipment. "Our rescue efforts were a little disorganized," admitted a spokesman for President Lee Teng-hui.

The next phase was to rebuild the 896 schools wholly or partially damaged by the quake. The government could not accept this burden alone and asked civil organizations to help. Tzu Chi offered to rebuild 20 schools, with a budget of NT$4 billion ($125 million), substantially more than its funds at that time. Finally, it increased the number to 52, with 50,000 students, and the budget more than doubled to NT$10 billion ($300 million). They included large city schools with several thousand students and small ones in mountain villages. While other institutions paid for schools and left the building to someone else, the foundation undertook the entire construction process, from fundraising to architectural design and building.

Cheng Yen stayed in Taichung to take charge of the reconstruction, the biggest building project in the foundation's history, which she called Project Hope. "The hope of a nation is in the talent of its people and the hope of this talent is in education," she said. "The hope of parents is in their children and the hope of children is in education. Each day, the reconstruction of the schools is delayed is one day that children cannot receive a normal education. Countless households will be affected. In such circumstances, I took the decision that Tzu Chi must play its role in this project."

Project Hope captured the imagination of the public. The foundation raised money from businesses, non-profit-making organizations, government agencies and millions of individuals in Taiwan and abroad. It selected more than 20 of Taiwan's best architects to design the schools.

Cheng Yen said hospitals and schools were the two structures that could not fall during an earthquake, because one treats the sick and the other serves as a place of refuge. She instructed that the new schools be built of steel-reinforced concrete, strong enough to survive another earthquake. This raised the cost and extended the building period. "We build everything the best we can because we hope the things we do today will last a thousand years," she said.

The schools were to reflect the local character, with features that have become typical of Tzu Chi buildings—low-key colors like white and gray, good natural ventilation, use of drains, pools and tanks to collect and reuse rainwater, use of natural light, planting of grass and trees and use of natural materials like wood and bamboo. Cheng Yen asked that old trees be preserved and not moved to accommodate the construction: instead, the buildings should be designed around the trees. She said air conditioners should be avoided, since they consume electricity and increase the outside temperature. Another feature was measures to reduce noise, so that students and teachers would not be distracted in their work. To improve safety, the architects separated cars and students, providing car parks and space for parents to pick up children in an area away from that used by the students. To allow the earth to breathe, the architects used, where possible, brick instead of concrete. "I hope that the schools will not only fulfill their function for the next 10–20 years and more but will also be a legacy to future generations," said Cheng Yen. "In 50–100 years, it may be impossible to revive village life but the schools built by Tzu Chi will show the culture and living style of their generation."

More than 200,000 volunteers joined in the work. They donated cement, steel, bricks and other raw materials, they worked as architects, engineers and interior decorators, paved brick paths and did landscaping. They brought meals, drinks and snacks to the construction workers. Those with cars provided transportation. Many took leave from their regular jobs to help. High school and university students also joined in. This mass effort had a knock-on effect in the local community, whose members offered their services, to help complete a facility vital to their society. It was this mass mobilization that enabled the foundation to complete the 52 schools within three years. On April 10, 2000, a middle school in the town of Fengyuan opened, the first of Project Hope.

On completion of the 52 schools it built, the foundation handed them over to the local government.

Tzu Chi's relief and reconstruction effort after the earthquake inspired thousands of people to donate money and greatly raised its profile in Taiwan and abroad, attracting tens of thousands of new members. It was a dramatic illustration of Buddhism in action, how a religious organization helped people at a critical moment in their lives— not monks in saffron robes reciting scriptures in a room full of incense but engineers and carpenters, housewives and shop assistants with their sleeves rolled up and shoes covered in mud, putting the finished touches to a new home and a new school.

14

ENVIRONMENT

*"If the earth follows its natural law, it can continue to support
a multitude of life forms. But the unbridled destruction caused
by man is driving the earth quickly to extinction. The avarice of
man is injuring the earth in a thousand ways ... Mother Earth is
wailing in agony. The earth has provided plenty of resources for
mankind to live on but man has used too many of them."*

—Cheng Yen

JUST AFTER FOUR O'CLOCK EACH MORNING, an 88-year-old woman
in Southwest Taiwan leaves her modest house and pushes a trolley
through the streets of her small town. Liao You-hsien picks up discarded
cardboard boxes, plastic and glass bottles, Coca-Cola cans and scrap
metal and loads them onto her trolley. At that hour the streets of Siluo,
a farming town of 40,000 famous for its soy sauce and fragrant rice, are
quiet and deserted. Liao walks slowly so as not to miss anything. When
it rains, she wears a cape and, in the heat of the summer, a round straw
hat. When the cart is full, she pushes it back to a small plot of land next
to her home, which she has turned into a collection centre.

This scene is re-enacted each morning in hundreds of cities and towns
across Taiwan, with some collectors older than Liao, into their 90s and
even over 100. "I have been doing this for more than 10 years," she
said. "When I went to Hualien, I heard the Master speak of the need
for recycling and decided that this was something I should do, to serve
the public."

She is one of more than 62,000 unpaid volunteers across Taiwan
who have turned recycling into one of Tzu Chi's core activities, with

4,500 centers across the island. Volunteers at these centers sort the goods into different materials and sell them to factories. The money they earn goes to the foundation's global television channel, covering a quarter of its annual costs. They see this donation as a "spiritual" recycling. The money goes toward helping the channel in its mission to "purify the heart of man," just as the volunteers aim through their recycling to "purify" the earth.

In Cheng Yen's thinking, the recycling serves two purposes. One is to diminish the waste of natural resources and contribute to saving the planet from destruction by man. The other is to provide people with an opportunity to practice Buddhism. She refers to the recycling centers as *daochang*, which traditionally meant a place where Buddhist rites were performed to save the souls of the dead. But Tzu Chi's credo is to practice Buddhism for the living, not the dead. So the centers have become, like a hospital, school, old people's home or refugee camp, a place where a person can gain merit by serving others.

Cheng Yen calls people like Madame Liao "elderly Buddhas" and praises them for giving their time and energy for a common good, when they could be more comfortable watching television and playing mahjong at home. The work is also an exercise in humility, doing a task which society considers demeaning. She believes that the greatest human obstacle is selfishness—be it arrogance or a sense of inferiority—which leads to isolation from others. Working amid the dirt and smell of a recycling center is a way for rich and poor, educated and uneducated, to overcome this self-centeredness and learn equality and a common purpose. "Doing recycling is true awakening. You must not fear the filth and smells but see them as sweet as candy. It is the best way to overcome arrogance and the ego," she says. So working in a recycling center is both a way to learn humility and equality and to help the environment.

But recycling would not be so popular if saving the planet was the only reason driving people like Madame Liao to go out at four in the morning into the street with their trolleys. It must offer other attractions. The centers serve as places of friendship and camaraderie, attracting those, especially retired people, who live alone or with time on their hands. It gives them a focus for the lives and diverts their minds from dark, sadder topics and anxieties. Many participants say recycling has rescued them from loneliness, stress and anxiety. It is a way to do exercise, stay in good health and meet people of all ages, from school students to centenarians. Like Tzu Chi as a whole, recycling is an activity that answers personal and social needs as well as serving a good cause.

For Cheng Yen, the need for recycling and better use of natural resources has become a major theme, not only in Taiwan but worldwide. She sees the issue in moral terms—the greed and waste of man is causing over-exploitation of natural resources, which are being used up faster than the earth's ability to regenerate them. "If we do not take care of the heart of man, the rate of destruction will accelerate. Our planet has become old, like man. Man is born, becomes old, sick and dies. Our planet also grows, lives, deteriorates and becomes nothing. Mankind is causing ceaseless destruction to the planet. Each year is worse than the one year before, moral concepts are worsening, which is really very frightening."

The event that sparked the environmental mission came on the morning of August 23, 1990, when Cheng Yen was invited to give a lecture in Taichung, the biggest city in Central Taiwan. That morning, she walked through the streets of a well-heeled district covered by discarded beer bottles, food containers, coke tins, paper cups and plastic bags swirling in the wind. It could have been the center of any large city in the developed world the morning after a Saturday night of revelry. She was shocked and angry to see so much litter in a prosperous place.

That evening, as the applause was dying down after her lecture, she told the audience to use the two hands they were clapping with to collect waste and recycle it. A month later, when she returned to Taichung, a young volunteer told her that she had acted on her words and visited local households and asked them to collect their waste paper, cans and bottles. Once a week, she went to pick them up and earned from the sale NT$5,000 ($150), which she donated to Tzu Chi. Then an entire village in the district did the same thing. Its residents sorted their waste and laid it in neat piles in front of the house of a local Tzu Chi commissioner, who sold it for NT$8,000 ($250).

Seeing the success of this initiative, Cheng Yen spread the idea to her disciples all over Taiwan, asking them to reduce the volume of waste and recycle it. It is an activity well suited to a mass movement like Tzu Chi. It requires a large number of dedicated and able-bodied people driven by a common purpose. It is something which everyone can do and does not require a university degree or specialized training. It has proved especially attractive to elderly people, who find that their work in collecting and sorting recyclable items to be valuable and appreciated. Initially, not all the members welcomed the idea, regarding the work as dirty, smelly and beneath them. Taiwan's climate includes a long, hot summer, high humidity and heavy rainfall, so that recycling means sweaty and uncomfortable conditions, especially if you have to wear protective clothing to ward off insects and infection.

Taiwan is a developed country: it is a society of "conspicuous consumption"—instant food and automatic machines that dispense canned and bottled drinks 24 hours a day—leaving enormous waste, in the form of paper cups, plastic containers of instant noodles and lunch and pizza boxes. It is also a society of "face," in which entertaining friends or clients means ordering too much food and drink, to show the warmth of your welcome and the depth of your pocket book. In 2006, the 23 million people in Taiwan spent $9 billion on dining out, and much of it was thrown away. "Face" also means extensive gift-giving, at Chinese New Year, birthdays, weddings and anniversaries, in which wrapping and presentation are as important as content. This means elaborate and expensive wrapping paper and boxes and gifts that the recipient does not need—he may give them to someone else or even return them to the store which sold them, receiving close to the original price. Selling new products is profitable but collecting old ones is not: few commercial companies are interested in recycling.

Taiwan's 23 million people drive 6.7 million cars and ride 13 million motorcycles. The island has 20 incinerators that can process 21,600 tons of garbage a day, more than 70 percent of its solid waste. The government's Environmental Protection Administration calculates that about 40 percent of the garbage is recyclable. It has 2,000 trucks that make visits twice a week to collect 30 types of waste materials, including lead acid batteries, fluorescent tubes, used clothes and small electrical and electronic appliances. In 2005, a total of 1.8 million tons of recyclable garbage was picked up, 23 percent of all solid waste collected.

But the volume of waste is too large for the government to handle alone. The capital, Taipei, generates more than 3,400 tons of garbage a day, of which about 60 percent is picked up by municipal cleaning teams. That leaves a large space for private initiative and action by civic and charity groups like Tzu Chi.

Within Tzu Chi, the movement has grown gradually. In 1995, volunteers in Taiwan were collecting 20,700 tons of material, and by 2001 the number had grown to 20,000 at 200 recycling stations and 1,200 collection points, collecting 71,700 tons. In 2007, the number of volunteers reached 62,126, who collected during the year 148,000 tons of material, including 96,000 tons of paper, 7,100 tons of old clothes, 11,000 tons of glass, 8,700 tons of plastic and 235 tons of copper.

The foundation calculates that the paper recycled is the equivalent of 1.9 million 20-year-old trees. Between 1992 and 2007, they estimated their recycling program had saved 15.9 million trees. The foundation designates two Sundays a month as "the day of volunteers in their district," when thousands go to clean the parks and the streets and collect waste. Its volunteers abroad have followed suit, doing recycling in the United States, Indonesia, South Africa, Malaysia, Thailand and other countries. The largest number is in Malaysia, with 6,528 volunteers and 606 recycling centers.

Many volunteers are middle-aged and elderly men and women. Chu Chang-yu, a 58 year-old working mother in Taipei, is a typical example. Her day begins at 5 AM, when she gets up and makes lunch boxes for her children. Then she goes to the company where she works as a delivery woman, taking its products to customers, until lunchtime. In the afternoon, she takes her barrow to the city's Chongshan and Datong districts where she collects waste for recycling until sunset, when she buys food for her family and goes home to make dinner.

"In 1990, I heard the Master's call to start environmental protection and have been doing it ever since. It is good for my body and my soul. It helps reduce the amount of rubbish and cleans my heart. I do not get tired, despite cold and wet weather. People think that what I do is exhausting but I feel very fortunate. This work is positive for life and there is no conflict with other people. I am like many other brothers and sisters who do this. We have a happy heart and do not feel tired. Over the long term, we have a sense of achievement," she said.

Lu Chen, 55, is in charge of a recycling center with 40 volunteers in Ba Da Lu, an upmarket street in the center of Taipei. The center, built on land donated by the government, is divided into two areas—one in which volunteers sort the goods that have been brought in and another where second hand products are sold. In the first, retired people sit next to piles of magazines and paper, which they go through and divide into white paper and paper with printing on it, putting them into neat piles.

"These old people like to come here," Lu explained. "Their children have grown up. They like to meet new people and talk to them. We listen to the speeches of Cheng Yen as we work."

Since the center is in a rich area, many of the goods on sale are high-quality, like branded clothes from Italy, France and the United States. It also sells imported china and furniture.

There is one section where the goods are not for sale—daily items, like baskets, hand-driven machines and clocks, used by people in

Taiwan half a century ago. Lu said that she wanted to display the items to show visitors an era where life was poorer and less convenient, a reminder of their wealth and good fortune today.

The volunteers include a chief executive and his wife, who arrive at the center in a chauffeur-driven Mercedes and swap their designer clothes for jeans, T-shirt and woolen gloves. While they sweat putting paper and glass bottles into plastic bins, their maid at home is busy cleaning the house. It is slow and tiring work. In the evening, the chauffeur returns to collect the couple and take them home. After hours amid the dust and garbage, they look at the maid with a softer and more forgiving eye.

Cheng Yen blames environmental degradation on the greed of man and his insatiable desire for more cars, more roads, more goods and more growth. The most extreme form of this greed is war. "War is not a natural disaster but a man-made one. Although it is the idea of a few people, its impact is very wide. If the head of a household has a peaceful heart, so his home will be peaceful. If the leader of a country has a broad heart, he will concede a little and tolerate a little." She was speaking after she learned of the U.S. attack on Iraq in March 2003, which left her deeply shocked and full of foreboding. She recalled the World War Two air raids she witnessed as a girl. "Once, when I was going home, I heard the air-raid sirens and everyone rushed for the bomb shelters. After the raid was over, I saw that the whole street had been flattened and that arms, legs and intestines were hanging on electric cables that were drenched in blood. One woman said: 'Mother Guan Yin (Goddess of Mercy), why could you not lead the bombs to fall on the sea?' An elderly woman replied: 'You cannot blame Guan Yin for not being effective. It is man who is not listening. The eyes of Guan Yin have wept so much that her eyes are dry and weeping blood.'"

She also remembers the thriftiness of her childhood. "When I was young, parents used to say that, if a piece of rice fell on the floor, the thunder of God would punish you." She told the story of a boy of 12 who ate what his mother left on her plate. "He said that this was because she had told him that, after you die, you have to eat all the food you have thrown away during your life before you can be reincarnated. He wanted to save his mother from this trouble."

The volunteers who work in developing countries see at first hand the imbalance between the consumption of the rich and the poor. Out of the world's 6.5 billion people, 1.6 billion are overweight and 850 million are starving. A study in October 2007 found that the average German family spent $509 a week on food, compared to $70 by a family in Egypt,

171

$41 by a family in Mongolia, $5.1 by a family in Bhutan and $1.3 by a family in a refugee camp in Chad.

The volunteers see the degradation of the planet through the increase in the number and scale of natural disasters they respond to. "During 1998 and 2002, we were very busy," said Hsieh Ching-kuei, director of Tzu Chi's humanitarian aid department. "We witnessed an increase in disasters, including typhoons, hurricanes, floods, earthquakes and tidal waves. Everyone said that they were the worst they had seen, such as in Papua New Guinea, the worst for 99 years. I had a strong feeling this could be global warming. This was confirmed by the United Nations Intergovernmental Panel on Climate Change report in February 2007, which said that human behavior was behind the increase."

In 2006, 110 inches of rain fell on Taiwan, an increase of 11 inches over 2005, but the number of rainy days fell by 12: when it fell, the rain was more intense, causing more damage, including landslides. "The same phenomena are happening all over the world," Hsieh said. "On September 3, 2006, two hurricanes hit Mexico and Nicaragua on the same day. Such a thing had never happened before. All these are warning signs for the whole world. In 2007, stocks of wheat hit a 57-year low, because of drought in major wheat-producing countries, and prices reached a 30-year high."

Hsieh knows the consequences of global warming better than most. He spends his life distributing aid to starving mothers and children and victims of natural disasters around the world, where a single loaf of bread and a sack of rice are greeted with joy and happiness. Then he flies home to Taipei where shops and restaurants discard plastic bags full of bread and rice at the end of each day, and rich housewives buy a Swiss watch for a price which could feed for a lifetime one of the families he had met a few days before.

For Hsieh, time is running out for mankind to save the planet. "We are past the 59th of 60 minutes. Either we change the way we live or we destroy ourselves. The cause of this degradation is unlimited human desire. We must eat less and wear less. We must wear simple clothes and spend less on style and fashion. We will use less material and can reduce meaningless economic activity."

For Tzu Chi, the solution lies less in government policies and action plans than in the hearts of individuals, to make them change their own lifestyle. "Global warming shows the need to purify the hearts of man," said Hsieh. "The world has 850 million people who are starving. But a recent report from Britain found that one third of the quantity of food is lost during the production process, while

30–40 percent of that which remains is wasted. We must reduce our desires and live a more simple life."

Cheng Yen, a devout vegetarian, sees consumption of meat as murder, a waste and as environmental degradation. "The resources needed to produce half a pound of beef, in terms of water, grass, grains and so on, could be used to feed 40 children who are starving. If we look at these figures, we see how many resources are used up by animal raising. We raze forests not only to make paper and furniture but also to raise cattle to feed ourselves. This has led to the destruction of many tropical forests."

The number of animals raised each year is almost 10 times the world's human population of 6.8 billion, including 60 billion chickens, 1.8 billion sheep, 1.3 million oxen and one billion pigs. Members of Tzu Chi regard eating meat as immoral and an inefficient way to feed humankind, because animals consume far more grains, grass and plants than the meat they become. If humans ate these grains and plants them-selves, instead of having them processed by animals, there would be a large surplus of food. In addition, the gas emitted by oxen accounts for 20 percent of the world's greenhouse gases.

Members of Tzu Chi aim to live in a simple way that consumes few resources and causes little waste. On foundation business, they wear a uniform, which, they say, saves the need for a large and expensive ward-robe, and that their material demands diminish after they become active in the organization. Needing less money is one reason why they are able to work as unpaid volunteers.

Members carry plastic chopsticks and plastic food boxes for their meals, to avoid the use of disposable wooden chopsticks. They wash the utensils themselves after the meal and use them again.

In its buildings, Tzu Chi implements environmental principles. They collect water—rain or washing water—and reuse it. They maximize the use of natural wind, to reduce the need for air conditioners, and sun-light, to decrease the need for electricity. Cheng Yen opposes the use of air conditioners since they transfer hot air from the interior to the outside, raising the temperature, which the natural environment cannot tolerate. In paving, they use individual pieces, with space between them, which allows water to seep into the earth, rather than concrete, which does not.

In 2000, its Hualien hospital received an award from Taiwan's Ministry of Economic Affairs for its energy-saving, its recycling of mate-rials and reduction of use of paper by using electronic messages and reusing paper except for confidential documents. It calculated that, by using their own eating utensils, Tzu Chi members at the hospital saved 570,000 plastic lunchboxes, cups and chopsticks.

At the headquarters in Hualien, staff use paper three times, first with pencil, then a ballpoint pen and finally a writing brush. In the early years of the movement, Cheng Yen rarely used clean white paper, preferring to write on the back of calendars that had expired.

PART FOUR

A TEACHER
FOR LIFE

15

RELIGIOUS BACKGROUND

"He spoke of mercy and benevolence, not love. She speaks of love. She was the one who put the theory into practice and many of the ideas were her own. Heaven exists now, not after death. If your heart is good, you see heaven."

—Rey Her-sheng, spokesperson for Tzu Chi

FOR CHENG YEN, TZU CHI is the rebirth of Buddhism, the resurrection of a glorious religion that had fallen into decline and irrelevance. Her aim is to put Buddhism back into the center of life and human society, to turn it from the chanting of scriptures in remote monasteries into a faith that touches people's lives every day. She has achieved this among the quarter of Taiwan's population who are Tzu Chi members and wants to spread her message around the world.

Cheng Yen belongs to a tradition of reformed Buddhism that began 80 years ago in China and has since flourished in Taiwan. Tzu Chi is the largest of several Buddhist organizations active in many sectors of Taiwan life, fulfilling the dream of those monks who launched the reformist movement in the 1920s. This has been impossible in China since the Communists took power in 1949. Buddhism suffered enormous damage during the Cultural Revolution (1966–1976), when Red Guards destroyed temples, killed monks and nuns and burnt the scriptures. While civil liberty has greatly improved since then, Buddhism, like other religions, remains subject to official control and supervision.

Tzu Chi practices "humanist Buddhism," a concept created by a Chinese monk named Tai Hsu (1890–1947). One of his followers was Yin Shun (1906–2005), a monk from East China who was to become the teacher of Cheng Yen. Yin Shun was born in 1906 in Haining in the Eastern province of Zhejiang. As a young man, he worked as a primary school teacher, studied Chinese medicine for three years and read the Bible. He found in it an emphasis on faith, hope and love that was missing in Confucianism and Taoism, but could not accept the idea that believers would live eternally and those who did not believe would be punished in the fires of hell. "So the matter of one's destiny is not decided according to human behavior but whether one believes in God or not," he wrote in his autobiography, *An Ordinary Life*. He was attracted to Buddhism, which he said was reasonable, comprehensive and full of hope, and became a monk in October 1930. A gifted student, Yin Shun was soon lecturing at the seminary where he studied and elsewhere. He found many monks ignorant of the intellectual richness of Buddhism, instead spending their days idling about or performing funerals for paying clients. He came to believe that Buddhism had become corrupted on its journey from India to China.

In 1949, he was forced by the Communist victory to move to Hong Kong, where, in the following year, he completed a biography of Tai Hsu and edited his complete works. In 1952, he moved to Taiwan and spent the rest of his life there. He was a prolific author and traveled widely in Asia, lecturing at academic and religious meetings.

For him, the moment of revelation came in a drafty cell in a mainland monastery. He was reading the Agama Sutras, the first scripture compiled by the Buddha's disciples 2,500 years ago, and came across this verse: "All Buddhas arise in the human world; no one achieves the status of Buddha in heaven." As he described it, this verse answered a question that had long troubled him and he wept uncontrollably. Buddhism was not something that dealt with the afterlife and another universe but was applicable to everyday human life.

He broadened Tai Hsu's idea of "humanist Buddhism" by saying not only that Buddhism was practiced in this world but also that anyone could become a Buddha. "Benefit others with all sorts of good deeds and do so without expecting any merits or blessings in return. The work of promoting the Buddha's teachings is not reserved for only monks or nuns. Lay people who have a profound understanding of Buddhism can also do so. A taxi driver once asked me how to practice Buddhism and I told him to act like a good Buddhist by driving mindfully. Perform your duties earnestly. It is as simple as that."

Plagued by bad health from an early age, Yin Shun was a scholar and teacher rather than an activist. He preferred solitude and quiet research to organization and social activism. It fell to one of his disciples, Cheng Yen, to establish an institution that would put his theories into practice.

The two met for the first time in February 1963 outside a bookstore in Taipei, where, at the age of 26, she had gone to a temple in the hope of being ordained as a nun. Told that she could not be ordained without a religious master, she left disappointed and went to the bookstore to buy the complete works of Tai Hsu, the work that Yin Shun had edited. At the time, Yin Shun was living above the store and Cheng Yen was surprised to see him standing there, waiting for a rainstorm to pass. Too nervous to speak to him, she asked another monk to approach him and see if he would accept her as a disciple. Yin Shun initially refused, responding that teachers should be familiar with those they sponsor, but after talking with her in person, he changed his mind. He said later that what convinced him was the fact that she had bought the complete works of his mentor, Tai Hsu. "The world is full of incredible coincidences," he said later. "The relation between us started with a book by my mentor. Our karmic relationship is very special."

Yin Shun's mission to Cheng Yen, "to serve Buddhism and all living beings" affected the young nun deeply.

"The words he gave me as my mission made my heart shake," Cheng Yen said. "It raised the quality of Buddhist teaching. Considering the state of Buddhism in Taiwan at that time, it was a heavy responsibility and mission."

The elderly monk continued to help and advise his disciple at critical moments. When she was setting up the Tzu Chi Foundation, he told her to consider carefully whether she would have the strength and the money to handle all the demands that would be made on it. In 1975, a typhoon blew off the tiled roof of the modest temple used by her and her disciples. When he found out, Yin Shun provided money for a new concrete roof. In the summer of 1979, when he visited her in Hualien, she told him of her plan to build a large general hospital. He said she could only achieve this objective with unwavering commitment, and promised his support. To help, he gave most of the money his supporters had given him, a substantial sum since he was at that time a better known religious leader than she. For 18 years from 1973, he gave her the use of his lecture hall in Taipei as a place to distribute relief supplies. He also contributed money to Tzu Chi's relief efforts after the 1999 earthquake in Taiwan, the 9/11 terrorist attack in New York and the Southeast Asian tsunami of 2004.

The relations between the two were not equal. He was one of the most famous Buddhist scholars in Taiwan and she a young nun with little formal training. He spoke Mandarin with a heavy accent of his native Zhejiang, which she and other Taiwanese found hard to follow.

Since it was impolite for a student to ask a teacher to repeat himself, it was easier for the two to communicate in written Chinese. "I regarded my teacher with awe and respect," she said. "I wanted to listen to him speak of Buddhism but feared that I would not understand his Zhejiang accent. That would be very impolite. If I spoke of what Tzu Chi was doing, I did not dare to talk too much, fearing that these mundane matters would disturb his serene heart. Over 40 years, each time I went to the West of Taiwan, I would visit my teacher, but our meetings were very short."

For the last six years of his life, Yin Shun suffered from serious diarrhea and stayed at the Tzu Chi hospital in Hualien for months at a time, attended by the best team of specialists it could muster. He became a beneficiary of the institution that he had helped to create.

This is how Cheng Yen remembered him after his death on June 4, 2005, at the age of 100:

"With the changing of time, the translated texts (of Buddhism) are often difficult for the average person to understand. Great Buddhist teachers are needed to transform classic Buddhist texts into teachings that can be applied to the modern day and used in everyday life. In the Venerable Yin Shun, we have such a teacher. Over 40 years ago, he instructed me that I must dedicate myself to working for Buddhism and for all living beings. Ever since then, I have endeavored to bring Buddhism into everyday life and show everyone that they can emulate and become bodhisattvas (enlightened beings).

"Though my Master lived past 100, his passing was only natural and inevitable, as death is but the natural course of life. Deeply I grieve but I am also very grateful for my Master for opening up a path of humanized Buddhism, so that the spirit of the Buddha's teaching may truly benefit people of this world. As his disciples, let us piously vow to continue on this path and let the Venerable's teachings live on forever in this world."

His funeral was a national event, attended by Taiwan's President, Prime Minister, Minister of the Interior, other legislators and leading religious figures from Taiwan and abroad, and by hundreds of monks and nuns.

Serving with Compassion and Insight

Tzu Chi belongs to the Mahayana, the "Great Vehicle" school of the religion, which is predominant in China, Mongolia, Japan, Tibet, Korea, Taiwan and Vietnam. It emphasizes the value of insight and compassion, with the bodhisattva who devotes himself to the service of others. He is the model for religious practice, rather than the person who cloisters himself to pursue his individual "liberation." The other great school of Buddhism is Theravada, which became the dominant form in Sri Lanka, Burma, Thailand, Laos and Cambodia. It advocates the meditative monastic life as the path to salvation and liberation, a path reserved for the few, the monks, who can give up everything to follow its austere practices.

In the Mahayanan tradition, the bodhisattva is an individual who works to liberate all beings from suffering. Cheng Yen sees her disciples as these bodhisattvas: "You can see Tzu Chi volunteers in every community in Taiwan. Their blue and white uniforms are to be found in the poorest villages in rural China. Thousands of Zulu Tzu Chi volunteers in South Africa give their love to tribal people, volunteers in Paraguay have built schools for aboriginal children among the native Indian tribes. Volunteers in Indonesia join together to clean the garbage of the Angke river in Jakarta, Tzu Chi members of the Islamic faith help in the aftermath of natural disasters. All these volunteers follow the principle of non-discrimination to love every race, nationality and religious group equally. We aim to inspire the rich to support the poor and expect those who are helped to support others."

Life of Yin Shun

In 1994, Yin Shun published his autobiography entitled *An Ordinary Life*. It was anything but ordinary.

He was born in the spring of 1906 to a farming family in Haining county in the Eastern province of Zhejiang, not far from where Tai Hsu had been born 16 years earlier. Two months premature, he was weak and suffered numerous illnesses during his life, especially diarrhea. A gifted student, he turned to Buddhism at the age of 20 and read its scriptures widely, although he could not understand much of what he read nor find in his hometown monks educated enough to explain it to him. In 1928 and 1929, he lost his parents and decided to become a monk, to try to acquire peace of mind. He went to study at a monastery in Putuo Mountain, in Zhejiang province. It was there, on October 11, 1930 that the abbot shaved his head and gave him the religious name of Yin Shun (which means Mark of Obedience). His unusual academic abilities soon brought him to the attention of Tai Hsu and he was invited to become a teacher and lecturer.

His autobiography describes the life of a scholar and teacher in East and Central China until the Japanese invasion at Marco Polo Bridge outside Beijing in July 1937. Like thousands of others, Yin Shun fled to Chongqing, in the Southwest, which became China's wartime capital. He called the next eight years the most difficult of his life and also the years that would decide his future. During that time he deepened his study of Indian and Tibetan Buddhism, which was to have a great impact on his future research and writing. His writing career started in 1942 with a treatise on Indian Buddhism and his last major academic work was in 1989, on the same topic. He wrote an astonishing seven million characters. His works have been widely read in Taiwan, China and among overseas Chinese. They include texts aimed at the general reader as well as the scholar.

The autobiography records his constant illnesses, especially diarrhea. At 26, he had an attack of it that left him unconscious. One day, as he was lying semiconscious and unable to sleep, he thought that sickness had become the normal state of his life: "With a little change in destiny, such a weak body can die. Living may not necessarily be happy. Death is like a friend we do not know well. If he comes, we will not welcome him but will not despise him either. If I can carry on, I will lie here for a few more days, get up and do what I have to do. I am a simple monk. . . A healthy person can, through a small karma, die suddenly. Death is very easy. But, in my experience, if you have not fulfilled your karma, then death is not so easy."

In November 1954, he was diagnosed with pulmonary tuberculosis. "At that time, there was no medicine to treat it. I do not know how I have been able to live so many decades. Sometimes the body was so weak that I did not even have the strength to read books." In 1971, he had two operations to clear obstacles in the small intestine and his life hung in the balance for 38 days: during his stay in hospital, his weight fell from 52 to 46 kilograms.

In the mainland, he was constantly short of money, paying inflationary prices caused by the Japanese invasion and civil war, and often had to rely on donations from the faithful and help from fellow monks. From 1952, Yin Shun became editor of a Buddhist magazine, *Hai Chao Yin* (Voice of the Sea Tide), which Tai Hsu had founded in 1921, a post he held for 13 years. He encouraged Buddhists to take an active part in social, cultural, educational and medical life. To promote the religious training of women, in 1957 he set up the Women's Buddhist Institute in Hsinchu, of which he became principal. This is one reason Taiwan has the highest proportion of women among the Buddhist clergy of any country in the world. Nuns account for about 75 percent of the 30,000 Buddhist religious on the island. Yin Shun worked hard to raise the intellectual quality and social status of Buddhist monks and nuns and earn the respect of the wider society. In 1961, he set up a lecture hall in Taipei, as a place to propagate Buddhism and edit his magazine. In 1965, he became the first monk to hold a teaching post at a university, teaching Buddhism in the philosophy department of China Culture University. In 1972, he received a PhD from Taisho University in Kyoto, the first monk from Taiwan to receive such an honor from a Japanese university, for his book, *Zhongguo chan zong shi* (The Zen History of China).

In 1994, he returned to the mainland for the first time in 46 years, visiting many of his former temples during a visit of 24 days. In 1997, his followers set up a foundation named after him in the town of Hsinchu, where he lived much of his life, to publish his works in Chinese and foreign languages in written and electronic form, give scholarships for the study of Buddhism and establish a Buddhist library. During his final years, he spent much of his time at Hualien, staying at the Abode, the home of Cheng Yen, or undergoing treatment at Tzu Chi's hospital. Cheng Yen set up a medical team to look after him and instructed them to spare no expense. In 1999, his diarrhea set a record, with 37 visits to the toilet in a single day. After 108 days of treatment in the hospital, he was allowed to leave. The doctors ordered that he be injected with medicine each day and they had it flown to wherever he was staying.

Tzu Chi held a 100th birthday party for Yin Shun on April 20, 2005. A month later, he was admitted to hospital where he spent most of his time asleep. On the morning of June 4, doctors told Cheng Yen that his condition had worsened. She hurried to his bedside and found that his heartbeat was below 42, against the normal range of 60–100. "I said to him: 'do not worry, we are here.' At that moment, his face had an expression as if he was saying goodbye. Then, in less than a minute, his heartbeat dropped from below 32 to zero." The chief doctor waited a minute and confirmed that the heart had stopped beating and the breathing had stopped. His disciples and the nursing staff in the room dropped to their knees and began to chant Buddhist sutras for the dead.

It is in part due to the work of Yin Shun that Buddhism in Taiwan has realized the vision of Tai Hsu to become an integral part of daily life. The island's Buddhist establishment includes more than 4,000 temples, 40 seminaries, five universities, three colleges, four high schools, 45 kindergartens, 30 nurseries, five orphanages, five retirement homes, one center for the mentally retarded, a dozen hospitals and clinics, 118 libraries and 28 publishing houses.

16

AT THE HELM

"Most people think of years. I think of seconds. Each day has 86,400 seconds. We organize our time very tightly and hope to use every second in our life."

—Cheng Yen

THE HOME OF CHENG YEN IS SO DISCREET that it is hardly noticeable. A low-rise building with a slanting roof sits on a narrow sliver of land between a mountain range and the Pacific Ocean. As they walk toward it, disciples of Tzu Chi feel the same excitement as Jews approaching the Wailing Wall in Jerusalem and Muslims who see the Ka'aba in Mecca.

The Abode of Still Thoughts has changed little since it was built in 1969, a small temple in the style of the Tang dynasty. Disciples board buses in the city of Hualien six miles away and ride North along a road close to the sea. As the city disappears, buildings and people become smaller, against the thunder of the ocean on one side and the soaring mountains on the other. The imposing landscape reminds them of the earthquakes and typhoons that strike this coast every year.

The buses turn inland, cross a railway line and pass rice and sugar fields before stopping in a large car park. There is still no sign of what they have come to see. They form a neat line and walk, two by two, along a narrow country road. Looming over them is the mountain range that runs North to South, the backbone of Taiwan. It has suddenly become quiet. The noise of the city has disappeared and the cars on the coastal road have become a murmur in the distance. Here the sounds are birds calling, the bubbling of water running along irrigation chan-nels and the rustling of leaves in the trees. A buffalo splashes in a pool of shallow water.

The disciples turn right at a crossroads and see for the first time on their left a small compound, with trimmed lawns and trees and a narrow path that leads them to the temple. The modest building has become the symbol of the foundation and the logo of its global television station. As they arrive, the disciples are welcomed by their "brothers and sisters," in blue and white uniforms, who clap as they approach and sing that this is home for all 10 million members worldwide. A nun with shaven head and long gray robe stands at the door of the temple and welcomes the visitors. Hualien is far from Taipei and Kaohsiung and even further from Kuala Lumpur, Capetown and Los Angeles: disciples from these distant places are thanked for their long journey. Cheng Yen says: "Welcome home."

The white temple has four round pillars supporting a curved roof over the entrance, with simple lines and no adornment. Passing through a pair of screen doors, the visitor sees three altars, with candles, flowers and a small holder for incense. Each altar has a gleaming white statue, of Buddha, of Guan-yin, the goddess of mercy, and Ti-tsang, the guardian of the earth. The wooden floor is spotless and shining, after hours of polishing. In front of the temple are lawns carefully laid out with trees, stones and pools. Behind them are fields where the nuns grow rice, fruit and vegetables for their own consumption. Next to the fields are sheds to store tools and equipment. The tranquility is only interrupted by the rumble of trains on their way up the coast to Taipei and the deafening sound of fighter jets in practice runs from their base in Hualien, the center of the Eastern command of the Taiwan air force.

Behind the temple are low-rise buildings that house offices, meeting rooms, dormitories, a restaurant, a bookshop and workshops where the nuns make candles, beans and other food items which they sell in Tzu Chi shops around the world. The style of the Abode is low-key and ascetic—wooden boards and panels, colors of white, gray and brown, with the scent of flowers and scrubbed floors and the noise of birds and the wind blowing in from the Pacific. The people who live and work here are nuns in their gray robes and Tzu Chi staff, dressed in the uniform of dark blue and white, suits for the men and long dresses for the women. People bow and smile as they pass. The ambience is discretion and good manners. The security guards are middle-aged men in gray suits, foundation members of long standing. The Abode is both the headquarters of a global enterprise with 10 million members and annual turnover of $300 million and a community of 150 nuns seeking peace and enlightenment away from the greed and extravagance of the material world. The name "Still Thoughts" comes from the name Cheng Yen gave herself when she was studying Buddhist scriptures.

After she arrived here in 1962, she adopted a spartan lifestyle for herself and her disciples, which has not changed—a 17-hour work day, sleeping no more than five hours a night, a strict vegetarian diet and no holidays. The waking gong sounds each morning at 3.50 AM. At 4.20 AM the nuns recite sutras for an hour in front of the three statues in the temple, followed by 10 minutes of meditation and a 30-minute religious lecture by Cheng Yen. They eat a simple breakfast at 6 AM.

At 6.50 AM, she holds a meeting with about 70 volunteers, from Taiwan and elsewhere in the world, in a meeting room next to the temple. They sit cross-legged on brown leather seats on the polished wooden floor, while she faces them, seated at a table with flowers. The room has wooden walls, with vases of flowers, religious paintings on the wall and a small white statue of the Buddha at the back. It has ceiling fans to keep the air cool. Cheng Yen gives an address of about 15 minutes. The room has television screens, which enable her to speak to doctors, nurses, patients and volunteers at Tzu Chi hospitals around the island. They report on operations and treatments and the stories of patients, happy and sad. The meeting is an opportunity for visitors and invited guests to give testimony and to show footage of the foundation's projects around the world. The meetings are carefully scripted and conducted with the slickness of a U.S. news show. For visiting members, this face-to-face meeting with their master is the high point of their journey.

The room is too small to accommodate everyone. Some must sit in three nearby rooms and watch on a large television screen. Her Great Love Television station, records the morning address and broadcasts it, with subtitles in Chinese and English, round the world in the evening of the same day. The address, *Renjian Pu ti* (Practising Buddhism), is re-broadcast four more times over the next 24 hours. It is the main link between her and her followers around the world.

After the meeting, Cheng Yen begins a day like that of a chief executive of a multinational corporation. She receives a flood of visitors—Tzu Chi commissioners, the full-time managers of her global enterprise who report to her on ongoing projects and future plans, at home and abroad; doctors and other medical specialists, local and foreign; religious peoples, including Buddhist, Christian and Muslim; and scholars and professionals. She plays close attention to the news, especially of natural disasters, and hears reports from members in the countries affected. They decide together whether and how Tzu Chi should assist the victims.

She avoids foreign dignitaries and journalists, unless they have a particular connection to Tzu Chi, like the presidents of El Salvador, Honduras and Nicaragua who came in person to thank her for building homes and schools and distributing food and clothing to victims of disaster in their countries. Since Taiwan's foreign ministry is proud of Tzu Chi, it sends foreign dignitaries to Hualien. She leaves it to her colleagues to receive them. As Tzu Chi expands in the world, so her workload becomes heavier. There are ever more projects to be discussed and more decisions to be taken.

Cheng Yen has no office of her own but shares a workroom with her colleagues, with a flow of people in and out. She prefers this collective atmosphere to the formality of a large office.

During meetings, a team of people surround her. There are secretaries, staff members from the departments concerned, an interpreter if there is a foreign visitor and chroniclers who record everything she says. Television cameras are another part of the scenery—excerpts from the meetings are broadcast on the foundation's channel, to let the members know what Cheng Yen is doing.

At midday, she enters the Abode's canteen for lunch with her disciples and visitors. She sits at the head table with senior colleagues and invited guests. At the other tables sit the 150 nuns of the community and Tzu Chi members. The food is strictly vegetarian, with no milk or dairy products. Cheng Yen eats little and leaves after several minutes.

She does not nap after lunch: she drives herself hard, battling fatigue and sickness. "A body that knows no exhaustion and a mind that knows only determination belong to a person's superior self. When the inferior self is forgotten and the superior self takes over, then a person can gain super energy and force himself or herself to go on."

The hectic schedule of meetings continues until 6 PM, after which she does not receive visitors. Eating dinner takes only a few minutes. With the time her own, she reads newspapers and e-mails, surfs the internet and watches television, both her own station and some of Taiwan's 80 other channels. One of her favorite programs, on her own station, is the evening drama, based on the life of a disciple whom she selects as a model: the drama department of the station turns it into a series.

The lights in the Abode go out at 9.40 PM, although residents can stay up if they wish, with a small light to read or meditate. Cheng Yen goes to bed between 10 PM and 11 PM in a small, plain room. She lives with two white cats, one a Siamese, one an Angora, gifts to her in 2002.

Like their master, they are vegetarian and do not even kill mice. They walk behind mice, following them but not too close: the mice do not try to run away. One is called Shan Lai, which means the "arrival of goodness," and the other Show, "double charm."

This intense schedule is only interrupted by visits to Tzu Chi institutions in Hualien, including its large hospital, university and primary and secondary schools. She will visit individual patients, meet doctors and nurses and give prizes to school and university students. She pays special attention to long-term patients and those with severe injuries. At Chinese New Year, she attends festival events, giving out red packets to thank people for their hard work. For anniversaries, performances and special events, she attends ceremonies at *Jing Si Tang* (Hall of Still Thoughts), the foundation's giant meeting hall in Hualien.

Cheng Yen also regularly telephones members on foreign assignments, to check on the state of the mission and discuss what more needs to be done. If she decides Tzu Chi should help the victims of a disaster, she calls a meeting, attended by officials from the aid department and the nuns who research the country involved. They contact members there or, if there are none, in the country that is nearest and decide what action to take. Her office is equipped with video link-ups, computers, mobile telephones and the latest in international telecommunications. She can call a meeting at any time and her staff is on call 24 hours a day.

Seventy-two at the time of writing, Cheng Yen maintains this punishing schedule despite poor health, that also prevents her from flying. Her inability to travel makes it the more remarkable that she has become the leader of a global movement. The Pope, the Dalai Lama and other major religious figures travel frequently to meet their followers face-to-face and spread their message. Instead, Cheng Yen has to rely on television, which is why Tzu Chi has invested so heavily in its own channel with expensive satellite signals that enable it to reach nearly all the countries in the world.

Television cameras are omnipresent in the Abode and follow Cheng Yen wherever she goes. Initially, she was very uncomfortable with the idea: nuns are trained to be modest and self-effacing. But the goal of becoming a major social movement in the world convinced her that television was the only way to reach a mass audience. If she cannot visit her members abroad, she must get close to them by showing them much of her life and that of her colleagues. So she has to put her modesty aside and get used to the glare of the cameras every day.

She is driven by an irresistible sense of mission. "Each day has 24 hours, which is not enough, because we never finish all we have to do. Whenever

I hear or see people in trouble, my heart is very worried and I want to do something as quickly as possible to help them. This is my daily lesson in practicing Buddhism.

"Life inevitably has setbacks and I also have moments when I lose heart and want to give up. Whenever I have this feeling, another voice arises in me and says 'No one is forcing you to do this. How did you start traveling this route?' Then I start to think of how it all began and of the difficulties. When I reflect on this, my heart will have a new spurt of unlimited energy.

"Sometimes I feel very tired but make my best effort to keep going. I am full of confidence in myself. During my lifetime, I will not change. . . In Tzu Chi, there is no retirement." Her sense of urgency is increasing. As each year passes, she feels that she has less time left to complete all that she wants to.

While she may not be able to go abroad, she spends a week every month visiting members and projects around Taiwan, traveling by train or mini-bus. During these visits, meetings start at 6 AM at breakfast and can run until 9 PM. While traveling, she wants the same access to global information she has at home, which means the same availability of internet, video and telecommunications.

Her colleagues say she maintains this schedule through self-control and will power. "At her age, her body is weaker than before but she uses her spiritual strength instead," said De Fan, the nun who has recorded her words every day for the last 13 years. "Her mind remains very sharp. She is calm and collected and so is able to decide things. She is learning all the time."

Cheng Yen says she manages the workload by compartmentalizing the issues in front of her. "Each moment I must concentrate on the matter in hand. I never think too far ahead. I start with the question and need in front of me and keep my mind focused on that and then deal properly with it. My heart is like a mirror. People come and their problem is reflected in my heart. When they leave, so their problem leaves my heart. Then I can quietly see the next person and deal with the next issue."

Asked if Cheng Yen lost her temper, De Fan said that she could be strict with her own followers, like a parent toward her children. "A look is enough. Otherwise, she is very calm and does not show her emotions."

Such discipline persuades thousands of her disciples to do the same—to work a seven-day week and take no holiday. "If the Master works like this, so should I," is a common reply when asked why they work such long hours. This is also the reason people leave jobs in Tzu Chi institutions—they feel that the intense schedule leaves them too little time for family or personal life.

This close relationship between her and her members is one reason for Tzu Chi's rapid growth. The members feel they are working not so much for Buddhism—a fine ideal but distant and abstract—but for an individual they admire and respect, someone close to them, a friend they want to be with and hear from each day. Her speeches and television broadcasts show this intimacy: she talks of everyday life, of children, families and the elderly, of work and leisure, of the pain and happiness of ordinary people, in a conversational style, like a friend more than a religious leader, using words that are accessible to the mass audience. She makes jokes and praises the accomplishments of her members, identified by name. She recounts the happiness and tragedies of the lives of ordinary people—fruit sellers, farmers, seamstresses and teachers— to which her listeners can easily relate. She speaks in a mixture of Taiwanese, the mother tongue of 80 percent of the island's population, and Mandarin, the common language of Chinese around the world. She does not speak a foreign language.

Her status and moral authority have reached a level that disciples often kneel or prostate themselves in her presence. Many disciples cannot control their emotions where they meet her face-to-face.

This is how Liu Su-mei, 53, head of the foundation's branch in Indonesia since 1993, described her encounters: "When I see her, I cannot express the troubles I have in my mind, which melt into insignificance compared to what she has done. The Abode, with the love and compassion of the nuns, brothers and sisters, is like a magnetic field. This feeling is a great motivation. Once we disciples come back from there, then the space in which we can grow naturally increases. Spending money on air tickets and going on holidays absolutely cannot compare with the benefit we receive when we go to the Abode."

Huang Rong-nian, 49, a corporate tycoon in Indonesia, who runs an agro-business with 35,000 employees, says that whenever he calls her, his face becomes covered with sweat: "Every time I call her, I feel very nervous. That is how it is with Tzu Chi people. No matter how big an entrepreneur, professor, lawyer or doctor they are, when they are in front of Cheng Yen, they drop all affectation and become like a child."

So, when she enters a room, those present stop what they are doing and acknowledge her, with a bow, kneeling or prostrating. Her presence dominates the Abode, which she created and sustains. She is the reason everyone is there.

Her disciples regard her as a remarkable human being but not divine. Asked how a woman who only completed primary school and had limited formal education in Buddhism could become the leader of a global movement, one member in Hong Kong said that she was born with wisdom from previous lives. "Look at Mozart. How could he learn to play music at the age of four and start composing at five?"

Chan Yee Chuck, a commissioner at the Hong Kong branch, said that Cheng Yen was human, like Buddha and like other people. "Everyone can cultivate themselves and become Buddha. As your level of cultivation rises, you sleep less and eat less. You appreciate more of what you eat. The food is very simple but you appreciate it more."

Life in the Abode

The Abode is a place of worship and home to a community of 150 nuns, as well as the administrative center of the foundation. From the beginning, Cheng Yen insisted that the community and the foundation be two different entities, with their own accounts and no financial relationship with the other.

In 1963, when she accepted her first disciples, she said that the community would follow the rule of Pai Chang, a famous Chinese monk in the ninth century A.D. who declared that a day without work was a day without food. The community was to be self-supporting and not rely on donations from the faithful, a practice approved by the Buddha himself and common among Buddhist temples and monasteries for the last 2,000 years. Her decision aroused strong opposition from other Buddhist communities, who asked how a young nun of low status could challenge their custom and tradition. She said that this was only the rule she was adopting for her own community and did not imply criticism of anyone else. So the Abode is different to most temples in Taiwan, Japan and the rest of the Buddhist world, which have used money given by the faithful to construct large and elaborate buildings, with extravagant decoration and gold-coated statues of the Buddha.

Since 1966, the community has supported itself without outside funds. It grows its own rice, vegetables and fruit—but without pesticide, which could kill insects. They have made children's shoes, toys, candles, gloves for the military, foodstuffs and other products, using some of the money for themselves and the rest for charity. The nuns live a busy and highly regulated life, like their Master. They rise early, at 3.50 AM, and attend the morning prayer meeting with Cheng Yen. For the rest of the day, they tend the fields, grow their own food and make candles, biscuits, popped rice, nutritional drinks and other items they sell at the foundation's shops. The Abode's shop also sells Tzu Chi books, tapes and souvenirs. The nuns run the canteen, clean the building and receive thousands of visitors every month. Some work as Cheng Yen's secretaries and advisors, responsible for different aspects of the foundation's work. Equipped with computers, mobile phones and blueberries, they belong to the twenty-first century information technology age.

De Fan has a master's degree from National Taiwan University, the country's most famous college. She is an example of a new generation of nun created in part because of Tzu Chi and its high proportion of women leaders. Of the 30,000 Dharma (Buddhist) masters in Taiwan, 75 percent are women, the highest ratio in the world and a number unprecedented in history. Most are highly educated, with degrees from foreign or domestic universities, and combine a religious life with a career in education, publishing, the media, charity or social activism.

Those who wish to live in the Abode must serve a two-year probation, to see if they can adapt to its rigorous conditions. It is not a decision to be taken lightly since it is a lifetime commitment. If they have good academic qualifications, Cheng Yen will ask if they have fully considered all the other career possibilities and rejected them. Those who are unmarried must have the agreement of their family, to pre-empt future quarrels about who is to look after elderly parents in the future. Those who are married must have the approval of their husband and children and ensure that they will be properly taken care of. The Chinese term for "nun" means "a person who leaves the home" and this is exactly what it is. The nun leaves her family and takes on a new name and a new family. She no longer belongs to her original family and her contact with them is limited.

"When I first came, I used to call my family often," said De Fan, who joined in 1996. "But then I called them less and less. For several years they have not come to visit me. We must love everyone, not only our family." Like Cheng Yen, they shave their head and wear a uniform of a plain gray smock and white leggings, with no makeup or ornaments. It is hard to tell what age they are.

Nuns can only leave the community with permission from their superior and must write a notice of their departure on a public blackboard. They can visit their family in special circumstances, such as illness. They are allowed to receive visitors and mothers are allowed to stay. One nun said that the first six months were the most difficult—rising so early in the morning and adapting to the spartan conditions of life. "My mother opposed my coming, fearing that life would be too harsh. She offered me NT$300,000 ($9,500) to stay at home and study. But now she sees that I am happy and accepts it. Here we support each other. We want to be with the Master."

In the earliest days, the community's focus was to provide aid to the poor and sick of Hualien. But, after the foundation was set up and began to raise money, the community became instead a spiritual center for Tzu Chi and its members. "The Abode is the home of everyone (in Tzu Chi)," said Cheng Yen. "When members from all over the world come here, it is up to the nuns to look after them. We provide spiritual food for them. When I see so many people coming here every day for meals, my heart is full of joy."

Life is a lesson in frugality. The complex has a single air conditioner, used not to cool people but the equipment that transmits and receives television signals. During the summer heat that averages 82°F with over 80 percent humidity, everyone else has to make do with ceiling fans and table fans they bring in themselves. In the winter, the only thing to do is put on more clothes and shut the window. Everyone has her own bowl and chopsticks, which they clean after use, to minimize waste and reduce work for those in the kitchen. Food is never wasted. What is uneaten is kept and served at the next meal. The complex collects the plentiful rainwater which falls on Hualien and stores it in an underground tank, to be used in the fields. To save power, they use electricity sparingly. Rooms are often dimly lit.

"During the summer, tens of thousands of households turn on their air conditioner, pushing hot air into the atmosphere, which is hard for nature to tolerate," Cheng Yen said in February 2007. "Many people trade in their own machines for new ones. This year alone, it will take more than 7,000 environmental protection vehicles to transport them all. People should not underestimate the value of what they do themselves. Small changes in our everyday lives can save resources and material."

The rigor of the community and the small size and simplicity of its temple impress members, who give them as reasons why they are willing to donate to the foundation. They contrast it with other temples in Taiwan, whose size and magnificence show that they spend their money in another way.

The rapid increase in the number of staff working at the Abode and of visitors forced Cheng Yen to approve a major expansion of the complex starting in 2006, the fourteenth and the biggest since its foundation. She postponed this decision for several years, because she considers hardship and inconvenience part of religious training and because she had grown attached to individual rooms and what had happened in them.

"Every place has its own soul. One day I heard the earth breathing, with a skin like that of human," she said in a program describing the redevelopment. When she saw things being demolished, she felt full of contradictions, because she wants them to be preserved or recycled. Her tone in the program was apologetic, as if she feared that people would think the nuns were abandoning their principles and spending money on themselves and not on the poor and needy.

But, in the end, the requirements of modernity and efficiency prevailed, for more and better equipped space for the staff and more comfortable facilities for visitors, including those who stay overnight, and so she approved the expansion. One of her responsibilities, as she is getting old, is to pass on a good and secure home to her disciples. The original temple will remain. But other rooms will be demolished, to make way for a large hall where all those attending the morning meeting will be able to see Cheng Yen in person, as well as new three-story buildings for offices and dormitories for visitors.

Nuns insist that it is they, and not the foundation, who are paying, in line with the principle of separate financing. They earn money from sale of their food products and candles in Tzu Chi shops around the world. They pay market prices for the building materials and a salary to the construction workers. When the work is finished, the amount of space in the Abode will have increased substantially, making a larger and more efficient building. But the new rooms will contain no air conditioners or heating fans. The space will be larger and more comfortable but the spirit of simplicity and frugality will remain.

17

INTO THE FUTURE

"The Master says that she must continue with her mission until her last breath and then come back to do the same job in her next life."

—De Fan, the nun who records Cheng Yen's words

THE QUESTION NO ONE IN TZU CHI likes to ask is what will happen after the passing of their Master. How will the movement survive the death of its founder and the person who guides her disciples every day?

Cheng Yen permeates everything. Her picture hangs on the walls of its branches in Taiwan and around the world, of its schools, and of the homes of her followers. When earthquake victims in Turkey or Pakistan received food and blankets, they saw on the Tzu Chi truck a photograph of the shaven Buddhist nun in distant Taiwan. When the hungry children of North Korea were given rice and jackets, they received a pamphlet, in Chinese and Korean, from Cheng Yen, expressing her love and concern for them. Every evening, the volunteers in Pyongyang called her from their hotel, to report on the day's work and ask her advice.

So it is with all sensitive missions to difficult and dangerous countries Cheng Yen takes personal charge and hears daily reports from her staff in the field. When she visited a housing project for evacuees from the September 1999 earthquake in Taiwan, she found that the streets were paved with asphalt and one of the bedrooms in the model house had no windows, two features which reduced the cost of the project. She declared the asphalt made the street feel like a refugee camp and that people should not live in windowless rooms. So the asphalt was dug up and the house torn down—future Great Love villages had tiled streets and all the rooms in the houses had windows. When she convenes a meeting at the Abode, the participants express their opinions. On issues of method and strategy, she accepts divergent views: but, on issues of principle, she makes the final decision and everyone accepts it.

Cheng Yen also plays a major role in the Great Love Television channel and the other media run by the foundation. The highlight is her daily 15-minute address, *Renjian Pu ti* (Practising Buddhism), which the station broadcasts five times during the day and is required viewing for her disciples. Other programs include discussions of her ideals and philosophy, her discourses on religious themes and dramas based on the real life of commissioners. The foundation's monthly magazine publishes an essay written by her, and a report of her activities and words day by day during the preceding month, including several pages of photographs. Its bookshops are full of books and essays she has written and of books about her. When she visits branches around Taiwan, thousands turn out, in the hope of glimpsing her in person. Ask the members about their work and they will recount stories and sayings of the Master. For many, it is the personal relationship with her, as teacher, counselor and mother-figure, more than a belief in the Buddhism she teaches, that is the basis of their devotion. They work for her as well as for the religion.

Most members joined because of an encounter with her, in person or through the television channel, a speech, a radio address or an article she wrote. For many who became full-time volunteers, it was the defining moment of their life. One woman, formerly a television reporter, described how she first heard Cheng Yen speak. Coming from a mainland family who spoke Mandarin, she had a poor understanding of Taiwanese, which Cheng Yen was using on that occasion. "I could not comprehend very well what she was saying but I was intensely affected. I started to shake and to weep. It was very emotional." She gave up her job at the television station and went to work for the foundation full-time. This is a common story, especially among those who left long-term careers and businesses to work for the foundation full-time and without pay.

Stephen Huang, who heads the international department, is a typical example. In April 1989, he went to meet Cheng Yen after the sudden death of his elder brother, 54, and talked to her for two hours. He was so moved that he sold the business empire he had built in California over two decades, to devote himself full-time to the foundation. His job requires him to fly around the world—about 100 flights a year—often to dangerous and unstable countries and live most of the year away from his family. He pays the travel and hotel bills from his own pocket. These volunteers speak passionately about the inspiration they draw from Cheng Yen herself and her example of self-sacrifice. They draw encouragement and support every day from meeting her and seeing her broadcasts, which drives them to imitate her life of 18-hour days, no holidays and limited time with their family.

So what will they do when their inspiration and guiding spirit has left them? Will they maintain the same level of commitment, the volunteers working a seven-day week without pay and the professionals earning a salary lower than in the outside world? And how about the millions of donors? Without the Master's persuasion, charisma and jokes will they be so generous? Will they still want to help victims of a flood in Argentina or Angola, countries they will never visit and with whom they have no connection?

Cheng Yen appears to have made the same decision as the Buddha, to name no successor. "A man is a man and should not be deified," she said.

Like the Buddha, she believes her legacy is her teachings, set out in dozens of books, television programs and DVDs, in addition to the 10-million army of members, Tzu Chi hospitals, schools and other institutions around the world, and the organizational structure she has put in place. Cheng Yen stresses she is merely the instrument who created the foundation and that the credit for its achievements belongs to the members. "I did not make Tzu Chi what it is today. Everything should be attributed to the hard work of all its members, commissioners, Tzu Cheng Faith Corps members and honorable board members. They contributed their great love to make Tzu Chi what it is today. It is not right to attribute all these accomplishments to me."

The foundation has established a committee of senior members responsible for overseeing a smooth handover after her departure. The four missions will continue to be run by the professional managers in place and her religious duties will be taken over by the 150 nuns who live with her in the Abode. Some already have senior management roles, in areas such as overseas aid, education and publishing.

Despite these careful preparations and the institutional structure, there is still a sense of unease and foreboding among her followers and the public at large on the question of Cheng Yen's passing. People fear that the light and the spirit may disappear. The members see in Cheng Yen an exceptional individual, whose like will not come again in their lifetime. The full-time volunteers believe that their lives have been transformed by knowing her. So, while the Buddha was correct to say that his teachings and not an individual were his legacy, in the case of Cheng Yen humans are following a person rather than a doctrine, a person they can see, touch and listen to.

To ask members about the passing of their Master is as painful as inquiring about the death of a parent or family member: inevitable, yes, but something best not thought about and left in a dark cupboard of the mind. They see her frail health and the medication tube sometimes attached to her arm. But they regard her as an exceptional individual who can draw on sources of willpower and determination unavailable to ordinary people. Hopefully, they say, Cheng Yen will be like her mentor, Yin Shun, who endured illness his whole life yet lived a long life from a sense of mission and the love and devotion of his disciples.

The relationship between her and her disciples is clearly intense and emotional. In May 2007, the foundation held many events to celebrate its forty-first anniversary. During one, she was sitting on a platform while her disciples entered. They knelt in front of her, their hands clasped in prayer, many weeping. "Do not worry, Master," they chanted. It was their way of saying that they would carry out her mission during her life and after. It was a poignant moment, the disciples hoping that their love and devotion would give her the strength to live longer: she was moved and uplifted by this support.

Lin Yang-gang, a former Minister of the Interior and a strong supporter of the foundation, summed up the disciples' sentiments when he said, "The lifespan of an individual is limited. The basic spirit and great enterprise [Cheng Yen] has set up will continue. She has not designated one successor but a group of people to take over. If she leaves, it would be a great loss. We hope that she lives to the age of 100."

Death is a constant theme in her books and speeches—the death of a young person from cancer, the passing of an elderly volunteer and the deaths caused by floods and other natural disasters. What counts is not the length of life but how it is lived: if a person performs good deeds and helps others, it is a life full of merit.

Cheng Yen speaks of "birth, growth, sickness and death" as the cycle of life for every human being as for all creatures and plants on the planet. She uses it as a theme of Buddhist scripture and a way to comfort the relatives of someone who has died. She tells them that the one they have lost is going through the natural cycle of events and will return to the earth in another reincarnation. When his time has come, then his family should let him go, be grateful for what he achieved during his life and not hold on their grief and dwell on what he might have done. "Release him," she says and get on with your life. She tells her disciples to accept death in their family and among their friends as the natural course of life, a cause for sadness but not for resignation—as if she was preparing them psychologically for her own departure.

In her daily talk on July 25, 2007, she spoke with profound admiration for a disciple named Chang Mei-ying, a teacher, who had just learned of the murder of her husband. A 55-year-old assistant professor of biology at National Taiwan University, he was cycling to his laboratory the previous morning when a drug addict, one of 9,500 prisoners released under a presidential amnesty eight days earlier, assaulted him. He sustained serious head injuries and died later that day. The assassin told police he had beaten the professor but could not remember why. Chang was grief-stricken by this senseless murder but found the strength to forgive the assassin and his family and hold no anger and resentment in her heart. Cheng Yen praised her as a model of someone who had experienced death so close to her and yet had accepted it. This was, she said, the true wisdom of a Buddha.

Cheng Yen sees her mission as lasting far into the future. "We build everything the best we can because we hope the things we do today will last a thousand years. We walk the path of truth. We build everything carefully, step by step, the best we can. We do not waste time, even a minute, because we hope the things we do today last forever."

Hence, the foundation builds hospitals, schools and other structures to withstand the earthquakes that frequently strike Taiwan. "Tzu Chi started from nothing but now the four missions are complete, in all the corners of the world. The sun never sets on Tzu Chi. It is a matter of cause and effect. One seed leads to more seeds. We all here have the same thoughts. We must recruit more members and work harder."

She wants the foundation to have a more international character, spreading from Taiwan into other countries and recruiting thousands of local people as members. As far as Cheng Yen is concerned, the work has only just begun and is without end. During the foundation's forty-first birthday celebrations, Cheng Yen looked back on what Tzu Chi had done and recalled the mission given her by her mentor Yin Shun in the spring of 1963 "to serve Buddhism and mankind."

"My master's words to me were very simple," she said, "but the path is infinite, stretching over 1,000 and millions of years, and countless numbers of people need our help and guidance. They cannot be quantified. No matter how big the population is the number is limitless."

De Min, a senior nun who lives with her in the Abode, put it more bluntly; "My dream is for everyone in the world to become a member of Tzu Chi."

However, some scholars are skeptical that Tzu Chi will be able to grow outside the Taiwanese community, who account for a majority of its members. "Tzu Chi welcomes people of all religions but it has a specifically Taiwan cultural flavor," said one scholar who preferred to remain anonymous. "Outsiders may not feel at home there. Since it grows through personal introductions and contacts, this growth is likely to be more of people of Taiwanese origin. In the United States, evangelical groups tend to be exclusionary and discourage their members from joining other organizations. The mainstream Protestant and Roman Catholic churches are more flexible."

Others also believe the foundation will be weakened without Cheng Yen's presence and charisma, saying that the rate of growth and the level of donations could fall without her leadership and media savvy. "Her integrity allows her to lead by example and her compassion allows her to affect people deeply with few words," writes U.S. scholar Charles Brewer Jones in his book *Buddhism in Taiwan*.

"The fact that, despite physical frailty and the handicap of being a woman, she has accomplished so much inspires followers to exert themselves to the utmost. Perhaps more than any other Buddhist leader in Taiwan, her followers seek to emulate her, in accordance with the dictum 'the Master's resolve is my resolve, the Buddha's mind is my mind.' Many identify with her to the extent that they value their relationship with her more than with their own families and some make vows to follow her from one rebirth to the next. . . It is a leadership style that relies heavily on Cheng Yen's personality and character and presages problems when she passes from the scene."

Cheng Yen, however, reflects little about the past or future. "I only want to grasp the present and do all I can. . . Life is limited. As long as we can talk and act, we should make use of our time to do good deeds. The future is a fantasy and the past is an illusion. We must project the love of this moment and carefully keep on fulfilling our duties at this instant. . . My mind would be in a state of confusion if I kept looking back on what I did and I would be in a state of delusion if I kept dreaming about the future. I must continue to seize this day, marching toward my goals in accordance with my blueprint."

APPENDIX

STILL THOUGHTS

Cheng Yen began her pastoral work giving advice to disciples who brought their personal problems to her. Since then, it has grown into a religious and moral vision of the world and a detailed set of principles for her disciples. It has become the philosophy of Tzu Chi, an addition to the house of Buddhism, a palace with a thousand rooms.

This philosophy was first contained in the three-volume *Jing Si* (Still Thoughts) *Aphorisms*, Cheng Yen's sayings recorded by her disciples and first published in 1988. The book has since been through many reprints, becoming a best seller in Taiwan and translated into many languages.

A Selection of Cheng Yen's Sayings

"We must realize that, from the day we were born as humans, we should be happy with our lives. We should learn from people like Lin Chen-chin. Some people asked him how he coped with both legs amputated. He replied: 'I am much luckier than those who have injured their spines.' We think that he is suffering but in fact he is not."

"Open the door to your heart. If you open the door, anyone can go in and out. On the other hand, if the door is too narrow, everyone will bump into it. . . Life is happiest when you are needed by others and can do things for others. . . A loving heart is the most beautiful thing in the world, while a lustful thought is the least beautiful thing in the world."

"When a person becomes bogged down in the pursuit of wealth and forgets to use his wealth properly to help others, he is eventually abandoned by others. His life becomes more lonely and miserable than that of a poor person. . . Some people are materially poor but spiritually rich. Though destitute, they are warm and loving. They always smile and talk pleasantly. Their lives are happy and full."

"We should speak kindly and gently to the poor and our attitudes should be humble and amiable. The poor need love even more than material goods. Love is shown in our attitudes, so do not be arrogant toward them, but be kind and amiable."

"To victims of disaster and poverty: you should first use gentle, kind and loving words to warm their helpless, frightened souls. Then slowly establish religious faith in them, for when their spirits have something to depend on, those people can cope with the difficulties they face. Our work is not only to give them material help. Soothing their souls is more important. Helping people is urgent, but helping souls is even more urgent."

"Fighting for the downtrodden and shouting about justice will make the situation even more complicated and confused. Many injustices are not as simple as they seem, so do not be too hasty to fight for justice, because you might just make things worse. . . A sense of responsibility is more important than a sense of justice. If everyone acts this way, then there is a possibility that society will become even more fair and just."

"Anger is a lack of responsibility toward yourself, fruitlessly exhausting your body's physical and mental energies. It is an inner force of destruction that confuses the mind and destroys one's problem-solving ability. Achieve a state of strong concentration and face reality. Do not let reality disturb your mind's clarity and peace."

"How to communicate? First, you must be calm and listen carefully, get rid of your own prejudices and have the wisdom to humbly accept other people's way of thinking. Then you can really communicate."

"Getting along with others is not based on one's appearance but on one's character. Good character is something we have to work at."

"Accepting the criticism of others is a kind of lesson. You should listen carefully and then behave prudently. You should eliminate arrogance, stubbornness and egotism so that you can cultivate morality and conduct yourself properly."

"Raising children is like growing trees. After you plant the tree, you must be careful not to add too much water or fertilizer or else the roots will quickly rot. Nature already has the proper amount of water, sunlight and air. It is the same way with children. The parents give birth to the child but heaven and earth nurture him. On the other hand, if you spoil the child, you will hurt him."

"The belief in supernatural powers is not part of Buddhism or Taoism. . . Most people feel anxious and do not fully comprehend the true meaning of religion, so they believe in divination from the gods. Buddhism is not a religion of worshipping idols. It is a religion that reforms human life and promotes science."

"To act like a Buddha is to give without asking for anything in return and to cultivate one's speech and conduct for the sake of all living beings. . . If you want to act like a Buddha, you must cultivate yourself to the point where, no matter what happens, you do not have the tiniest complaint."

"The Pure Land is here and now. The purpose of moral cultivation is not to go to the Pure Land after passing away but to go to the Pure Land while alive. It is to become pure and compassionate in one's present life."

"Believing and worshipping the Buddha is believing in the Buddha's character and life goals. When we turn and examine our basic natures, we come to believe that everyone has the same perseverance as the Buddha. One only needs to be mindful to bring forth one's true nature."

"The true Path is not reached by reading sutras or listening to sermons . . . One must put what one has learnt into practice. Only through actual practice can one understand the true Path."

INDEX